W9-ACG-081

Conjuring the Folk

Conjuring the Folk

Forms of Modernity in African America

David G. Nicholls

Ann Arbor

THE UNIVERSITY OF MICHIGAN PRESS

2003   2002   2001   2000   4   3   2   1

A CIP catalog record for this book is available from the British Library.

Library of Congress Cataloging-in-Publication Data

Nicholls, David, 1965–
    Conjuring the folk : forms of modernity in African America / David
G. Nicholls.
        p. cm.
    Includes bibliographical references and index.
    ISBN 0-472-11034-9 (alk. paper)
        1.   American literature—Afro-American authors—History
and criticism.   2.   Literature and folklore—United States—History—
20th century.   3.   American literature—20th century—History and
criticism.   4.   Modernism (Literature)—United States.
    5.   Afro-Americans in literature.   6.   Afro-Americans—Folklore.
    7.   Folklore in literature.   I.   Title.
PS153.N5 N53 2000
810.9'896073—dc21   99-050557

For Tom and Natalie Nicholls

Contents

Acknowledgments   *ix*

1   Conjuring the Folk   *1*

2   Modernism and the Spectral Folk:
     Jean Toomer's *Cane*   *21*

3   Folklore and Migrant Labor:
     Zora Neale Hurston's *Mules and Men*   *43*

4   The Folk as Alternative Modernity:
     Claude McKay's *Banana Bottom*   *63*

5   Rural Modernity, Migration, and the Gender of
     Autonomy: The Novels of George Wylie Henderson   *85*

6   The Folk, the Race, and Class Consciousness:
     Richard Wright's *12 Million Black Voices*   *113*

7   Conclusion: Local Histories and
     World Historical Narrative   *131*

Notes   *135*

Select Bibliography   *157*

Index   *171*

Acknowledgments

This book project has been sustained by a number of enabling individuals and institutions. It began as a dissertation in the English department at the University of Chicago, where it was guided by Kenneth Warren and Loren Kruger; I am grateful to both of them for their careful readings of the work in progress as well as for their encouragement at every stage of the project. As I began the study, conversations with a number of scholars helped me to define its scope and to find sources I had not considered: I am particularly appreciative for suggestions made by Benedict Anderson, Lauren Berlant, and Katie Trumpener. A number of public forums provided an opportunity to try out the arguments of the chapters, and comments from the audiences there often yielded the impetus for strategic revision: I am grateful to audiences at the Chicago Humanities Institute, the African-American Studies Workshop at the University of Chicago, the Midwest Modern Language Association, the Twentieth-Century Literature Conference at the University of Louisville, and the American Studies Seminar at the Université d'Ouagadougou. During those years in Chicago Aditya Behl, Mark Morrisson, Laura Reed-Morrisson, Pamela Robertson Wojcik, and Angela Sorby read portions of the work and offered their insights on the argument as well as on the processes of researching and writing generally; their friendship has sustained me and this project since my departure.

At the University of Michigan the community of scholars at the Center for Afroamerican and African Studies (CAAS) provided a welcoming and supportive environment in which to transform the study into a book. I am particularly grateful to Simon Gikandi, Earl Lewis, and Patsy Lewis for their comments on some of the chapters. Audiences at CAAS's Faculty Colloquium Series and the African Peoples in the Industrial Age Working Group provided helpful responses to my work as well. CAAS's administrative staff helped me in myriad ways: thanks are due to Gerri Brewer, Tammy Davis, Elizabeth James, Sharon Patton, Camille Spencer, and Evans Young. During this period Cynthia Wilson of the Tuskegee University archives helped me with my research on George Wylie Henderson; information in the archives there enabled me to find Roz Allen, Henderson's stepdaughter, who graciously gave me access to his papers. David Ebershoff was a gracious host during my visits to see her and other resources in New York City. Correspondence with Barbara Foley and Robert Hemenway helped me to tie up some loose ends.

During 1998–99 I returned to the University of Chicago to put final touches on the book as a guest of the Center for the Study of Race, Politics, and Culture. I thank the center for its hospitality; I particularly appreciated the administrative support of Evalyn Tennant and Julia Nitti during my time there. I also welcomed the assistance of Rick and Pamela Robertson Wojcik, who helped keep me housed in various ways during this time.

I am happy to acknowledge generous financial support for this work. A Jacob K. Javits Fellowship from the United States Department of Education funded most of my doctoral education, including the first year's work on the dissertation. A summer research fellowship from the Mellon Foundation allowed me to develop my dissertation proposal, while a Mellon Dissertation-Year Fellowship enabled me to finish writing the dissertation. Two graduate scholarships from Bowdoin College, the Nathan Webb Research Scholarship in English and the Wilmot Brookings Mitchell Graduate Scholarship, provided additional support throughout my graduate education. And a Rockefeller Humanities Fellowship funded the year of postdoctoral research at the University of Michigan. I am grateful to all of these institutions for having faith in me and in this project.

Editors and peer reviewers from a number of venues have had a shaping influence on this book. At the University of Michigan Press LeAnn Fields shepherded the manuscript through the review process; I am grateful to her, the board of the press, and the anonymous reviewers for their insights and support. George Hutchinson, who chose not to remain anonymous, provided extremely thorough, intelligent, and supportive commentary in his reader's report; this book has benefited enormously from his careful attention to it. Chapter 3 first appeared in slightly different form as "Migrant Labor, Folklore, and Resistance in Hurston's Polk County: Reframing *Mules and Men*"; it is reprinted from *African American Review* (1999). Chapter 4 was also published in the *Journal of Modern Literature* (1999). Reprinted with permission of Indiana University Press. The two block prints by Lowell Leroy Balcolm are reprinted from *Ollie Miss*, by George Wylie Henderson, by permission of Roslyn K. Allen.

Several individuals have had an important, though indirect, influence on the development of my work here. Three extraordinary professors at Bowdoin College—Joseph Litvak, Gayle Pemberton, and Marilyn Reizbaum—taught me lessons that continue to motivate my work. My extended family always took an interest in what I was doing and never complained about how impractical it was. Finally, I want to acknowledge the enabling support of my parents: my education has been as much their project as my own.

1

Conjuring the Folk

In his 1940 memoir, *The Big Sea*, Langston Hughes wrote that "the ordinary Negroes hadn't heard of the Negro Renaissance. And if they had, it hadn't raised their wages any."[1] Hughes's comment suggests a critique of the Renaissance by noting the divide between the artistic activities of black elites and the lot of the working black masses. Despite Alain Locke's expectation, expressed in the opening essay of *The New Negro,* that artists of "the present generation will have added the motives of self-expression and spiritual development to the old and still unfinished task of making material headway and progress," the latter task remained unfinished for elites and masses alike when the movement lost momentum with the fall of the stock market in 1929.[2] But, while the Renaissance failed to deliver on the promise to improve the lot of the "ordinary Negroes," to use Hughes's term, a good deal of the art produced in the period sought to bring the black masses into representation. Locke himself attributed much of the energy behind the movement to the "migrant masses" who flooded Harlem and other urban centers during the period: "In a real sense it is the rank and file who are leading, and the leaders who are following. A transformed and transforming psychology permeates the masses."[3] Many artists, themselves recent migrants, sought to capture this energy by bringing popular forms like spirituals and folklore into new aesthetic settings and by telling stories about ordinary Negroes. Thus, while the Renaissance artists may be said to have failed on the promise to improve the economic circumstances of the black masses, it was not because they ignored them. Rather, many of them attended to the divide between elite culture and popular culture by translating across the divide.

The dynamic relation between metropolitan artistic culture and its popular referents is the central problem addressed in this book. In particular, I take up one of the more persistent tropes in this dynamic, the *folk,* and explore its workings in African-American literary culture during the period between the world wars.[4] Poets, novelists, folklorists, photographers, sociologists, and historians all engaged the discourse on the folk in their work. I trace the discourse on the folk through a number of formal settings in this study, devoting chapters to Jean Toomer's experimental collection of poetry and vignettes, *Cane* (1923); Zora Neale Hurston's ethnography, *Mules and Men* (1935); Claude McKay's naturalistic romance of post-emancipation Jamaica, *Banana Bottom* (1933); George Wylie Henderson's female Bildungsroman about an Alabama sharecropper, *Ollie Miss* (1935), and its sequel concerning her migrant son, *Jule* (1946); and Richard Wright's photo-documentary history, *12 Million Black Voices* (1941). In each case I examine the ways in which the folk is mediated through literary forms.

The discourse on the folk was widely available to those who had followed the debate among black intellectuals concerning the proper role of labor in advancing the "race." At the turn of the century W. E. B. Du Bois wrote in *The Souls of Black Folk* that "the training of the schools we need to-day more than ever,—the training of deft hands, quick eyes and ears, and above all the broader, deeper, higher culture of gifted minds and pure hearts."[5] Du Bois's advocacy of higher education for the "Talented Tenth" was meant to create a vanguard of intellectuals who would enable the race to progress economically and culturally.[6] In contrast, Booker T. Washington, who rose to prominence as a spokesman for the black agrarian class in the post-Reconstruction South, sought to instill in this class self-reliance and "the dignity of labour."[7] For Washington the folk were to be educated for a trade in which they could earn an honest living; their aspirations were to be humble. Worried about the fate of urban migrants, Washington wished that he could remove them from the city and "plant them upon the soil" in the Southern countryside from which they had departed.[8] Washington expended considerable effort in discouraging blacks from migrating; Du Bois, by contrast, urged blacks to refuse the national imperative to "be content to be servants, and nothing more" and encouraged elites to deliver the masses from unrewarding labor.[9]

But, despite the efforts of black intellectuals to shape migration and labor patterns at the turn of the century, the black masses had mostly voted with their feet by the end of World War I. The years between the wars saw dramatic changes in the economic and social organization of life in African America. Broadly speaking, the mechanization of agricultural labor and the growth of industrial production, along with persistent racial injustice and the hope for improved living conditions, encouraged black Southerners to seek a new life in urban centers. Through the Great Migration approximately five million blacks moved to the cities of Chicago, New York, Detroit, and the like between the start of World War I and 1960. While many blacks remained in the South, African-American literary culture in this period tended to emanate from metropolitan centers and was frequently produced by recent migrants. Much as Locke had suggested, cultural life in the period was energized by migration. By the 1925 publication of *The New Negro*, migration had decisively reorganized contemporary African America.

The practice of conjuring up an African-American folk thus produced a compelling vision of collective origins for metropolitan African Americans. As millions of black Americans left agricultural settings to pursue employment in urban centers, the *folk* seemed an appropriate term to describe these masses of former sharecroppers and farmhands who were moving across the landscape. Additionally, in homology with narratives of European national development, the folk provided the telos in narratives that sought to describe the development of the race into modernity.[10] As Benedict Anderson has argued, novels, newspapers, and other printed narrative forms provide an "imagined linkage" between disparate individuals through which they can imagine a shared temporality; such was the case with metropolitan representations of folk life.[11] I have chosen the folk as a topic for extended study not only because it is one of the most salient figures of the period but also because the topic tends to animate broader interpretive questions about the relation between literature and modernity.

My aim in this opening chapter is to develop a historicist method for interpreting the literary mediation of the folk in this era. I begin by considering the role the folk plays in critical histories of African-American literature, paying particular attention to the development of vernacular criticism in the 1980s. Following the post-structuralist critique of vernacular criticism, I explore the possible responses to the (largely unfulfilled) call by the post-structuralist critics for a historicist criticism. Hazel Carby and Robin Kelley have recently argued that the historical conditions giving rise to modernity also provoke the discourse on the folk. I examine recent work in post-colonial studies that relates modernity to modernization and that argues for a recognition of "many modernities," to use the words of one argument, in place of the global modernity assumed by the European Enlightenment.[12] With this sense of multiple destinations in mind, I seek to locate the folk through a brief discussion of two major poets of the era, Sterling Brown and Langston Hughes. This inquiry leads me to define a method of historical description that relates the ideological and narrative dimensions of form to contextual information so as to advance an understanding of the mediation of the folk in metropolitan art.

The Post-Structuralist Critique of Vernacular Criticism

Literary histories that address texts authored by African Americans have typically relied upon canonical, or tradition-centered, narratives for their coherence. In such narratives the folk has often been portrayed as the wellspring from which literary culture has flowed. Major studies such as Robert Bone's *Negro Novel in America* and Bernard Bell's *Afro-American Novel and Its Tradition* use the folk as an organizing trope.[13] In general, these studies have treated the folk as an assumed category of person rather than as a contested vision of collectivity. Consequently, the tradition-centered approach tends to underplay social conflict in pursuit of a neatly unfolding narrative of collective development and achievement. This practice gained momentum in the 1980s with the advent of vernacular criticism, by which critics attempted to identify the unique formal attributes of this literature to show how they form, across time, an African-American tradition. Frequently, the vernacular tradition also found its origins in the folk, conceived here as the authentic voice of the unconscious of the race. As I have suggested, this critical enterprise has recently come under scrutiny from post-structuralist critics, who have noted that for the vernacular critics the folk operates as an unmediated category. This critique forms an important precursor to my work in these pages, and for that reason I want now to rehearse the post-structuralist critique of vernacular criticism.

In her study of essentialism in contemporary literary theory, Diana

Fuss has observed that vernacular theory has been preoccupied with the folk as the origin of authentic African-American discourse. Fuss directs her attention to recent work by Henry Louis Gates Jr. and Houston Baker Jr.:

> What makes the vernacular (the language of "the folk") so powerful a theme in the work of both Gates and Baker is precisely the fact that it operates as a phantasm, a hallucination of lost origins. It is in the quest to recover, reinscribe, and revalorize the black vernacular that essentialism inheres in the work of two otherwise antiessentialist theorists.[14]

As a corrective scholarly exercise, Fuss suggests that we produce historical accounts of the sign *race*, noting that "such historically specific studies remind us that racial categories are politically shaped, that 'race consciousness' is a modern phenomenon, and that the very meaning of 'race' has shifted over time and across cultures."[15] In Fuss's revisionary account the folk could then be seen as a hallucinatory effect produced by a modern phenomenon, race consciousness.

As I have already suggested, there is good reason to critique the claims for folk authenticity in vernacular theory. In *Modernism and the Harlem Renaissance* Baker locates an authentic African-American voice in the folk when he contrasts Du Bois's *Souls of Black Folk* and Washington's *Up from Slavery* with respect to voice: "Washington remains the spokesperson *on behalf* of the folk (who, really, are not a FOLK in his account); Du Bois, by melodious contrast, lifts his voice and transmutes his text into the FOLK's singing. If Washington provides a speaking manual, then Du Bois offers a singing book."[16] Du Bois, who was educated in Europe and at Fisk University and received a Ph.D. degree from Harvard, would seem to be an unlikely candidate to sing the unmediated voice of the folk. Nevertheless, in Baker's description the narrator of *The Souls of Black Folk* acts as a spiritual channel through which the collective voice may be heard:

> The narrator's cultural performance, therefore, can give life to a sign ("folk") that connotes a pretechnological but nonetheless vital stage of human development toward ideals of CULTURE. A FOLK is always, out of the very necessities of definition, possessed of a

guiding or tutelary spirit—an immanent quality of aspiration that
is fittingly sounded in its treasured rituals, in its spirit houses or
masks of performance.[17]

Although Baker notes that *folk* is a sign and thereby suggests that he
takes the folk to be constructed through language, he never develops
this position with any consistency. He historicizes the folk ("The folk
not only come to the domain of culture but also refigure the very notion
of 'culture' for the modern world")[18] and shows how the 1920s generation of the Harlem Renaissance had to use standard forms, rather than
"unadorned or primitive *folk* creations,"[19] to prove their artistic merit,
but he sees in later work of the 1930s a return "to rendering the actual
folk voice in its simple, performative eloquence."[20] In the final pages of
Baker's book he turns to a discussion of the "genuine cultural authenticity" of African-American expressive culture[21] and calls attention to
the "traceable ancestry that judged certain select sounds appealing and
considered them efficacious in the office of a liberating advancement of
THE RACE."[22]

As Fuss has noted, Baker's concern with recovering the vernacular
roots of African-American culture is shared by Henry Louis Gates Jr.,
whose insistence on attention to formal analysis is often accompanied
by a yearning for these roots. For example, in a discussion of his strategies for editing the *Norton Anthology of African-American Literature* Gates
admits that "my own biases toward canon-formation are to stress the
formal relationship that obtains among texts in the black tradition—
relations of revision, echo, call and response, antiphony, what have
you—and to stress the vernacular roots of the tradition."[23]

In her response to Gates's remarks on canon formation, Barbara
Johnson argues that "the terms 'black' and 'white' often imply a relation of mutual exclusion. This binary model is based on two fallacies:
the fallacy of positing the existence of pure, unified, and separate traditions, and the fallacy of spatialization."[24] And she further examines the
term *vernacular*, noting that its Latin root means "a slave born in his
master's home"; she concludes that "the vernacular is a difference
within, not a realm outside."[25] Johnson would have us see that "black"
and "white" literatures are mutually intricated, rather than mutually
exclusive, and she would urge us to see the vernacular as located
within that intrication, rather than in a separate realm of black differ-

ence. Moreover, as Kenneth Warren has argued, there are dangers in centering a criticism and a politics on black difference: "as an interpretive and political strategy vernacular critique entails serious liabilities, not the least of which are the depoliticization of black cultural discussion and the tendency to suppress and discredit internal dissent."[26]

As with most attempts to construct a canon around the notion of tradition, vernacular criticism claims to honor history by dehistoricizing the texts it celebrates. It posits African-American folk expression as the authentic origin of a cultural tradition and includes texts that repeat its figures of speech and formal patterns in its canon. If we accept the charges that Fuss, Johnson, and Warren have leveled against vernacular criticism—namely, that it posits an essentialist origin, it reifies tradition, and it can operate to suppress dissent—we can return to Fuss's request for "historically specific studies" with a sense of urgency.[27] The critique of vernacular criticism from the standpoint of post-structuralism leads us to consider the folk as a historically contingent constituency. For Fuss this revelation might allow us to exorcize the "phantasm," or "hallucination," of the folk as produced, in her account, by modern race consciousness.[28] Such an exorcism does not go very far toward offering a historical account of folk aesthetics in this period. Moreover, it raises bell hooks's worry that "a totalizing critique of 'subjectivity, essence, identity' can seem very threatening to marginalized groups, for whom it has been an active gesture of political resistance to name one's identity as part of a struggle to challenge domination."[29] In place of a totalizing critique of the folk as phantasmatic essence, we can offer historically specific studies that acknowledge the numerous representations of the folk in this period.

The Folk, Modernity, and Historicism

How do we specify the historical contingency of texts addressing the folk? Hazel Carby's work on this topic attempts to answer the question by relating the folk to a specific mode of production. Making much the same critique of vernacular criticism as the post-structuralist critics, she argues that "the critical vernacular itself dissolves historical difference."[30] In "Ideologies of Black Folk" Carby writes:

A mythology of the rural South conflates the nineteenth and twentieth centuries and two very distinct modes of production, slavery
and sharecropping, into one mythical rural folk existence. Of
course, the ideological function of a tradition is to create unity out
of disunity and to resolve the social contradiction, or differences,
between texts. Consequently, not only are the specificities of a
slave existence as opposed to a sharecropping existence negated,
but the urban imagination and urban histories are also repressed.[31]

For Carby an appreciation of the differences between modes of production will lead us to see the literature of the folk as "romantic"[32] and
"outside history,"[33] and it will direct attention to the "transformative
power of both historical and urban consciousness."[34] The critical focus
on the folk, Carby would conclude, has occluded important historical
distinctions concerning modes of production in the rural South and has
neglected the history of migration and urbanization in the early half of
this century. For Carby, too, the folk are to be regarded as something of
a hallucination, a romantic mirage that must be demystified so that critical attention may be paid to the nitty-gritty of urban history.

   Carby uses historical information to deflate the utopianism of folk
romance. But even if one were to grant that the discourse on the folk is
fundamentally ahistorical, how would one explain the historical contingencies that give rise to this discourse? As my earlier comments have
indicated, the *literary* representation of the folk is necessarily linked
with urbanization. Robin Kelley reminds us, for example, that "'folk'
has no meaning without 'modern.' Unless we deconstruct the terms
'folk' and 'authentic' . . . and see 'modern' and 'traditional' as mutually
constitutive and constituting, we will miss the dynamic process by
which culture is created as well as its relationship to constantly shifting
experiences, changes in technologies, and commodification."[35] Carby,
too, would see the discourses on authenticity and tradition as arising
out of the dynamic cultural processes of modernity, although her conclusion suggests that aesthetic treatments of the folk attempt to cloud
historical recognition through romantic rhetoric. I will adduce some
examples later of folk romances that form historical analyses of modernity and modernization. For now, however, I want to examine the concept of modernity so as to extend Carby's and Kelley's inquiries concerning the historical underpinnings of folk discourse.

   The experience of modernity may be chiefly understood as a form of historical consciousness by which the subject experiences the present in relation to a mythic past so as to speculate about the future.[36] Perry Anderson has noted that modernity is "neither economic process nor cultural vision but the *historical experience* mediating one to the other."[37] The underpinnings of this historical experience have come under scrutiny in recent years, for, while the historical experience of modernity may be described as a formal cognitive relation, this kind of historical cognition itself arises out of a specific context. Recent post-colonial criticism has come to identify this context, broadly, as that of Enlightenment rationality and economic imperialism: Dipesh Chakrabarty has noted in "Postcoloniality and the Artifice of History" that, "if a language, as has been said, is but a dialect backed up by an army, the same could be said of the narratives of 'modernity' that, almost universally today, point to a certain 'Europe' as the primary habitus of the modern."[38] In mediating between the economic and the cultural, the modern subject rationalizes that relation and thereby projects an autonomous self. This ideal of autonomy corresponds to European expectations for modern citizenship, through which individuals have rights, equality, and freedom.[39] In addressing what he calls "the problematic of nonmetropolitan histories,"[40] Chakrabarty discovers a "transition narrative" in which "the overriding (if often implicit) themes are those of development, modernization, capitalism."[41] These narratives of transition expect the same ending: the realization of autonomous, modern citizenship in capitalist democracy. Histories that do not match this outcome read as stories of failed development or unfulfilled promise.

Chakrabarty reads the links between modernity, modernization, and narrative as productive of a "politics of despair" for those who would pursue nonmetropolitan historiography: "This is a history that will attempt the impossible: to look toward its own death by tracing that which resists and escapes the best human effort at translation across cultural and other semiotic systems, so that the world may once again be imagined as radically heterogeneous."[42] Some recent work in post-colonial studies has sought to interpret the heterogeneity of the modern world by opening up consideration of multiple modernities rather than just one. In their introduction to *Modernity and Its Malcontents* Jean and John Comaroff demonstrate that the concept of modernity is a legacy of classic social theory, which held the consensus that "modernizing social forces and material forms would have the universal effect of eroding local cultural differences," and they note that this consensus held for optimistic capitalists and dismayed supporters of local autonomy alike.[43] The Comaroffs argue that modernization has not effected a homogeneous global culture but has instead fostered "many modernities" in which expansive markets, mass media, technological change, and hegemonic ideologies have shaped, and in turn are shaped by, various local cultures.[44] They maintain that "modernity— itself always an imaginary construction of the present in terms of a mythic past—has its own magicalities, its own enchantments."[45] The Comaroffs' account complements Chakrabarty's critique of the Enlightenment origins of the modern subject (and the modernization narrative), while it also multiplies the locations of modernity to account for the radical heterogeneity—the many modernities—that Chakra-barty seeks to uncover.

In this new interpretive context it is possible to reexamine modern representations of the folk. Under the theory of one, global modernity such engagements with the folk would of necessity be situated at the telos of the transition narrative of modernization (in essence, as the premodern) or would be read as stories of unfulfilled development. But in a world with many modernities it is possible to see a folk ideal of subsistence farming as offering one route to political modernity and economic autonomy. In his recent remapping of the political geography of black culture in *The Black Atlantic*, Paul Gilroy observes that "modern black political culture has always been more interested in the relationship of identity to roots and rootedness than in seeing identity as a process of movement and mediation that is more appropriately approached via the homonym routes."[46] Gilroy stresses routes over roots in order to explore migrancy, hybridity, and transnational discourse as a counterculture to the modernity offered by essentialist, nationalist models for understanding race and culture.[47] His taxonomy between rooted identity and a fluid, migratory identity is useful as we consider the circumstances under which folk aesthetics developed in African-American literature in the early twentieth century. The antinomy between roots and routes that Gilroy proposes has a metaphorical affinity with the options available to agricultural laborers in this period: rootedness implies a fixed, sufficient relation to the land through subsistence farming, while its antinomy stresses migrant labor as a route toward gaining a wage with which to participate in a wider market. The latter, modernized agriculture, in which labor is rational-

ized and cash crops are grown for circulation in a global commodities
market, offers workers the least sure route to autonomy (crops and
markets fail, and the worker may starve in the field or be forced to
move), yet it also offers the freedom of greater mobility. Subsistence
farming, by comparison, promises the worker a sense of autonomy,
both economic and political, while fixing the worker geographically;
some narratives route black protagonists toward the rootedness of this
mode of production by suggesting that it best accommodates these
requirements for modern citizenship. To those seeking autonomy
through agricultural production, subsistence farming was seen as a
workable option and not simply a return to an idyllic past. This fact
complicates the transition narrative of modernization by showing that
supposedly superseded modes of production may yet yield political
modernity. In this heterogeneous context, then, an engagement with
the folk may address political and economic needs in the present.

Locating the Folk

In the previous two sections I have dissected two master narratives
about the folk. The first, vernacular criticism, used the figure of an
African-American folk to fix the origins of an authentic literary tradition; this master narrative was shown to dehistoricize the works in its
canon, to reify black expression by recourse to an essentialized notion
of race, and thereby to minimize political differences among African
Americans. The second, the transition narrative of development, was
seen to universalize what is a Eurocentric ideal of selfhood, economic
change, and national citizenship. In both cases our critical dissection
provoked a need for a revised critical method: the post-structuralist critique of vernacular criticism led us to need historically sensitive studies
of the folk that emphasized the contingencies determining its formations; the post-colonial critique of the transition narrative of development led us to look for how the folk emerges in a world with multiple
modernities. At issue, then, is the inadequacy of master narratives
when compared with the varied locations of folk-centered cultural formations. A brief look at two of the major poets of the period, Sterling
Brown and Langston Hughes, will reveal how various can be the
results of an artistic engagement with the folk. Brown and Hughes are
often paired in literary histories of the period, but, as these examples

will show, their poetic presentations of folk materials and lives convey different understandings about the prospects for political modernity in the agrarian South.

In Brown's *Southern Road* (1932) the poet reveals a landscape through which black Americans move restlessly. The "Odyssey of Big Boy," for example, describes the life journey of a male migrant worker whose career takes him through a dozen states (North and South) and as many physically demanding jobs. In "Long Gone" the speaker is a railroad man who, departing, explains to his lover that "it jes' ain' nachal / Fo' to stay here long."[48] He is, by nature, restless:

> I don't know which way I'm travelin'—
>   Far or near,
> All I knows fo' certain is
>   I cain't stay here.
>
>   (9, ll. 29–32)

This may be so because of the nature of the worker and his work, but Brown's collection also suggests that travel on the Southern road is no leisurely stroll down a country lane. The poem "Southern Road," after all, is based on a chain gang song. To be sure, there are routes with utopian destinations—in "Mecca," for instance, the Northern city is pictured as "the promised land" for two recent migrants (109, l. 9). And other urbanites pine for "de country" (105, l. 3), as does the speaker with the "Tin Roof Blues":

> Leave 'is dirty city, take my foot up in my hand,
> Dis do-dirty city, take my foot up in my hand,
> Git down to de livin' what a man kin understand.
>
>   (105, ll. 7–9)

The preponderant mood in *Southern Road,* however, is anti-pastoral. In "Convict" Jim is on the chain gang and spends "Daytime on the highways, / Nights in hell" (93, ll. 11–12); as he works on the gang, he looks at his home of Shantytown, "the longed for heaven / He's returning to" (94, ll. 27–28), and sees:

> Sleeping hounds everywhere,
> Flies crawling thick;

Grown ups drunken
And children sick.

(93, ll. 17–24)

This country scene is a pastoral "heaven" only in the ironic sense.
Brown's Southern road takes us to quagmires where African Americans get caught in "filth and squalor / And miseries" (94, ll. 23–24).
This sense of the Southern earth as quicksand comes through again in
"Riverbank Blues," in which the speaker warns against getting too
firmly rooted at the river's edge because "muddy water roundabout a
man's roots, / Keep him soaked and stranded and git him weak" (99, ll.
7–8). Ostensibly, the poem addresses the complacency of those who
waited too long to escape the devastating 1927 flood of the Mississippi
Valley. But the speaker hears an inner voice that reaches beyond this
circumstance to draw a larger moral about rootedness:

"Man got his sea too lak de Mississippi
Ain't got so long for a whole lot longer way,
Man better move some, better not git rooted
Muddy water fool you, ef you stay. . . ."

(100, ll. 29–32)

Clearly, Brown stresses routes over roots (to use Gilroy's terms) in this
poem. This stress is amplified by the ambiguity of the collection's title:
the *Southern Road*, as Vera Kutzinski has pointed out, is a "kinetic
trope" that links the symbolic landscapes of North and South without
exactly establishing either as the definitive point of departure or destination.[49] This movement between symbolic landscapes is underwritten
by Brown's poetic practice, in which folk dialect and forms like the
blues ballad are transformed into written verse.

Of course, Brown was not the first African-American poet to use
dialect and oral forms in his written verse: nineteenth-century poets
such as Paul Laurence Dunbar had achieved great popularity from the
practice. Thus, when we see that Alain Locke declared Brown to be "the
New Negro Folk-Poet," we should read particular stress on the words
new negro.[50] The modernity of Brown's verse has often been noted.
While a number of critics have tried to put Brown's restless folk into a
tradition-centered model,[51] many recent critics have described his
poetic technique in terms of modernization.[52] Kimberly Benston, for

example, argues that Brown did not write so much to recreate the past as he did to imaginatively reconstruct the present through inherited forms:

> Instead of cultivating nostalgic apparitions or resurrecting conventional images, Brown turned to the past to create a new yet tradition-inspired word-as-voice in which artist and audience, envisaged and repeated, partake equally in the poetic process. Brown's revisionary encounter with folk forms turns finally on the pointed reminder that "dialect" means a talking between subjects.[53]

Brown's poetry seeks routes for talking between subjects and places, not the purity of "racial" roots; neither form nor content is especially settled, as the blues verses that warn about rootedness in "Riverbank Blues" make clear.

Langston Hughes is also well-known for using the blues in modern poetic settings. As Robert Stepto has observed, "In the field of blues poetry, Brown matched Langston Hughes step by step, or innovation by innovation,"[54] especially with respect to form. Hughes, who praised "the low-down folks, the so-called common element" in "The Negro Artist and the Racial Mountain" (1926),[55] made it a particular project to bring those "folks" into representation. As Arnold Rampersad has put it, "Hughes worked to link the lowly blues to formal poetry in order that its brilliance might be recognized by the world."[56] In some ways this project was more appropriate for him than for Brown: Brown had grown up on the campus of Howard University, where he eventually taught for many years after training at Williams and Harvard; Hughes moved between working-class and intellectual circles frequently, leaving classes at Columbia University, for example, to work as a sailor. What, then, would be the routes and destinations that Hughes would feature in his poetic engagement with the folk?

Langston Hughes's poetry represents the broad range of attitudes regarding the geographical destinations of the routes available to African Americans in this period. Poems like "Daybreak in Alabama" (1940) and "Carolina Cabin" (1947) celebrate the simple, pastoral beauty of the South; others, like "Share-croppers" (1935) and "Georgia Dusk" (1955), detail the hard labor and violence that characterize this region:

> Sometimes a wind in the Georgia dusk
> Scatters hate like seed
> To sprout its bitter barriers
> Where the sunsets bleed.[57]

Often, the bitter harvest in the South leads blacks to migrate North: in "The South" (1922), for example, the South is a "dark-eyed whore" who spits in the face of the black speaker, who determines to "seek the North— / The cold-faced North" because she is "a kinder mistress."[58] The poet in "The South" would rather stay in his home region, but other poems on migration, like "One-Way Ticket" (1949) and "Bound No'th Blues" (1926), are less equivocal about their speakers' preference for the outbound destination. A number of Hughes's works on recent migrants in the city, however, express ambivalence about the outcome of migration. These include "Migration" (1923), about a "little Southern colored child" who is taunted by his white and colored schoolmates because of his darkness, and several of the poems in *One-Way Ticket* (1949)—notably "Restrictive Covenants," "Visitors to the Black Belt," and "Juice Joint: Northern City."[59] The migrant's disappointment in the North and nostalgia for the South comes forward most forcefully in some of Hughes's blues poems, especially "Po' Boy Blues" (1926), "Evenin' Air Blues" (1941), and "Homesick Blues" (1926). In his 1939 collaboration with Richard Wright, "Red Clay Blues," the migrant returns to the fields of Georgia:

> Pavement's hard on my feet, I'm
> Tired o' this city street.
> Goin' back to Georgia where
> That red clay can't be beat.[60]

The tactile pleasures of sinking one's bare feet in the earth lead the migrant to "want my little farm back";[61] clearly the migrant wants to grow more than the bitter harvest Hughes would later feature in "Georgia Dusk." Perhaps he even had in mind the metaphorical harvest celebrated in "Freedom's Plow" (1943). This long, jingoistic poem, performed on the radio with musical accompaniment and published as a pamphlet, narrates the history of the United States as the nurturing and development of the "seed of freedom."[62] Beginning at a very basic level

with the statement "When a man starts out to build a world, / He starts
first with himself,"[63] the poem enjoins the collective words of black
slaves to voice the national imperative to keep sowing the seed:

> A long time ago,
> An enslaved people heading toward freedom
> Made up a song:
>   *Keep Your Hand On The Plow! Hold On!*
> That plow plowed a new furrow
> Across the field of history.
> Into that furrow the freedom seed was dropped.
> From that seed a tree grew, is growing, will ever grow.
> That tree is for everybody,
> For all America, for all the world.
> May its branches spread and its shelter grow
> Until all races and all peoples know its shade.
>
> KEEP YOUR HAND ON THE PLOW!
>   HOLD ON![64]

Obviously meant to inspire Americans during World War II, the poem
makes a standard link between individual effort, agricultural labor,
and political modernity: if Americans work hard and tend their fields
well, they will eventually achieve the freedom they desire.

My survey of Hughes's poetic treatment of the folk ends with his
emphasis on rootedness, an emphasis that differs markedly from the
preponderance of routes in Brown's poetry and an emphasis that
diverges from other routes and attitudes one finds reading through
Hughes's canon itself. Hughes's folk are quite literally all over the map,
formally and ideologically; looking for Langston, as the title of Isaac
Julien's 1989 film puts it, will lead one in many different directions.[65]
My point here is that cultural formations engaging the folk resist the
master narratives of vernacular criticism and the transition narrative of
development. The mediation of the folk varies by author and within the
canon of each author: the locations of the folk are multiple. Through
examination of the formal and ideological contingencies shaping these
works, we can discover the ways in which they allow readers and writers to speculate about aspirations for political modernity as well as to
respond to the pressures of modernization under global capitalism. By

situating these works in this speculative context, I mean to open up a consideration of their political instrumentality.[66] The vernacular critics have depoliticized these writings by suggesting that their chief mission is to act as contributions to a tradition centered on the romance of racial origins.[67] A non-canonical, historically based method will allow us to consider the alternative modernities these works entertain, while it will also draw attention to the linguistic and formal innovations these writers used to conjure up their aesthetic visions of the folk.[68]

Forms of Modernity in African America

The forerunning critical meditations have led me to formulate the method and scope of this book. Having freed the folk from fixed meanings in the master narratives of vernacular criticism and economic development, I began to view the discursive possibilities of the engagement with the folk with fresh interest. As I read through the works of Jean Toomer, Arna Bontemps, Jessie Fauset, Nella Larsen, Claude McKay, Zora Neale Hurston, George Wylie Henderson, George Lee, Langston Hughes, Countee Cullen, Rudolph Fisher, Richard Wright, Ann Petry, and others, I began to see meanings about the folk that were not conceptually available to me using the two master narratives. Indeed, aesthetic settings of the folk vary tremendously across genre and across the political spectrum. What emerges from my reading is not a coherent tradition but a discordant and engaging conversation on the question of modernity in African America. My critical task is to find ways to let that conversation be heard.

Given Perry Anderson's definition of modernity as "neither economic process nor cultural vision but the *historical experience* mediating one to the other," I intend to investigate the problem of modernity in these texts as one of mediation.[69] How, I wonder, did these mediators of the folk relate economic change in the era to their cultural visions for African-American modernity? These metropolitan artistic works represent highly formalized mediations of historical experience. Drawing generally on Fredric Jameson's study of the "ideology of form" in *The Political Unconscious* and on Hayden White's analysis of "the content of the form" in historical narrative, I will pay particular attention to how the formal expectations of genre shaped the mediation of the folk in various instances.[70] Additionally, recognizing that the tropes of *modernization* and *development* to which the folk is often related imply stories of change, I will look carefully at the narrative situation of the folk within these forms. These narrative presentations of the folk sometimes draw on the master narratives of tradition and development; often, however, they resist or transform those broader narratives.

This book will unfold as a series of historicist interpretations of the literary mediation of the folk. Having surveyed the archive of folk-centered works, I have selected texts to represent a range of genres, authors, and geographical locations. A comparative assessment of the discursive situation of the folk will reveal the many positions available in the conversation about African-American modernity. My selection has also been determined by an interest in seeing how economic process is related to cultural vision through these mediations; I have chosen texts that thematize that relation. My method of historical description will be to relate the ideological and narrative dimensions of form to contextual information gleaned from research in sociology, labor history, literary critical history, and anything else that comes to mind; these descriptions will be woven into close readings of particular works. This method attempts to survey the historical field shaped selectively by these conjurings of the folk.

Such a survey can never be definitive, however. In considering these various forms of modernity in African America, I have not sought to define a new master narrative on the folk. My goal, as I have said, is to let the conversation on the folk be heard. In refusing to make a definitive and comprehensive account, I take some courage from recent comments by Myra Jehlen on the problem of historicism:

> There is no reason outside of the historian's sense of authority why historical narratives need resolve into single accounts. A scholarly history can be structured, rather than by a unified logic of its own, by an exposition of the known, the known in different versions, and the perhaps irrevocably unknown. The goal of a critical analysis is at any rate not a solution in the mathematical sense; rather, critics and historians produce useful descriptions or redeployments of texts and materials such that they are more accessible to being thought about.[71]

The interpretive analyses to follow make these texts, and the issues they raise, more accessible to being thought about. On the face of it, this is not a particularly ostentatious goal. Given the demonstrated weaknesses of vernacular theory and modernization theory for describing artistic engagements with the folk, however, this is a goal that needs urgently to be met. Moreover, given the persistence of folk-centered narratives of national and cultural development around the globe, this critical engagement with the problem is one that can have far-ranging consequences.

2

Modernism and the Spectral Folk: Jean Toomer's *Cane*

Jean Toomer's *Cane* (1923) repeatedly addresses the status of life in the rural South, less to inquire whether agrarian culture could be maintained than to pay tribute to its passing. Indeed, Toomer would refer to the book as a "swan-song"[1] for the African-American folk, indicating that he took folk life to be vanishing and worthy of a final artistic expression: "the Negro of the folk-song has all but passed away," he would tell Waldo Frank.[2] In *Cane*'s first section, set in rural Georgia, we encounter a poem in which the speaker is an auditor to the singing of both the soil and a "song-lit race of slaves."[3] In "Song of the Son" the son is a migrant, now returned to the place of his birth in the South. The second stanza presents the son speaking in apostrophe to the land, his parent:

> O land and soil, red soil and sweet-gum tree,
> So scant of grass, so profligate of pines,
> Now just before an epoch's sun declines
> Thy son, in time, I have returned to thee,
> Thy son, I have in time returned to thee.
>
> (14)

The son returns to a denuded pastoral scene "in time," but by this he does not mean he is in time to stop the milling of its forests. Rather, he is in time to catch the "plaintive soul" of the soil transmuted into a song that rides through the valley on pine smoke (14, l. 14). The son's relief is that he has not missed the brilliance of a sunset, the setting of the "song-lit race of slaves," and his motivation for seeing this spectacle is primarily aesthetic. This motivation is underscored in his second apostrophe, which he makes to "Negro slaves," whom he likens to "dark purple ripened plums" (14, l. 16). Since they are ripened and the tree has grown bare, he is happy to find that one plum and its seed have been saved for him. This seed will turn into "a singing tree" in the final stanza of the poem (14, l. 20), "Caroling softly souls of slavery" (14, l. 21). The folk in this poem has a spectral presence, for the souls of former slaves are transformed into the voice of a singing tree caroling an "everlasting song" (14, l. 20).[4] The landscape at the end of "Song of the Son" holds only an ornamental plum tree that sings instead of bearing fruit.

The son's return to the Southern countryside resembles the sojourn Toomer took to Sparta, Georgia, in 1921. Toomer spent two months as a substitute principal for a Negro agricultural and industrial training school there, and his encounter with students and sharecroppers led him to begin writing *Cane* while taking the train home to Washington, D.C.[5] While he may well have expected to have encountered a timeless rural South, Toomer discovered a Georgia in the midst of great economic change, as "Song of the Son" suggests. In his recent historical account, *Rural Worlds Lost: The American South, 1920–1960,* Jack Temple Kirby describes the state of affairs in Georgia's black belt:

> By the 1920s its lands were badly worn and eroded and infested with the dreaded boll weevil. Planters cut and sold their second-growth pine, leaving nothing of value on the land. They then began to withdraw, abandoning their property to the poor, or more commonly, to banks and insurance companies. . . . [W]here slaves first planted cotton, the plantation had broken down. This South was no longer modern in any sense.[6]

But if soil exhaustion and the boll weevil had rendered the South "no longer modern," Kirby shows us that "roughly between 1920 and 1960 the American South was modernized; it was not developed."[7] By this he means that, while paved roads, farm machinery, supermarkets, and the cash nexus reorganized agricultural labor and markets, there was no concomitant effort to ensure economic autonomy and political modernity for the agricultural workers who were displaced in this period. Accordingly, most displaced workers either migrated or lived in poverty. But when Toomer came to Hancock County in 1921, what we see now as a massive historical change was only beginning. Hancock County's population had been relatively stable from the turn of the century through 1920 but diminished by 29 percent between 1920 and 1930;[8] neighboring Greene County recorded its largest population to date in 1920, before losing nearly half of its black population by 1930.[9] Consequently, while a poem such as "Song of the Son" aims to lament the end of an era, it would seem to do so prematurely. Toomer's intervention on the scene of the changing Georgia countryside is curious, for he imagines the people who attend his school and work the nearby fields as spirits who will live on through their songs. This curious attitude arises out of an ambivalence toward the prospects for cultural and agricultural sustenance in this landscape. In some of the other works in *Cane* I will discuss, the "ripened plums" Toomer sees would be read as an agricultural metaphor for the fertile cultural circumstances here (14, l. 16): a bountiful harvest would give rise to joyous singing in the community. Here, however, the plum's seed produces disembodied songs from the antebellum era; the land sustains neither agricultural nor live cultural production. As we will see, *Cane* ambivalently entertains the possibility for black Southerners to achieve economic autonomy and political modernity in the modernized South, for the book seems both to honor rural life and to hasten its passing.

The "Identity through Form" Argument and Modernist Pastiche

Cane's engagement with both modernity and modernization has been at once the book's most attractive and elusive feature. Because the book addresses daily life in the rural South at the beginning of its transformation, it has about it the air of portent, of bearing witness to the passage of history. The book offers both the speculative pleasures of nostalgia and the certainty of historical testimony after the fact of modernization. Toomer's use of modernist formal gestures, such as imagism and pastiche, has underscored his interaction with the metropolitan literary culture of the 1920s and has contributed to *Cane*'s reception as that paradoxical entity, the modernist classic. *Cane* can be seen as both an interpretation of the modernization of African America and as a product of that very transformation, for *Cane* would seem to enact the process by which metropolitan cultural forms came to predominate: Toomer published a modernist book that included lyric poems about folk songs. In short, *Cane* is a particularly attractive work for readers attentive to the economic and cultural changes affecting African America in the 1920s.

But, as I have suggested, *Cane*'s position on modern culture has also been a frustratingly elusive feature of the book. *Cane*'s modernism—its lack of a coherent formal affiliation or overarching point of view—has made it difficult for readers to name the book's position on modernity. Most scholars have turned to Toomer's own writing on the book and to biographical information about the author to build up analyses that show how *Cane* is an allegory of the author's achievement of "identity through form."[10] Here *Cane* is a transitional space in which the author achieves "wholeness" through redemptive contact with the past. Nellie McKay, whose *Jean Toomer, Artist* is the most sophisticated and extensive articulation of this argument, describes Toomer's trip to Georgia and its generative effects: "He was moved by the folk spirit and the folk as by nothing else before, and he felt that he had found the missing element that he needed to harness his creative talents: a self-confirming sense of wholeness."[11] McKay's analysis, like that of many other critics, is both intentionalist and New Critical: it accepts the author's statements about his intentions for the book and uses these statements to demonstrate how the book fulfills his aspirations for a unified form, an organic whole. By accepting these assumptions, these scholars tend to subsume the book's engagement with modernity to their preoccupation with the artist's consciousness, as in Bernard Bell's description of the book as a poetic *Künstlerroman*.[12] McKay, for instance, locates modernization in Toomer's consciousness, arguing that "the external pressures that created the black folk culture also prevented it from comprehending its own historical and cultural significance. That was the responsibility of those who came later, those sufficiently removed from its influence to temper vision with objectivity and who were yet close enough to feel racial and/or emotional kinship with it."[13] McKay's assumptions lead her to the questionable conclusion that members of the African-American folk were incapable of self-consciousness. Further, her analysis would suggest that the value of a work like *Cane* lies in its contribution to a progressive teleology of racial development, of the coming-into-consciousness of modern African-

American subjectivity. The identity through form argument understands the book's engagement with modernity and modernization only as an enabling aspect of the artist's cognitive development.

When the identity through form argument addresses the formal qualities of *Cane,* it usually attempts to derive the transition narrative of modernization from the book's division into three sections, assigning each a position in various theories of historical, intellectual, and psychological development. Thus, Bernard Bell argues:

> Part 1, with its focus on the Southern past and the libido, presents the rural thesis, while Part 2, with its emphasis on the centers of commerce and the superego, offers the urban antithesis. Part 3 then functions as a synthesis of the earlier sections with Kabnis representing the black writer whose difficulty in resolving the tension of his double-consciousness prevents him from tapping the creative reservoir of his soul.[14]

This schematization of the book through Hegelian, Freudian, Gurdjieffian, and Du Boisian paradigms is compatible with the New Critical underpinnings of the identity through form argument in that it sees the movement of the book as progressing toward wholeness.[15] While the incorporation of the "rural thesis" and "urban antithesis" into the identity through form argument complicates our understanding of the book's relation to its historical moment, this gesture fails to capture the full resonance of *Cane*'s engagement with history because the argument is fundamentally committed to proving that the book is a unified and fully formed masterpiece. Indeed, this argument collapses the multiple histories of rural and urban lives presented in *Cane* into one history, the history of the artist and his search for a satisfyingly complete expressive form.

One way to read history back into *Cane* is to address its status as pastiche.[16] The pages of *Cane* present multiple forms, including poetry, fiction, and drama. Rather than seeing Toomer's incorporation of rural and urban settings into *Cane* as productive of a synthetic dialectic striving toward wholeness, we might instead see the book as presenting multiple settings through which to interpret the changes affecting 1920s America. *Cane* understands that the widespread effects of this historic change occurred in different sites and that they could be interpreted through different forms of representation. My introductory reading of "Song of the Son" has suggested one way in which aesthetic form mediates historical change in the book: Toomer presents a lyric poem in which the speaker returns to a denuded Southern landscape in time to catch the plaintive songs of a spectral folk. *Cane*, as pastiche, presents many other settings through which to understand economic and cultural change, and yet these multiple settings do not simply provide a benign plurality of points of view. Rather, Toomer's book settles on a pattern of interests. As we will see, this pattern emerges as a preoccupation with male subjectivity, with female reproductive crisis, and with the tension between the crowd and individuality.

Abundance and Scarcity in the Georgia Landscape

In *Cane*'s first section we witness a Southern landscape perpetually at dusk, hazy with the smoke from the many timber mills converting the forest into a salable commodity. "Georgia Dusk," a poem that immediately follows "Song of the Son," situates dusk at the end of the workday at a sawmill and shows how both dusk and the mill have transformed the countryside. This transformation is described in the third and fourth stanzas:

> The sawmill blows its whistle, buzz-saws stop,
> > And silence breaks the bud of knoll and hill,
> > Soft settling pollen where plowed lands fulfill
> Their early promise of a bumper crop.
>
> Smoke from the pyramidal sawdust pile
> > Curls up, blue ghosts of trees, tarrying low
> > Where only chips and stumps are left to show
> The solid proof of former domicile.

                                                                      (15)

The ghostly trace of the forest, blue smoke, wends its way through the detritus of its own destruction. Both dusk and the "blue ghosts of trees" inspire the voicing of memory by the landscape and its inhabitants (15, l. 14). Hence we see "some genius of the South" (15, l. 6) "Surprised in making folk-songs from soul sounds" (15, l. 8), while we also hear "the men, with vestiges of pomp, / Race memories of king and caravan, / . . . / Go singing through the footpaths of the swamp" (15, ll. 17–20). The "dusky cane-lipped throngs" (15, l. 28) are accompanied by "the chorus of the cane" (15, l. 23) and the strumming of pine needles. In "Georgia Dusk" a collective voice arises out of the terrain and its populace that bears witness to its passing. The speaker in "Georgia Dusk" is an appreciative but relatively detached auditor to the chorus of its "throngs."

"Georgia Dusk" relates a conflicted message about the country-side's productivity. While the spectral folk we heard singing through a tree in "Song of the Son" is now pantheistically heard through pine needles and cane, the landscape here is not so barren as in the other poem.[17] Instead, we read that the "plowed lands fulfill / Their early promise of a bumper crop" (15, ll. 11–12), and night is portrayed as a "barbecue" (15, l. 4) and "a feast of moon and men" (15, l. 5). The land would seem to provide an excess of food even as the mills were stripping it of its trees. The fecundity of the land here contributes to the sense in the poem that dusk is a time of leisure. The whistle has blown, and work has stopped; it's time to sing and eat. This time is, then, "an orgy for some genius of the South" (15, l. 6), while it is also the opportunity for spiritual recreation, as the speaker suggests when he calls on the singers to "give virgin lips to cornfield concubines" (15, l. 27). But, if the land were so abundant, why bother to do the work of cutting down the trees to sell them on the lumber market?

Arthur Raper's classic 1936 sociological account, *Preface to Peasantry: A Tale of Two Black Belt Counties*, gives us another view of the Georgia Toomer encountered in 1921. One of the counties Raper studies, Greene County, is only ten miles to the north of Sparta, and they share the same climate, agricultural resources, and cultural dynamics. Raper demonstrates that the collapse of the black belt plantation system "leaves in its wake depleted soil, shoddy livestock, inadequate farm equipment, crude agricultural practices, crippled institutions, a defeated and impoverished people."[18] He argues that the collapse provides a preface to peasantry rather than to independent farming, since the workers who inherit the remains of the plantation do not have enough personal or natural resources to sustain themselves. They are consequently open to exploitation as sharecroppers. Raper's sociological analysis concludes that in Greene County in the 1920s and 1930s,

while a few rural families . . . live well enough, the vast majority
have but little money; that they buy much of their food, and many
of them are dependent upon landlords for subsistence while growing a crop; that they produce only a small proportion of the meat,
milk, eggs, and cereals which they need for their own tables; that
they live in unattractive and uncomfortable dwellings; that they
have scant household furnishings and but little reading matter;
and that they own and work with the crudest kind of agricultural
tools—in short, that they maintain a very low plane of living.[19]

This plane of living was precarious and susceptible to collapse. Greene
and Hancock Counties had been largely unaffected when the boll weevil invaded their cotton crops in 1916, and speculators thought that the
area was "weevil-proof" and invested most of the area's wealth in cotton crops over the following years. When the weevil returned in 1921,
the year of Toomer's trip to Sparta, it was not so gracious; a "severe
plunge of agricultural prices in 1920" did not help matters.[20] "The year
1921, with very low prices added to the weevil devastation, was a particularly bad one in all parts of the cotton region," concluded one econ-
omist.[21] Land value diminished, credit evaporated, and the economy
collapsed. Hungry and out of work, 43 percent of Greene County's
black population left. In response to the economic crisis, landowners
turned to the forest as the last salable commodity: "By 1923 sawmills
were puffing away all over the county. They had become Greene
County's major source of income. From the car windows of the Atlanta-
Augusta train, as it ran across the county, one could see a score of sawdust piles in 1925."[22] One can imagine Toomer enjoying a similar view
on his travels to Sparta and back. *The History of Hancock County* reports:

> The lumber industry has always been profitable in the county, but
> it was most prosperous from 1920–27. During this period there
> were 50 to 75 sawmills in operation in various parts of the county.
> . . . In late years, since most of the original timber had been cut,
> pulpwood has been the main item in this industry.[23]

Yet even this sector of the economy was under stress in 1921. Barbara
Foley's recent research indicates that a depression in the lumber industry closed several mills and provoked layoffs.[24]

If Raper's account of the black belt during the 1920s explains the place of the sawmill in "Georgia Dusk," it also raises questions about the feast available to the throngs in the evening. Certainly, Toomer was misreading the scene before him. And yet the inconsistency Toomer presents between a fecund Georgia landscape and the stubble of a countryside literally going up in smoke is also endorsed, in part, by Raper. At the end of his study Raper holds out the possibility that "peasantry in America" could also offer autonomy for former black belt sharecroppers.[25] He explains that a constructive land policy for the area will not try to rejuvenate the plantation system but will succeed

> if it enables the poorest farmers to build up the soil, to own live-stock, to raise vegetables and fruits for their own tables, to coöper-ate with their fellows making their purchases and in producing and marketing crops—in short, if it enables the landless farmers to attain ownership on an adequate plane.[26]

This never happened, as Jack Temple Kirby has shown us. But at the time Toomer was writing the possibility existed, and this may con-tribute to an explanation of the inconsistency in Toomer's attitude toward agricultural production in the South, for he would seem to cel-ebrate the fecundity of the farm and its promise of economic autonomy and political modernity, while he also proclaims its doom under mod-ernization.

This inconsistency may be mapped across the remainder of the poems in Cane's first section. Some poems, like "Reapers" and "Cotton Song," present scenes of agricultural work without adding the dimen-sion of temporal change. Indeed, in "Reapers" Toomer presents the repetitive motion of "Black reapers" (5, l. 1) swinging their scythes "one by one" (5, l. 4), and, when the scene is interrupted by the blade of a mower cutting a field rat, the poem stresses the continuity of the work: "I see the blade, / Blood-stained, continue cutting weeds and shade" (5, ll. 7–8). Likewise, "Cotton Song" is a work song in which the speaker invokes his fellow workers to "roll, roll!" (11, ll. 8, 20) as they work: "Come, brother, come. Lets [sic] lift it; / Come now, hewit! roll away!" (11, ll. 1–2). But, while "Cotton Song" represents agricultural labor as a repetitive and continuing activity, "November Cotton Flower" notes the presence of the boll weevil and the effects it has on the crops:

> Boll-weevil's coming, and the winter's cold,
> Made cotton-stalks look rusty, seasons old,
> And cotton, scarce as any southern snow,
> Was vanishing
>
> (6)

The poem continues to describe how drought dried up the streams and sent birds into wells in search of water. When the cotton suddenly blooms out of season, "Old folks were startled" (6, l. 10), and the sudden beauty of the event urges fearlessness on those who had lived with the doom of the failed crops. In contrast, then, to "Reapers" and "Cotton Song," this poem presents the field as a site of crisis, and it shows that site transformed by sudden beauty. "November Cotton Flower" shows both agricultural crisis and the potential of renewal.

Male Migration and Female Reproductive Crisis

Where the poems in the first section vacillate between celebrating the fecundity of the land and pronouncing it barren, the poems and vignettes in this section are far more consistent when it comes to the topic of women's reproductive prospects. The poems I have discussed so far have generally been enunciated through a man's lyric voice: "Song of the Son" presents the subjectivity of a migrant man, while "Cotton Song" addresses fellow laborers as "brother" (11, l. 1). Two poems present flat descriptions of women as a catalog of traits, and these poems emphasize grotesque and corpselike features. In "Face" a woman's brows are "recurved canoes / quivered by the ripples blown by pain" (10, ll. 5–6), while the flesh of her face resembles rotting fruit:

> And her channeled muscles
> are cluster grapes of sorrow
> purple in the evening sun
> nearly ripe for worms.
>
> (10)

While the poem's understatement conveys pathos for the woman, it also imparts the message that she is nearly done for. "Portrait in Georgia" also uses the method of cataloging traits—both poems begin with

"Hair—" (10; 29)—and continues the practice of portraying woman as corpse. Here each trait of a white woman's body is revealed as an element of a black man's lynching: "her slim body, white as the ash / of black flesh after flame" (29, ll. 6–7). This is a coupling that will result not in reproduction but death.[27] Women's flesh in these two poems is either rotting or burned up and both scarred and "blown by pain" (10, l. 6). These poems help set the context for the vignettes, in which six women are portrayed in various situations of social and reproductive crisis. Given the prevalence in folk aesthetics of linking the figure of the mother with agrarian labor so as to secure the perpetuity of peasant life, we might expect the women here to be strong maternal figures working the land.[28] As we will see, none of these women is featured in such a vision, for in *Cane* the folk world is not expected to survive the onset of modernization.

The opening story of the book, "Karintha," begins with an invocation that serves as a call to witness:

Her skin is like dusk on the eastern horizon,
O cant [sic] you see it, O cant you see it,
Her skin is like dusk on the eastern horizon
. . . When the sun goes down.

(3)

The story repeats this invocation midway through its narrative and again at the end, and we can see the intervening fictional prose as filling in the context for Karintha's association with the dusk. Karintha has been beautiful since birth, and men are anxiously waiting to mate with her, an ominous sign: "This interest of the male, who wishes to ripen a growing thing too soon, could mean no good to her." The scene in "Karintha" could be played against the backdrop of "Georgia Dusk," and it would seem that Karintha will become one of the "cornfield concubines" referred to in the last stanza of that poem. Indeed, we encounter a sawmill in this poem, and the smoke provides a contrast to the "wild flash" of Karintha at twelve: "At sunset, when there was no wind, and the pine-smoke from over by the sawmill hugged the earth, and you couldnt [sic] see more than a few feet in front, her sudden darting past you was a bit of vivid color, like a black bird that flashes in light." But her wildness is portentous: Karintha lives in a two-room home, and she "had seen or heard, perhaps she had felt her parents loving," and we discover that "the soul of her was a growing thing ripened too soon" (4). In other words, she starts gratifying men's desires, and in so doing she brings in a lot of capital: "Young men run stills to make her money. Young men go to the big cities and run on the road. Young men go away to college. They all want to bring her money. These are the young men who thought that all they had to do was to count time." Karintha gets pregnant. After she has a child on a bed of pine needles in the forest, the smoke from the smoldering sawdust pile at the nearby mill thickens, suggesting that the child has been burned there as well. The scene in Karintha recalls the smoky landscape that animates the spectral folk to sing in "Georgia Dusk." The smoke "curls up and hangs in odd wraiths" and was "so heavy you tasted it in water," and a song urges spiritual redemption: "Smoke is on the hills, O rise / And take my soul to Jesus." This tale presents a rural woman who has ripened on the vine, and it blames this spoilage on both the woman's desire for capital and the broad network of exchange by which young men can go off to get capital for her. The story intermingles the child's soul with the smoke from the burning sawdust, linking the fate of the forest with the child's; it would seem that the dusky beauty of Karintha warns of the setting of an era.

As the sun sets on Karintha, the young men continue to circulate in the world. The women in *Cane*'s first section are stuck in the past, reserved for the admiration of returning migrant men, and they generally do not survive the move from country to city.[29] The narrator of "Fern," an African-American man from the North, considers bringing Fern back North with him but quickly notes "the futility of mere change of place": "Besides, picture if you can, this cream-colored solitary girl sitting at a tenement window looking down on the indifferent throngs of Harlem. Better that she listen to folk-songs at dusk in Georgia, you would say, and so would I" (17). "Fern" tells of the migrant's fascination with a woman whom no man can satisfy. She is presented as a transparent eyeball, for "the whole countryside seemed to flow into her eyes," and one night when he takes her into the canebrake she falls into a religious trance. She speaks in tongues and sings as a Jewish cantor, then faints. This episode serves to further mystify the woman, while it also provokes gossip: although the narrator is not forced to leave town, he decides to do so after experiencing some insinuating stares. As he leaves, he positions Fern as a permanent fixture of the countryside: "From the train window I saw her as I crossed her road.

Saw her on her porch, head tilted a little forward . . . , eyes vaguely focused on the sunset. Saw her face flow into them, the countryside and something that I call God, flowing into them" (19). He concludes the story by noting that she is still living there, further emphasizing her immobility.

As I noted earlier, the women in the first section are in various states of social and sexual crisis. The heroine of "Becky," for example, is a white woman with two Negro sons; she is "islandized" by her community in a shack between a road and a railroad track (7), where she is ostracized and yet supported by the anonymous charity of passersby who leave food and prayers in her yard. One day a train rumbles by and the chimney of her house collapses, killing her; her sons had wandered off long before, "drift[ing] around from job to job" (8). While this story continues the pattern of stressing women's immobility in comparison to men, at least one story ends with a man's entrapment and lynching. The final story of the section, "Blood-Burning Moon," has a black man kill a white man in rivalry for a black woman; predictably, the killer is lynched by a white mob. More than the other elements of the first section, these stories emphasize the agony incumbent upon sexual relations across race in Jim Crow society. Where "Karintha" links the heroine's fall to her desire for capital and where "Fern" fixes its heroine as a spiritual medium, these stories blame social ostracism and its extreme, the mob, for women's reproductive crises.

The first section of *Cane* presents a Georgia with an unpromising future. The persistence of smoke denotes the depletion of the last salable commodity in this area, while the infestation of the boll weevil, as noted in "November Cotton Flower," threatens the area's agricultural economy. Toomer's occasional praise of the fecundity of the land and the cultural wealth of the folk songs produced by its workers suggests that he sometimes yearns to endorse the ideal of independent farmers Raper put forth at the conclusion of *Preface to Peasantry*. But Toomer also insists on the depopulation of the landscape, in part by making the singers of folk songs a spectral presence that reveals itself pantheistically through a singing tree, pine needles, the wind in the cane, and blue smoke and in part by demonstrating in various ways that women cannot provide children in this landscape. The presence of male migrants returning for a visit suggests what Raper confirms empirically: 43 percent of black Americans left Greene County between 1920 and 1930.[30] While many migrants were economic refugees who moved

to the closest town that could provide work and food, many others set
their hopes on urban life and moved to big cities like Chicago and New
York.

The Urban Crowd and the Drone's Fantasy

Washington, D.C., also attracted its share of migrants from the South,
and, when Toomer returned home from his sojourn to Sparta, he had a
deeper appreciation of the origins of the "wedge of nigger life" on the
city's Seventh Street (41).[31] "Seventh Street" is the opening sketch of
Cane's second section, which is set primarily in Washington, and the
wedge cuts through the wood we saw being milled in the South: "black
reddish blood into the white and whitewashed wood of Washington.
Stale soggy wood of Washington. Wedges rust in soggy wood . . . Split
it! In two! Again! Shred it!" Urban blacks, the sketch argues, have
money to burn, and this allows them to add vitality to a blanched
Washington culture: "Money burns the pocket, pocket hurts, / Boot-
leggers in silken shirts." The second section of *Cane* will not endorse
cheap amusements as the route to happiness, however. Instead, the section repeats a scene in which the speaker yearns for the pastoral landscape from which the "stale soggy wood" comes, and it imagines this
departure as an escape from the urban crowd.

Midway through the second section of *Cane* we encounter a lyric
poem whose speaker enjoys a reverie in which he takes flight from an
urban crowd and wings himself into the embrace of a farmyard flower.
In "Beehive" the speaker is a drone who distinguishes himself from the
black masses swarming through an urban nightclub district. The drone,
perhaps the insect world's most notorious flâneur, drinks with his fellow bees, while he also abstracts himself from the scene and into an
agrarian landscape. The poem reads as follows:

> Within this black hive to-night
> There swarm a million bees;
> Bees passing in and out the moon,
> Bees escaping out the moon,
> Bees returning through the moon,
> Silver bees intently buzzing,
> Silver honey dripping from the swarm of bees

Earth is a waxen cell of the world comb,
And I, a drone,
Lying on my back,
Lipping honey,
Getting drunk with silver honey,
Wish that I might fly out past the moon
And curl forever in some far-off farmyard flower.

(50)

The drone's abstraction from the scene takes him to a pastoral utopia in which he can "curl forever" in the petals of a flower. Never mind that it is the female worker bee, not the drone, who gleans pollen and nectar for the hive; Toomer's error here simply underscores the drone's intention for leisure and his inattention to the collective needs of the hive.[32] Significantly, the poem stops when the bee comes to rest in the flower; solitude, rather than connection with a rural collectivity, is the aim of the fantasy.

For the migrant man in the North the "mass-heart of black people" (52), as the narrator of "Theater" describes an audience, presents the threat of constraint and isolation. I have shown how the crowd in "Beehive" gives rise to the drone's fantasy of solitude in a pastoral setting. In "Box Seat" Dan Moore is a migrant who feels equally isolated from the middle class and the urban crowd. When Dan goes to visit his love interest, Muriel, in a middle-class house, he feels a sense of paranoia:

> The house contracts about him. It is a sharp-edged, massed, metallic house. Bolted. About Mrs. Pribby. Bolted to the endless rows of metal houses. Mrs. Pribby's house. The rows of houses belong to other Mrs. Pribbys. No wonder he couldn't sing to them. (60)

The opening of the story asks us to "stir the root-life of a withered people" by calling people from their houses, and associates the virgin with domesticity: "Dark swaying forms of Negroes are street songs that woo virginal houses" (59). But the urban throngs do not play a role in freeing residents from their putatively withering lives. Instead, they are subject to the spectatorial relations of mass entertainment. Dan follows Muriel to a vaudeville performance at the Lincoln Theater. Clearly, his paranoia is not relieved here: "The seats are bolted houses. The mass grows denser" (64). Dan sees Muriel, and he sees her as a "sweet, tame woman in a brass box seat," and he reads her willing confinement to the form of mass spectatorship as evidence that he is a "slave of a woman who is a slave" (66). The audience enjoys the grotesque spectacle of dwarfs boxing, and Muriel fights her revulsion in order to accept a rose from a bloodied dwarf. At the moment when Muriel capitulates to the audience's nudging to accept the rose, Dan breaks the frame of spectatorship to yell, "JESUS WAS ONCE A LEPER!" (69). His statement is meant to urge Christian acceptance of the grotesque figure of the bloodied dwarf. But, instead, the audience reads his intrusion as a denial of their pleasure in grotesque spectacle. Consequently, they turn on Dan, and their "gaping faces strain towards him." In "Box Seat" consciousness is constrained both in the isolation of a feminine domestic space and in the reified pleasures of mass entertainment. Dan walks away from both in disgust, relieving his paranoia through solitude.

"Bona and Paul," a story in which Paul is a migrant from the South living in Chicago, also dwells on the problems of courtship in an urban setting. Paul, who is dark-skinned, goes on a date with white-skinned Bona at the Crimson Gardens, a white nightclub. Toward the beginning of the story, Paul prepares for his date in his bedroom. His room has two windows, and "Bona is one window. One window, Paul" (73). Paul looks west from his window and sees the South:

> Gray slanting roofs of houses are tinted lavender in the setting sun. Paul follows the sun, over the stock-yards where a fresh stench is just arising, across wheat lands that are still waving above their stubble, into the sun. Paul follows the sun to a pine-matted hillock in Georgia. He sees the slanting roofs of gray unpainted cabins tinted lavender. A Negress chants a lullaby beneath the mate-eyes of a southern planter. Her breasts are ample for the suckling of a song. She weans it, and sends it, curiously weaving, among lush melodies of cane and corn. Paul follows the sun into himself in Chicago.

This passage is remarkable in part because Paul's fantasy literally turns the earth on its axis, so that the sun sets in the South. In this way the passage continues the practice of the first section in seeing the South at dusk. The Georgian landscape in Paul's window is fertile, filled with wheat, pines, cane, and corn. The woman, too, is fecund, breaking with the first section's preoccupation with women's reproductive crises.

And yet this woman is not nursing a child but a song, and she weans the song from her breast to send it weaving, like the smoke smoldering in the hills of "Georgia Dusk" and "Song of the Son," through the fields. Similarly, Paul is weaned from his nostalgic projection and "follows the sun into himself in Chicago." He faces the other window, Bona's window, and "with his own glow he looks through a dark pane." This look is ominous, for it foreshadows the scrutiny white customers in the nightclub will pay to his dusky complexion. In contrast to "Box Seat," in which a black crowd proves suffocating, this story displays a white crowd as the source of alienation. But, like the drone in "Beehive," Paul experiences a nostalgic projection of a rural utopia, and this experience in "Bona and Paul" provides a contrast to the alienation of an urban scene in which racial difference is a source of scrutiny and shame.

Where the first section of the book conveys a conflicted understanding of the fertility of the Southern landscape, such that it is both barren and depopulated and yet holds the possibility of renewal and sustainable peasant autonomy, the second section of *Cane* does not hold out hope for sustenance in the countryside. Here the South supports the prospect of pastoral solitude, as in the drone's fantasy, but this abundance is also something from which one must be weaned, as Paul understands. This section advocates a speculative return back to agrarian life rather than actual migration. As an argument that this world will not sustain its workers, Toomer provides the poem "Harvest Song," for example, as a bleak counterpoint to the earlier "Cotton Song." This poem is told through the voice of a reaper who cannot eat the harvest he has exhausted himself to reap. Where "Cotton Song" stressed the repetitive nature of field work, the importance of collective camaraderie, and the eventual redemption of the workers by God, "Harvest Song" presents a lone worker who is not likely to survive under current conditions:

> I am a reaper. (Eoho!) All my oats are cradled. But I am too
> fatigued to bind them. And I hunger. I crack a grain. It
> has no taste to it. My throat is dry . . . (71, ll. 26–28)

This poem reminds us that if the rural South is utopia, as "Beehive" and "Bona and Paul" have encouraged us to see it, it is a lost utopia even for those who work there. In the second section the pastoral South offers a point of contrast through which to develop an argument against the crowdedness of urban life; while the section does not praise modern life in the city, it does not offer the prospect of return to rural life either.

New Dawn, Everlasting Song

If the second section of *Cane* would seem to draw the shades decisively, though wistfully, on the vision of rural life Paul saw in the sunset from his Chicago apartment, the third section of the book will return us once again to the Georgia countryside. The third section consists of a closet drama, "Kabnis," in which Ralph Kabnis is a mixed-race Northerner returned to a small Georgia town to teach in a Negro school. Toomer, we will recall, had traveled to Sparta to work in such a school in 1921, and we can safely assume that the situation inspired the premise for this story, as the trip had inspired much of *Cane*. Like the first section of *Cane*, "Kabnis" expresses an ambivalence about the fertility of the Southern landscape. In the first segment of the drama Kabnis has insomnia, and his restlessness brings him out of his cabin, haunted by his surroundings and the spectral presence of folk songs, to beg for salvation:

> Dear Jesus, do not chain me to myself and set these hills and val-
> leys, heaving with folk-songs, so close to me that I cannot reach
> them. There is a radiant beauty in the night that touches and . . .
> tortures me. (85)

Kabnis feels out of touch with his environment, in part because he is a Northerner, and this leads him to pine nostalgically for the North, while he also contrasts his situation to the supposed immediacy rural blacks feel for their surroundings:

> Christ, how cut off from everything he is. And hours, hours north,
> why not say a lifetime north? Washington sleeps. Its still, peaceful
> streets, how desirable they are. Its people whom he had always
> halfway despised. New York? Impossible. It was a fiction. He had
> dreamed it. An impotent nostalgia grips him. It becomes intolera-
> ble. He forces himself to narrow to a cabin silhouetted on a knoll
> about a mile away. Peace. Negroes within it are content. They

farm. They sing. They love. They sleep. Kabnis wonders if perhaps they can feel him. If perhaps he gives them bad dreams. Things are so immediate in Georgia. (86)

If Kabnis had "halfway despised" the urban blacks from the North, he now projects the first nostalgic vision in the book of that setting. As an antidote to this "intolerable" nostalgia that cannot be satisfied, he proposes instead to find the immediacy and peace of the content Negroes in the cabin. To fully appreciate the "radiant beauty" of the landscape (85), he must be unchained from himself.

In the drama Kabnis becomes rather more unhinged than unchained. He becomes terrified of lynching, a terror made palpable when, during a Sunday morning chat with other middle-class men, a rock hurtles through the window with the message "You northern nigger, its [sic] time fer y t leave. Git along now" (92).[33] Kabnis's fear drives him to seek spiritual comfort in alcohol, and he is consequently fired by the principal of the school because, according to the principal, "the progress of the Negro race is jeopardized whenever the personal habits and examples set by its guides and mentors fall below the acknowledged and hard-won standard of its average member" (95). Where Kabnis had tried to console himself earlier that his status as a middle-class Northerner would protect him from lynching, he now loses that status as well as any assurance that the status would have protected him. Fired, he becomes an apprentice blacksmith, and he discovers the condescension whites convey toward laborers as he struggles to learn on the job. He continues his descent, literally, in a drunken party in the basement of the shop. Here he denies his black lineage and berates an old man, Father John, a mystic. Kabnis is contemptuous when Father John declares, after years of silence, that the sin the white folks committed during the era of slavery was to make the Bible lie. Kabnis wants "somethin new and up t date" (116), and calls the old man a "fakir" (117). After Kabnis trudges up the stairs to return to work in the shop, we are asked to see Father John and Carrie, a devout woman who cares for him, in a circle of light streaking through the "iron-barred cellar window": Father John and Carrie share out-of-date beliefs that imprison them in the shop's cellar. The slow pace of work in the blacksmith's shop indicates that this trade is out-of-date too; Kabnis will find nothing new there. But Toomer does not close this hopeless scene by dimming the lights; rather, the narrator presents the image of a South-

ern landscape at dawn, a departure from the prevalent image of the
South at dusk:

> Outside, the sun arises from its cradle in the tree-tops of the forest.
> Shadows of pines are dreams the sun shakes from its eyes. The sun
> arises. Gold-glowing child, it steps into the sky and sends a birth-
> song slanting down gray dust streets and sleepy windows of the
> southern town.

While Kabnis himself does not become "unchained" from his ambivalence about his racial heritage and his place in the South, the story
endorses the possibility of a new dawn for the South through pastoral
renewal.

"Kabnis" returns us once again to a conflicted vision of Southern
prosperity. Where the second section of *Cane* had been fairly decisive
about the fate of Southern agrarian life, the concluding scene of "Kabnis"—and of the book as a whole—asks us to contemplate the prospect
of a new day for the South. For Arthur Raper this new day would
emerge from a constructive land policy and the development of peas-
ant-owned, self-sufficient farms. But Toomer urges spiritual rather
than material renewal in *Cane,* and the final scene characteristically features a "birth-song" rather than an actual efflorescence of life. Just as
the woman whose "breasts are ample for the suckling of a song" in
Paul's vision of the rural South (73), the sun too sends out a song, and
here we can remember the singing of the caroling tree in "Song of the
Son" as lyrics that haunted the modernized landscape.

It is telling that when Toomer settles on an image of a productive
Southern landscape, the landscape's chief product is a new song. While
Toomer's project was to articulate a swan-song for the folk, the book
also served as an invocation in the most literal sense: as so many critics
have noted, *Cane* served as a touchstone for many writers of the New
Negro movement and after who chose to produce more folk-based aesthetic works. This was not the project Toomer would choose for himself, however; like *Cane* itself, Toomer was preoccupied with spiritual
matters after quitting his work in the South. *Cane's* engagement with
the prospects for political modernity in the context of modernization
gives us an intricate, if sometimes inconsistent, picture of the transformation of the Southern landscape as well as an understanding of the

psychological experience of migration and dislocation.[34] His text helps us to understand the rich cultural products of a once-rich agricultural region. As an intervention into the economic consequences of modernization, however, *Cane* presents a dubious legacy: *Cane* conjures up a spectral folk singing an "everlasting song" when the daily needs of rural Southerners were both dire and immediate (14, l. 20). As the next chapter will reveal, black workers in the South did not sing songs and tell tales simply to produce an aesthetic spectacle of their heritage; rather, folklore and singing provided a language of dissent by which these workers could comment on their plight during this era.

3

Folklore and Migrant Labor: Zora Neale Hurston's *Mules and Men*

In a recent article proposing a rethinking of the historiography of black working-class politics in the Jim Crow South, Robin Kelley has suggested that the historian's attention should shift from a focus on political leaders to a consideration of "everyday acts of resistance" carried out by working people.[1] Taking the cue from such scholars as James C. Scott, Michel de Certeau, and Eugene Genovese, Kelley sets out to find the "hidden transcript" of a "dissident political culture" in the urban South during the 1930s and 1940s.[2] He explains his rationale for doing so:

> Beneath the veil of consent lies a hidden history of unorganized, everyday conflict waged by African-American working people. Once we explore in greater detail those daily conflicts and the social and cultural spaces where ordinary people felt free to articulate their opposition, we can begin to ask the questions that will enable us to rewrite the political history of the Jim Crow South to incorporate such actions and actors.[3]

Kelley's article discusses forms of resistance as they occurred at home, at work, at play, and in the public at large so as to force a reconsideration of how action in daily life contributed to political change in the South.

My aim in this chapter is to use Kelley's study of working-class resistance to launch a revisionary reading of the narrative frame of Zora Neale Hurston's *Mules and Men* (1935). Kelley's article itself

43

begins with an epigraph from Hurston's book in which she debunks the "seeming acquiescence" of the smiling Negro laborer.[4] In Hurston's collection of folklore, I will argue, the hidden transcript of everyday resistance is exposed through the narrative frame with which she surrounds her transcription of folk tales. This articulation of resistance through folklore is most evident in the middle pages of her book, in which Hurston describes her visit to a lumber camp in Polk County, Florida. In this section Hurston at first experiences the workers' efforts to resist her intrusion on the scene because they think she is a detective. As she gains their acceptance, however, she is able to record their tales. She displays the migrant laborers telling tales on the job, and in so doing she shows how the tales form a discourse of dissent relating to the conditions of labor in the company town. When Hurston is accepted in the camp, her narrative voice shifts from first-person singular to the third person. As her authorial presence recedes, the narrative shows us how folklore could be used as a form of resistance in the Jim Crow South. In contrast, then, to the spectral folk of Toomer's *Cane*, Hurston's folk employ folklore as a living language of dissent.

Autobiography, Ethnography, and the Narrative Frame

Hurston's narrative frame has long been a topic of study for readers of *Mules and Men*, and it is worth considering the critical history on this topic before pursuing a revisionary reading of it. Rather than present a compendium of folk tales collected from the field, Hurston weaves the tales into an overarching narrative featuring her travels to her hometown of Eatonville, Florida, to neighboring Polk County, and to New Orleans. Since the link between these three sites is her traveling, observing self, most studies of the book's narrative frame have centered on the relation between autobiography and ethnography in the text. Her biographer, Robert Hemenway, spells out the questions that animate this line of inquiry:

> Is *Mules and Men* about Zora Hurston or about black folklore? If the former, the self-effacement makes the reader want to know more about what was going on in her mind, more about her reaction to

the communities that embraced her. If the latter, there is a need for folklore analysis.[5]

Hurston's text would seem to blend aspects of the autobiographical travelogue with aspects of the ethnographic study. Hemenway's questions suggest that the expectations of both genres remain unmet in *Mules and Men;* her narrative frame, he argues, frustrates the reader's attempt to understand her relation to the folk she is describing.

Hurston's frustration of generic expectations has been a source of excitement for many feminist scholars. Cheryl Wall claims that "the subtext of *Mules and Men* is the narrative of a successful quest for female empowerment,"[6] while Priscilla Wald claims that Hurston was "uniquely situated to explore the critical possibilities of marginality."[7] These arguments take Hurston's departure from traditional folkloric form as subversive, even if such subversion is submerged, subtextual, and marginal.[8] Barbara Johnson has complicated this approach, noting that "one of Hurston's most memorable figurations of the inside/outside structure is her depiction of herself as a threshold figure mediating between the all-black town of Eatonville, Florida, and the big road traveled by passing whites."[9] As Hurston mediates between these two spheres, Johnson argues, she also complicates the inside/outside opposition, yielding "difference as a suspension of reference."[10] In all of these accounts Hurston's presence in the book is shown to trouble the ethnographic endeavor. Her troublemaking is shown to be inspired by her marginality and her feminism in these arguments.[11]

Hurston's formal innovation has recently provoked a great deal of discussion among scholars whose primary interest is in folklore and ethnography. Some critics, citing an aspiration for science and objectivity in folklore studies, have seen Hurston's narrative frame as compromising the book.[12] Many others have seen Hurston's break with scientism as exemplary given the postmodern critique of ethnography. Sandra Dolby-Stahl, for example, has argued that Hurston attends to the concerns articulated in the collection *Writing Culture:* "Long before Clifford and Marcus and other contemporary scholars brought such concerns out into the light of day, Zora Neale Hurston showed us how a good writer does it best—with a writer's skill *and literary objectives* taking precedence over the conventions of scholarship."[13] Dolby-Stahl argues that Hurston submerges technical jargon in dialect, making her scientific analysis more amenable for a literary audience, thus slipping in an argument in the subtext. Other scholars have read Hurston's use of "literary" devices as a way of experimenting with ethnographic form; her self-reflexive gestures deconstruct ethnographic authority, introduce multiple, partial truths, and trouble the academy's relation to minority ethnographers.[14] These analyses of the narrative frame of *Mules and Men* as secretly subversive are homologous with the feminist arguments about the book I have discussed.

My brief synopsis of the extant work on Hurston is meant to show that the critical exploration of Hurston's narrative frame has focused almost exclusively on the relation between autobiography and ethnography. While this interpretive work has done much to question the certainty of the ethnographic encounter and to raise important questions about gender, it has tended to oversimplify the role of the narrative frame in *Mules and Men*. This oversimplification, I will argue, has led readers to miss the book's presentation of everyday forms of resistance in the Jim Crow South.[15] For example, in an article that is largely critical of Hurston's interpretation of the folk, Hazel Carby has written that "Hurston's representation of the folk is not only a discursive displacement of the historical and cultural transformation of migration, but also is a creation of a folk who are outside of history."[16] Carby's overall project is to demystify the romanticization of Hurston's engagement with the folk by some feminist and postmodern scholars, a project with which I sympathize.[17] But I am reluctant to conclude, with Carby, that Hurston's presentation of the folk is indicative of a "romantic and, it must be said, colonial imagination."[18] This conclusion is most plausible if one looks only at moments when Hurston finds herself in identity with her subject, as in her investigation of her hometown. Instead of viewing Hurston's work as enacting a "discursive displacement of the historical and cultural transformation of migration," I will examine the ways in which Hurston places migrant laborers *within* history through the Polk County section of *Mules and Men*; the section on Polk County, which has not received much critical attention to date, has the most to say about the link between folklore and resistance. My reassessment of Hurston's narrative frame will move beyond the relation between autobiography and ethnography to consider how she presents the relation of the teller to the tale within the company camp.

A "Small Empire": Polk County, Florida

Hurston's departure from Eatonville, Florida, to the neighboring Polk County marked a journey from a small town in which blacks held political office to a company work camp in which migrant workers from throughout the South labored for a wage in a highly regulated living environment. Polk County promoted corporate truck farming as an investment opportunity. The county's publicity department promoted the region as a "small empire" in which investors could expect to profit from agricultural and mining resources that could be sold throughout the eastern corridor (see fig. 1).[19] "Imperial Polk," as the county commissioners described it, "stands today as an empire within herself, far more than self-supporting," and its truck farms produce an abundance "causing the balance of trade, at the end of each year, to be greatly in her favor."[20] The promotional pamphlet emphasizes the county's transportation infrastructure, boasting of "the most complete system of modern highways to be found in any county in the South": a two-page photographic spread labeled "Highways and Motoring" displays the vanishing point of paved highway after paved highway, noting that "our system of highways is both a business asset and a most integral part of your pleasure."[21] For Hurston, however, this pleasure may have been somewhat muted, for, as the pamphlet reminds the reader, Polk County was segregated. These reminders nevertheless boast of the modern infrastructure available, unevenly, to blacks and whites. In a collage of institutional buildings, a picture of the wooden Negro Hospital is shown far beneath a photograph of the brick County Hospital (see fig. 2), and a paragraph on public schools notes that "there are 92 schools, 65 of which are white."[22] Using the promotional material provided by the county, Hurston might have motored straight to the local golf course in search of material; the only African Americans pictured in the pamphlet are caddies.

Hurston knew better, of course. When she sees "a huge smokestack blowing smut against the sky," she knows she'll find a source for folklore, and she enters the grounds of the Everglades Cypress Lumber Company in Loughman.[23] In contrast to her earlier excursion into Eatonville, in which the town and its inhabitants occupied a relatively autonomous and closed cultural sphere, Hurston has launched a collecting tour in the lumber camp because it brings together black Amer-

Fig. 1. A twenty-four-page brochure published by the county's publicity department encouraged investors to move to the area by citing its agricultural resources and modern highway system. Cover of *Polk County, Florida.* (Courtesy of the University of Chicago Library.)

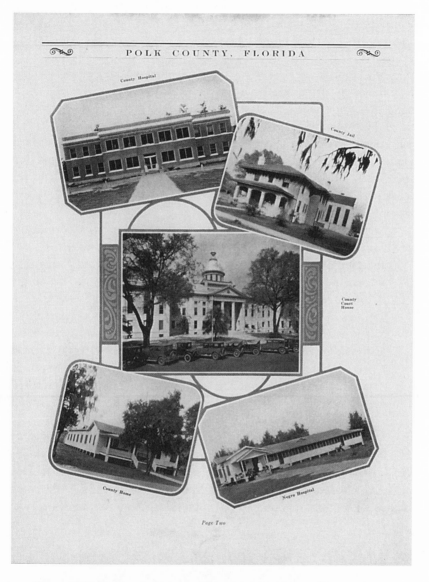

County Hospital

County Jail

County Court House

County Home

Negro Hospital

Fig. 2. Polk County boasts to prospective residents of its modern facilities while stressing their segregated status: the brick County Hospital is displayed at the top of the page, the wooden Negro Hospital at the bottom. *Polk County, Florida,* 2. (Courtesy of the University of Chicago Library.)

icans from numerous locations: "I saw at once," she observes, "that this group of several hundred Negroes from all over the South was a rich field for folk-lore" (60). Logging camps were typically staffed by migrant laborers. A 1931 study demonstrates that due to the exhaustion of much of the Southern timber supply, the one hundred thousand African-American timber workers were exceptionally mobile when Hurston visited Loughman: "In the past few years as the forests have been cut out the movement of Negro workers from one southern state to another in search of work in the lumber camps has increased."[24] This study notes that black workers usually held the least attractive positions:

> Negroes predominate in the turpentine camps of Georgia and Florida where exploitation of the workers is notorious. Mexican and Negro workers only are employed in the insect ridden cypress swamps. To cut cypress, the workers must wade in humid swamps, often up to their hips in water, and must live with their families in house boats built over the swamps. Living quarters for Negro workers are "match-box" shacks or box cars, segregated from white workers in the towns and in the camps. Negro lumber workers share the lot of all other Negro workers in the South, in that they are discriminated against in the types of jobs given them, are paid lower wages and provided inferior housing conditions and poorer schools for their children.[25]

Hurston could have expected to gather material from semi-skilled workers from throughout the South in this camp; rather than seeking an untouched and exotic cultural sphere, she examined the camp because it brought together strands of folklore from different sources.

The Hidden Transcript and the Disappearing Narrator

How does Hurston experience and transcribe the hidden transcript of everyday resistance if she herself is an outsider? As I suggested early on, Hurston encounters resistance from the workers on the job when she first arrives.[26] In these early scenes at the lumber camp her narrative persona is present as a clumsy "I" who can't quite fit in: she drives a fancy car, she wears expensive clothing, and the workers suspect that she is a detective. She explains what she had to do to become part of the "inner circle": "I had first to convince the 'job' that I was not an enemy in the person of the law; and, second, I had to prove that I was their kind" (65). As she gains their trust, her narrative persona shifts more easily between first and third person. Finally, when she follows the men on the job, her narrative persona practically disappears; instead, she situates her transcribed tales in relation to conditions on the camp. Hurston learns to overcome resistance by fitting in, and her studied invisibility enables her to display folklore's power as a discourse of dissent.

The major event leading to her acceptance in the camp is her contribution to a group performance of "John Henry," a track-laying ballad. The ballad dramatizes a competition between John Henry, who is an excellent spike driver, and the steam drill his boss has procured to replace him; John Henry keeps up with the drill for an hour, until he collapses of a heart attack. The song is a parable of the manual laborer's plight under the industrial organization of work: "I'll hammer my fool self to death," John Henry sings repeatedly (56). By contributing verses to the performance, Hurston demonstrates that she shares a cultural language with the workers on the job. The form of the ballad allows her to occupy the same subject position as the others when she sings her piece, while the refrain allows all of the singers to come together as one. "John Henry" exemplifies the living language of dissent that folk songs provide. As she notes in her glossary, the song's syncopation fits the rhythm of spike driving, and this suggests that the song's origin is as a work song. In the context of the workplace the song has operated as an articulation of beleaguered resistance to the hard work of laying down track. But Hurston does not sing the song with railroad workers: the context for this performance is a payday party, a social event that celebrates the receipt of wages. Here the song serves as a reminder of workers' alienation under capitalism and of the ever-present threat of replacement by machines, while John Henry's story also serves to contrast with the workers' attitude on the job: John Henry dies in his attempt to best the machine, while the workers in the camp find ways to avoid labor.

Hurston's joining in the performance of "John Henry" marks a moment of transition in her narrative performance in the Polk County section of *Mules and Men*. Although the break is not decisive, one can detect a shift in her narrative voice from the first person to the third person. Her narration before the song concerns herself and her efforts to fit in. After she has occupied the singer's position in the ballad, however, she seems to slip more easily between first and third person. And, as I have earlier suggested, when she turns to describe the telling of tales on the job, she frequently slips out of view entirely.

Hurston presents the telling of tales in the Everglades Cypress Lumber Company as performing everyday acts of resistance, and she investigates the telling of tales both on the job and during leisure time. In each context the tales reference the presence of company supervision in the daily lives of the workers. On the job the tales concern work and labor relations: I focus on tales about the meanness of bosses, the origins of work, and the advantage of stubborn literal-mindedness as a form of resistance. During leisure time the workers tell tales, sing, and dance; I examine how the company both supervises and profits from the workers' time off at the juke joint. Both on the job and off, Hurston shows us, the workers use folklore as a form of resistance to the company's considerable power over their lives.

Folklore and Resistance on the Job

Hurston determines to join the swamp gang on the job one day in order to gather more tales. As she narrates her discoveries on this day, Hurston lays out the relation between work and leisure in the camp, while she also shows how the workers employ folklore in order to interpret that relation. Hurston's study of the workday begins at dawn; she shows how the camp is transformed from its silent "dawn gray" into a frenzy of activity motivated by the fear of repercussion from the boss (66): "Grab your dinner-bucket and hit the grit. Don't keep the straw-boss waiting" (67). The unusual circumstances of this day allow Hurston to record a number of comments and tales about the meanness of bosses. This morning the straw boss, whom Hurston identifies as a poor white section boss on the railroad, keeps the workers waiting at their appointed meeting spot. This unusual delay allows the workers the opportunity to express their resentment for their supervisors even as they speculate on the cause of the delay: one worker cynically observes that it "must be something terrible when white folks get slow about putting us to work" (68). Another speculates that the boss is sick, but this theory is rejected: "Man, he's too ugly. If a spell of sickness ever tried to slip up on him, he'd skeer it into a three weeks' spasm." The gang continues to compete for the most disparaging tale about a boss. At one point Hurston brings together stories from disparate geographical origins to show how conversation among the migrant workers accumulates into an argument for the meanness of bosses. One worker tells of a boss from "Middle Georgy" who "was so mean dat when the boiler burst and blowed some of the men up in the air, he docked 'em for de time they was off de job" (69), while worker Tush Hawg attests to a boss on the east coast who "was so mean and times was so hard till he laid off de hands of his watch." In this section Hurston does not enter the action or participate in the tale telling; she is an omniscient observer whose reaction to the tales is subsumed in such approving phrases as "Everybody laughed" (68). Despite the laughter, Hurston's portrait of the beginning of the workday shows the pastoral worker's camp transformed into the site of contestation between black workers and their white bosses. In the context Hurston develops here, the competitive practice of woofing among the workers serves to build a collective discourse of resentment for the straw boss in this camp and in other working camps across the South.

Hurston does not get to observe and record work on the swamp gang, however, for logging has been suspended this day to allow the train to go to the Everglades to pick up a track gang. The workers erroneously conclude that they will have a day off; their conclusion is rejected by the foreman, who tells them to go check at the mill for work, thus giving rise to the aforementioned discourse on the meanness of bosses. But the change in plans allows us to see that a day off is a rare pleasure, just as it allows us to traverse the camp to another labor site. And, as the workers trudge off to the mill, two of the workers exchange folk tales on the origins of work that serve to explain their current predicament.

These tales place the allotment of work within a social hierarchy in which race and (sometimes) gender determine who has leisure and who is expected to do the hardest work. The first tale, "Why the Sister in Black Works Hardest," is related by Jim Allen; it is a creation myth that begins with God's creation of "de world and de varmints and de folks" (74). According to this tale, God completes his creation of the world by placing a bundle in the middle of the road. The bundle sits in the road for a thousand years before arousing human curiosity, but when such curiosity is aroused a division of labor is devised to determine what is in the bundle. The character called Ole Missus asks her husband, Ole Massa, to pick up the box and see what is inside. But the box appears to be too heavy, so he tells "de nigger" to get the box. He, in turn, tells his wife to get it, and "she run and grabbed a-hold of de box and opened it up and it was full of hard work." While the tale concretizes the origin of work by describing it as an object that can be concealed in a bundle, it also explains the social context by which the worker is compelled to do her job. The tale also offers an ironic exposition of the lure of the gift by conflating the gift with work: "de nigger 'oman" who opens the box does so with great enthusiasm, as if the box contained a gift. Jim Allen's tale analyzes labor by relation to race and class and offers an ironic conflation of the pleasure of the gift with the burden of hard work. The chain of deferrals begins with the leisured white woman, who relies upon the wealth and prestige of her husband; in her social context she has the least work to do. Her husband, who owns a slave, also avoids the onerous gift of work by asking the black man to satisfy his wife's curiosity. The black slave, in turn, is able to put the duty off on the black woman. In essence, the tale shows that it is the social hierarchy itself that creates alienated labor: by satisfying everyone else's curiosity and easing their burdens, the black woman assumes the greatest labor in this story.

Another worker, Jim Presley, objects to Jim Allen's tale and provides an alternative explanation for the origin of work in his tale, "'De Reason Niggers Is Working so Hard.'" Presley's tale shares much with Allen's tale; the two are variations on a theme. Presley's tale again presents the conundrum of the mysterious bundle, but this time God sets two of them on the road. The bundles are five miles down the road, and a white man and a black man race to get to the bundles. The black man runs fastest and gets there first, and he grabs the larger of the two bundles before the white man can get it. This is an unfortunate choice, for the larger bundle contains "a pick and shovel and a hoe and a plow and chop-axe," whereas the smaller bundle contains "a writin'-pen and ink" (75). Presley's tale again relates a division of labor according to race (if not gender) through a drama in which God's bundle serves to trick the black man into receiving the unpleasant gift of hard work. This moral is emphasized in the closing line of the tale: "So ever since then de nigger been out in de hot sun, usin' his tools and de white man been sittin' up figgerin', ought's a ought, figger's a figger; all for de white man, none for de nigger." This bleak conclusion emphasizes how the betrayed promise of God's bundle has resulted in the social exploitation of black labor.

In addition to tales on the meanness of bosses and the origins of work, Hurston witnesses a number of tales about the power of dissemblance in labor relations during her day on the gang. Deliberate literal-mindedness, lying, and foot dragging have been consistently useful tools for African-American workers who sought to assert some control over their work environment. In the antebellum era, Eugene Genovese has argued, these tactics asserted accumulative pressure on the institution of slavery:

> The slaves struggled to influence their own working conditions. Their actions did not challenge slavery *per se*, nor were they often meant to, any more than striking workers often mean to challenge the capitalist system. Yet, in an important sense the slowdowns and resistance to overwork contributed more to the slaves' struggle for survival than did many bolder individual acts that may have reflected a willingness to attack slavery itself.[27]

These tools have been codified in folktales concerning Ole Massa and John, whose origins are certainly in the antebellum era. The tales encode lessons about how to resist mastery. They remain powerful pedagogical tools in the different working conditions of the logging camp. Without imposing her own narrative voice, Hurston transcribes the men's stories as they relate them to one another. In between the stories she describes the men's worries about getting caught by the boss telling tales on the job, and she also shows how the men slow their pace both to allow for more storytelling and to keep from getting to the mill. Hurston's juxtaposition of the narrative content of the tales with the actions of the tellers suggests that the lessons of the tales have been absorbed into the tellers' behavior.

Unlike the tales chronicling the creation of work, in which God's gift tricks the African American into acquiring the burden of work, the tales about Ole Massa and John turn the tables for the African-American figure. John, a slave, is a trickster figure who finds ways to undermine the authority of his white master, Ole Massa. Typically, John tricks Ole Massa by adhering to a stubborn literal-mindedness, a literal-mindedness that flatters the master in his expectation that his slave lacks both wit and guile. One tale in particular, "The First Colored Man in Massa's House," shows how John exploits his master's misapprehension of his cunning in order to defeat Ole Massa. As Black Baby tells the story, John is the first colored man in the country, and Ole Massa exploits John's putative lack of linguistic skills by giving him the wrong name for selected items in the house: he tells John that the fireplace is his "'vaperator," the cat is "his round head," and the barn is "his mound" (79). When the cat catches fire from the fireplace and runs to the barn and sets the straw on fire, John runs to Ole Massa's room and relates the story in the language his master has given him. His master cannot comprehend John's message, so after several repetitions John relays the message using the correct language. By this time, the tale suggests, the fire is well under way in the barn. By playing stupid, John is able to outwit his master.

This pattern persists in the rest of the Ole Massa and John stories related this day. In "Ole Massa and John Who Wanted to Go to Heaven" Ole Massa tries to outwit John by showing up at his doorstep dressed up as God and telling him he has arrived to deliver John to heaven; John plays into the ruse by feigning fear of God until Ole Massa is coaxed into stepping far enough away from the door to allow John to bolt past him. In the "Deer Hunting Story" related by Will Richardson, Ole Massa and a slave go hunting for deer. The slave is instructed to shoot the deer after the master scares them into the slave's range of fire. The deer runs past as the slave waits, but he does not shoot; queried on his inaction, the slave responds that he had not seen any deer: "All Ah seen was a white man come along here wid a pack of chairs on his head and Ah tipped my hat to him and waited for de deer" (75). Again, the slave's supposed guilelessness undoes the master's plan.

As I have suggested, Hurston's descriptive narrative of the men on the job signals the danger the men feel as they tell these stories of dissent. The bulk of the stories concerning Ole Massa and John are told by the swamp gang as they walk from the appointed meeting spot to the mill (see, e.g., fig. 3). After the first tale concerning Ole Massa and John ("Ole Massa and John Who Wanted to Go to Heaven") is told, Hurston's narrative voice laughs and comments, "If the foreman had come along right then he would have been good and mad because he could tell their minds were not on work" (72). The workers deliberately slow their journey to the mill in order to have the time to tell more tales, and the worry caused by this tactic is on the minds of most of the swamp gang: Jim Allen notes a need for haste before he tells his story about the origin of work, Gene Oliver asks his coworkers to hush so he can tell "What Smelled Worse" before they get to the mill, and Hurston notes that "we were at the mill at last, as slow as we had walked" (84). When they neglect to inform the mill boss of their arrival so that they can tell more tales, the tales are then framed with their expressions of worry concerning this breach of decorum. Presumably, there are at least two reasons to worry about being discovered exchanging tales: they are not working, and they are also telling stories that are disparaging about white overseers. Clearly, then, the narrative frame presents a context for the stories that suggests their volatility in the present work camp; Hurston anticipates Vladimir Propp's desire to read such stories not as "living antiquity" but, rather, as adapted commentary to present conditions: "Historical study should show what happens to old folklore under new historical conditions and trace the appearance of new formations."[28] Hurston's text shows us a palpable discourse of dissent working within the company town.

Folklore and Recreation in the Company Camp

Hurston's text also explores the extent to which leisure time in the camp is regulated by the company. To exchange tales on the job the men stole time from the bosses by dragging their feet. When the men have time off from work, they persist in telling stories at the fishing hole. Their time is no longer "stolen" from the company here, although the company is not far from their minds. Cliff Ulmer notes: "We ain't off lak dis often. Tomorrow we'll be back in de swamp 'mong de cypress knees, de 'gators, and de moccasins, and strainin' wid de swamp boss" (114–15), and, when another of the gang wonders what the swamp boss is doing while the men are fishing, Cliff professes not to care. The men are intent on sharing stories, many about "varmints"; others take the form of brags about the relative fecundity of pieces of farm land owned by "my ole man" (101). Since the workers live in company-owned shacks in a corporate compound, their brags about fertile farm land are out of place. Here their values correspond to an alternative modernity in which their prosperity is tied to their own property rather than to the company.

Fig. 3. "Sawmill Workers Waiting for a Motor to Cool, Childs,
Florida, January 1939." Photograph by Marion Post Wolcott.
(Courtesy of the U.S. Farm Security Administration Collection,
Prints and Photographs Division, Library of Congress, LC-USF
34–51043-E.)

Men's leisure time on the camp allows them to brag about their fictive property; in this sense the time represents a moment of free self-
expression for them. But many of the women in the camp feel that the
men's free time is time stolen from them; the women hope for attention
and household chores from the men. Mrs. Bertha Allen wants her husband Jim to do yard work, but he resists, reminding her that the yard
and their shack belong to the company. His power to refuse indicates

that the division between leisure and labor in "Why the Sister in Black Works Hardest" persists. This is signaled not only by Bertha Allen's request but also by Big Sweet's intrusion at the fishing hole. Big Sweet is the vociferous girlfriend of Joe Willard, and her intrusion is mostly felt as the inappropriate interruption of men's leisure time. Joe complains, "We git a day off and figger we kin ketch some fish and enjoy ourselves, but naw, some wimmins got to drag behind us, even to de lake" (124). In this section the men's leisure time fishing provides Hurston with the opportunity to record more tales. It also provides us with an opportunity to understand leisure's rarity and its relation to gender difference.

If the company's presence is felt by the men at the fishing hole, its regulation of all of the workers' leisure time is especially marked at the juke joint (see, e.g., fig. 4). When we enter the juke joint with Hurston, we are led to believe that we are entering an autonomous cultural zone for the African-American workers in the lumber camp: we hear blues on the piano, we see couples dancing, and we watch various games in progress. Hurston's transition from the previous chapter, in which we have heard a traveling preacher's sermon, into the present one signals that the juke joint is part of life on the job: "The little drama of religion over, the 'job' reverted to the business of amusing itself" (143). Hurston calls amusement a business in part because the juke joint is where much of one's paycheck is spent, and because the juke is itself run by the company. Consequently, the same paranoia the swamp gang felt while they exchanged tales is felt by all of the workers in the juke joint:

> Somebody had squeezed the alcohol out of several cans of Sterno and added sugar, water and boiled-off spirits of nitre and called it wine. It was dealt out with the utmost secrecy. The quarters boss had a way of standing around in the dark and listening and he didn't allow a drop of likker on the job. (144)

One would be arrested and sent to jail in Bartow if caught with liquor. There is a high rate of murder on pay nights in the camp, and the banishment of alcohol is designed to prevent the loss of too many workers in this manner. In this scene we witness a knife fight that is broken up by the quarters boss, who is predictably lurking in the shadows. He throws the knife-wielding Ella out of the juke, reminding her that she is not on the job and that "this place is for people that works on this job"

Fig. 4. "A 'Juke Joint' and Bar in the Vegetable Section of the Glades Area of South Central Florida, February 1941." Photograph by Marion Post Wolcott. (Courtesy of the U.S. Farm Security Administration Collection, Prints and Photographs Division, Library of Congress, LC-USF 34–57086-D.)

(152). While Hurston shows the workers enjoying a lively night life, she also shows how their amusements are closely watched and regulated by the company.

Hurston's presence on the job, at the fishing hole, and in the juke joint is mostly hidden by her omniscient narrative voice. While her first days in the camp were characterized by her clumsy, obtrusive "I," her acceptance in the community allows her to transcribe the hidden transcript of everyday resistance in the camp. She records this not only by writing down the folktales that she hears but also by setting the scene for each performance through the framing story of a day on the job. My focus on this aspect of the narrative frame in *Mules and Men*, and on the middle section in particular, is meant to provoke a new evaluation of the book's understanding of the exercise of power in African-American folk communities. The feminist and postmodern investigations of Hurston's politics have typically focused on the ways in which the author is an embodiment of gendered and racial marginality; most of these analyses have rested on her troubling of the relation of authorial self to the ethnographic other. While these arguments have identified one important aspect of her engagement with issues of power, they have missed seeing the ways in which her text displays folklore's function as an everyday form of resistance in the Jim Crow South. This may be so because Hurston's authorial self is nearly invisible in this section, receding from the clumsiness of her first-person presence into the cover of omniscience. Indeed, given her oft-quoted claim that "I do not belong to the sobbing school of Negrohood who hold that nature somehow has given them a lowdown dirty deal," it is perhaps surprising that she allows the message of resistance to difficult conditions to come through.[29] While it is difficult to reconcile her complex and often contradictory political views, it seems clear that her silent framing of these stories of resistance should be taken into any accounting of them.

Hurston's achievement in this book comes into relief through comparison with her treatment of the same material in a later musical, *Polk County*. Subtitling it "A Comedy of Negro Life on a Sawmill, with Authentic Negro Music, in Three Acts," Hurston reworked her Polk County fieldwork for production on the Broadway stage with Dorothy Waring in 1944.[30] Here, however, Hurston and her collaborator frame folklore and blues as commercially viable entertainment rather than as modes of resistance in the lumber camp. Hurston, the ethnographer, is replaced by the character of Leafy Lee, a wandering woman from New York who makes her way to Polk County to learn the blues so that she can return to the city and become famous; she encourages other characters to follow and make money in New York.[31] In the musical Leafy learns "John Henry" from Big Sweet and the others in the camp; the song culminates in an ensemble chorus in which Leafy joins and demonstrates that she is learning how to be a blues singer, in contrast to Hurston's demonstration of insider status when she sings "John Henry" in the ethnography. And Leafy does not go on the job with the men as Hurston did; that scene is cut entirely. The commercially attuned *Polk County*, which nevertheless was never produced, demonstrates ways in which Hurston could have diminished the political implications of folklore in the lumber camp in *Mules and Men*. If

Hurston sought to present folklore in a "colonial," "romantic" context, it is perhaps here that she did so, and not in *Mules and Men*.[32] Of course, as the next chapter will show, even a romantic engagement with the folk can offer its share of resistance to colonial power; this does not seem to be the case, however, with *Polk County*.

If the folk are now inside history in *Mules and Men*, what claims can be made about the efficacy of their language of dissent? In Hurston's narrative the white bosses rarely come into contact with the acts designed to resist their power. While the work of the company is certainly slowed by the gang's foot dragging, and the quarters boss expends a lot of energy supervising the juke joint, Imperial Polk County never seems greatly threatened by the tales its migrant laborers tell. But, as Genovese, Kelley, and others have argued, daily acts of resistance build communities and prepare the foundation for greater social change. In making the case for including such acts in the historical analysis of politics, Kelley writes: "I am not suggesting that the realm of infrapolitics is any more or less important or effective than what we traditionally consider politics. Instead, I want to suggest that the political history of oppressed people cannot be understood *without* reference to infrapolitics, for these daily acts have a cumulative effect on power relations."[33] The workers in the camp contributed to the political struggle for power in the Jim Crow South. Hurston's contribution in *Mules and Men* was not so much to write a book about herself and her own struggle for power, as the critical literature would suggest, but to transcribe the hidden transcript of resistance that obtained in the performance of folklore on the job.

4

The Folk as Alternative Modernity: Claude McKay's *Banana Bottom*

Claude McKay's final novel, *Banana Bottom* (1933), enacts a speculative return home to Jamaica for the self-exiled author. The facts of the novel's production suggest the international scope of McKay's career abroad: he wrote the book in Tangier and published it in New York for a predominantly American audience. McKay's early involvement in the Harlem Renaissance, his editorial work in London for the *Worker's Dreadnought* and in New York for the *Liberator*, his celebrity in Soviet Russia, and his years in Europe imply a broad engagement with the workings of the twentieth century as well as a strong interest in Marxist aesthetics. In his 1937 autobiography McKay describes himself as an "internationalist," explaining (with some levity) that "an internationalist was a bad nationalist"; he was also a self-described "peasant become proletarian," which gave his internationalist label a distinctly Marxian inflection.[1] So, while *Banana Bottom* argues for a return to folk roots and a celebration of the anti-modern, it does not do so for the sake of nostalgia alone; rather, McKay returns home in this novel to offer a careful analysis of the modern global economy and Jamaica's place within it.[2] In *Banana Bottom* McKay argues for the rejection of colonial cultural ideology—most notably, Christianity—and the return to folk roots as a route to autonomy for Afro-Jamaican peasants. Such autonomy is imagined not only as an alternative modernity to the modernity of the colonial mission but also as a form of resistance to the vagaries of the global commodities market and to the incursions of low-wage immigrant labor (the novel frequently insists upon the superiority of the

Afro-Jamaican peasant laborer in contrast to the newly arrived East Indian and Chinese workers). *Banana Bottom* argues for the authenticity of peasant culture so as to advance a secondary argument for Afro-Jamaicans to participate in the peasant appropriation of economic capital.

In *Banana Bottom* the ideologeme of the *folk* is situated at the axis between two generic imperatives.[3] In one, that of the folk romance,[4] the village of Banana Bottom represents the purportedly timeless values and collective identity of Afro-Jamaican peasant life; here the folk are economically self-sufficient and culturally regenerative, and any change is part of the synchronic cycle of daily life. In the other the folk drives the machinery of a naturalist plot;[5] the novel traces the inexorable fall of Bita Plant from her position as a highly educated Christian missionary in the town of Jubilee to her marriage with a peasant farmer in her native village. Bita's decline is often described by the narrator as motivated by her unconscious or instinctive feeling for her folk roots. But Bita's decline does not find her debased or in a state of monstrosity, as the naturalist plot might suggest; rather, in succumbing to the diachronic pressures of psychological determinism, Bita finds herself savingly inserted into the utopian world of the folk romance. By surrendering to instinct, Bita discovers the autonomy by which she can be true to herself and to her Afro-Jamaican community, perpetually.

Because the novel represents political affiliations through psychological categories, most critics have understood the novel to be about Bita's crisis of personal identity. These readers have assessed Bita's final position as either liberating or as too ideal to be plausible. Those critics who praise the book generally conclude that Bita is liberated by her return home. Kenneth Ramchand has praised Bita's "final liberation and embrace of the folk," noting that her "self-assertion takes the form of immersion."[6] George Kent sees Bita learn "how to make her Western education work harmoniously with the soulfulness of her roots. . . . Bita is able to resist [her education] and to opt for the warmer and more spontaneous celebration of life available in the village."[7] Critics who are unhappy with the book complain that Bita's fate is unrealistic. Michael Gilkes has charged that the novel "reads like a case of special pleading for an indigenous, rooted Black Consciousness."[8] Bita "finds a place that is truly 'home' by finding a 'solution' (the inverted commas suggest themselves) to the familiar West Indian dichotomy" of Western education and local roots.[9] Gilkes sees Banana Bottom as "an

idealized 'home,' a folk-centered community in which the black or colored West Indian can live in harmony with himself and others."[10] Leota
Lawrence is equally unhappy with the novel, dismissing it as naive and
unrealistic. She complains: "As much as one would wish to commend
McKay for the positive portrayal of his heroine and the rural folk as a
whole, Bita's is merely a romanticized version of West Indian womanhood. . . . McKay can be indicted for romanticizing his heroine and his
world of Banana Bottom."[11] She concludes that "anyone who knows
anything about West Indians would agree that McKay's Bita is a
romanticized version of West Indian womanhood."[12] Whereas Ramchand and Kent see Bita as achieving liberation through her assertion of
personal identity, Gilkes and Lawrence complain that such an assertion
of identity is unrealistic, if not undesirable. These readers share an
eagerness to follow the naturalistic drive and see Bita reach the state of
self-consciousness that is regarded as most instinctively true, but they
differ as to whether the novel's conclusion as romance is plausible or is,
instead, an instance of false consciousness that would more suitably
have been resolved in the terms of realism.

The question of the degree to which the folk is a true or a fantastic
entity has been the subject of debate in West Indian literary history generally. In a 1972 essay Gordon Rohlehr contests George Lamming's
position that the West Indian novel is "the people's speech, the organic
music of the earth."[13] Lamming has contrasted the West Indian novel
with the English novel, which he claims is preoccupied with the concerns of the middle class in England. The West Indian novel, he says,
has brought back to reading "lumps of earth: unrefined, perhaps, but
good, warm, fertile earth."[14] Rohlehr seeks "a more pliable theory . . .
one which can accommodate the interplay between country, town and
big city, between peasant, artisan and city-slicker or factory worker,
and between the ill-defined classes of the West Indies."[15] Lamming,
according to Rohlehr, has presented an overly synchronic view of folk
culture, one that does not comprehend its place in the dynamic activity
of West Indian culture generally. Rohlehr advocates a view of the culture in constant flux: "West Indian society is in fluid motion, and often,
oscillation, between the two extreme poles of the folk-urban continuum, [which] makes it difficult to define one's terms."[16] Both Lamming
and Rohlehr take the position that the folk is a real entity in the culture;
Rohlehr simply advances a more nuanced understanding of that reality. His understanding bears considerable explanatory power with

respect to *Banana Bottom*, in which most of the constituencies he cites are represented. But Rohlehr's model is useful for us only on the level of reflection theory: it suggests that the world in which Bita operates corresponds to the real world of Jamaica, but it cannot explain why Bita is drawn inevitably to affiliate with the collective identity of the folk as a romantic act of personal liberation.

Peasant Freeholds and Economic Capital in Post-Emancipation Jamaica

Thomas Holt's recent history of Jamaica gives us some leverage on this question. In *The Problem of Freedom* Holt shows how the emancipation of the slaves in Jamaica posed a problem for the British colonials who still sought to maintain their interests in the Jamaican economy. The British granted Jamaicans individual autonomy but sought in various ways to curtail their economic activity. The growth of a peasant economy throughout the nineteenth and early twentieth centuries, to the extent that by the 1930s between 60 and 80 percent of the population lived as peasants, produced a nightmare for British plantation owners, who lost a cheap labor pool, and a conundrum for contemporary interpreters and later historians, who sought an explanation for the change. Some interpreters, Holt tells us, saw the rise of the peasantry as actually a cultural regression, since, as the argument goes, "ex-slaves were culturally endowed with relatively simple aspirations that could easily be satisfied in a tropical environment and worked just enough to gratify immediate desires."[17] Others defined the change as driven not by character but by economic conditions: the new peasants capitalized on the chance for a better life by working for themselves rather than for a wage on the estates. But this interpretation assumes that the former slaves would make choices based solely on economic incentive, without regard to cultural ideals. Ultimately, Holt concludes, peasant freeholds formed near plantations, and peasants moved between maintaining their own gardens, selling the surplus in local markets, and devoting time to estate labor when they chose, while sometimes forming as part of a "militant agricultural proletariat, utilizing all the tools of labor agitation, including strikes, slowdowns, and sabotage to extract concessions of better pay and working conditions from the estates."[18] The rise of a peasant society in Jamaica was not fueled by cultural regression or economic determinism; instead, Afro-Jamaican peasants positioned themselves to take advantage of the remains of the plantation system by creating an alternative modernity in which they could accumulate their own property and sustain their livelihoods through the cultivation of their own lands.

Holt's description of post-emancipation Jamaica gives us more leverage on the question of freedom in *Banana Bottom* than does Rohlehr's offer of a dynamic folk-urban continuum. By emphasizing freedom as a problem, Holt presents the folk as a chosen affiliation rather than as a pole of meaning in a continuum or as a premodern state that will eventually be superseded by modern life. Sidney Mintz's seminal description of the "rural" Caribbean as a by-product of "'industrial' colonies" suggests as much: "The ruralness of the region . . . is not the ruralness of tribal horticulturalists, or of ancient agricultural civilizations, but the consequence of an industrial system that happened to be based on agriculture rather than on factories."[19] And in "The Agricultural Show," a story included in his 1932 collection, *Gingertown*, McKay himself describes the acquisition of peasant freeholds as the product of "tenacious" activity (rather than as the expression of an inherent teleology of development); in this story a ninety-six-year-old peasant remembers a series of political and economic structures in Jamaica: "He was full of memories about the land; of the old slave days when sugar-cane was king of colonial products, of its displacement by and the spread of the banana; of the rebellion of the slaves, the half-freedom of the slaves, the full freedom of the slaves; of the deterioration of land values, the importation of indentured Indian coolies to take the place of the slaves, the decline and agony of the great plantations, and the grim, tenacious acquisition of small landholdings by the freed slaves and their children."[20] Holt, Mintz, and McKay all suggest that the folk operates as an alternative figuration within the discourse on Jamaican modernity.

In this context we can see peasant life as a form of resistance to British colonial rule and a significant staking out of economic autonomy. The novel displays the consequences for not following this strategy. Early on we are presented with background on a failed coffee collective that engendered antipathy for the colonial missionaries. When the Reverend Angus Craig noted that poor peasants were selling their coffee during the flush season when the price was low, he organized a pool so that they could collectively wait out the market until the price rose. This strategy of organizing around one commodity fails, however: the market price falls and the peasants do not believe that the market was beyond Reverend Craig's control, and they resolve not to follow his advice in the future. But the real lesson of this episode, the novel eventually argues, is that dependence on one commodity puts the peasants at the mercy of the global commodities market. The choice of the folk as an affiliation, however fantastic or romantic the choice is presented to be in aesthetic form, is ultimately also a political choice and not mere nostalgia. The imagining of a synchronic folk world bespeaks a certain intransigence to the modern marketplace. An affiliation with the folk also represents a rejection of the autonomy offered by the colonial mission in this novel, in which colonial ideology is shown to deny religious freedom; the autonomy Bita acquires is that more commonly associated with political modernity under democracy, which, according to Selwyn R. Cudjoe, underwrites many of the narratives of resistance in Caribbean literature.[21] For Bita the solution to the "problem of freedom" is to return home and settle in with her folk. Her personal liberation is also a political affiliation. But in coming to understand Bita's choice we must also confront its greatest paradox. We must ask why her political liberation is also her deepest instinct.

Sex, Gossip, and Christian Redemption

When Bita is drawn back into her native self, she is said to recover both her memory of childhood and her true sexuality. As the novel opens, we witness Bita's return to the town of Jubilee from England, where she has been educated for seven years. Bita's education has been sponsored by local Christian missionaries, who intervened when they heard the news of Bita's rape by the village musician, Crazy Bow. The narrator insists that the rape is the consequence of play between the two that escalated into sexual intercourse. But village gossip and Christian moral doctrine convert the accident into a crime of lunacy for Crazy Bow and a moral blemish from which Bita must recover. Malcolm and Priscilla Craig, the town missionaries, take on Bita as an experiment, and we witness Bita return to the town as highly educated and morally purified, an example of what the novel's psychological schematization would see as the ability of civilization to repress one's base unconscious desires. The Craigs watch proudly at Bita's "welcome home" party in the first scene, for she is "the transplanted African peasant girl that they had transformed from a brown wildling into a decorous cultivated young lady."[22] Sexual repression and an education in English civility conjoin on the route to elevate Bita. Consequently, the road home will prove difficult, for the return to uncivilized folk life will be linked here with a fall into atavism.

McKay is at pains to demonstrate that the rape was more an accident than an act of violence, and consequently he is able to use the event to show how public discourse can reshape extramarital sex as a scandal worthy of sanction. His narration will not investigate Bita's point of view concerning the rape and its consequences; in this sense McKay's attitude toward Bita's rape resembles the detached, experimental attitude exhibited by the Craigs—an attitude his narrative aims to critique. Where McKay creates a silence about Bita's inner experience of these events, however, he also explores how various constituencies in her community seek to define the experience for her.[23] Indeed, the novel will offer a sympathetic portrait of Crazy Bow, and it will argue that Bita suffers more from the social reaction to the event than from the event itself. We are told by the narrator that Crazy Bow "was harmlessly light-headed and none could imagine him capable of any natural aberration" (9). Although he is twenty-five to Bita's twelve years of age, their friendship is generally considered to be motivated by mutual kindness. When they romp on the banks of the Cane River, Bita becomes "bewitched" by Crazy Bow's fiddling and climbs on top of him; "Crazy Bow was blinded by temptation and lost control of himself and the deed was done" (10). McKay gives us the sense that both parties blundered into the situation. But the event is quickly reinterpreted through public opinion. When Bita's Anty Nommy sees blood on her shift, she takes Bita to the village midwife, Sister Phibby Patroll, also known as the "village looselip." Soon the whole countryside knows, and Crazy Bow is arrested and sent to the madhouse. The story of Bita and Crazy Bow is a "toothsome tale" because Bita's father (14), Jordan Plant, is a leading peasant, and his daughter is expected to advance out of peasant society into the professional class. There is humor in her tale for those whom she would leave behind, for "before she was thirteen she had fallen into the profound pit that yawned between the plane of the peasantry and higher achievement." Bita is thus taunted in a popular folk ballad, which McKay repeats several times in the novel:

You may wrap her up in silk,
You may trim her up with gold,
And the prince may come after
To ask for your daughter,
But Crazy Bow was first.

Thus, in the first instance, Bita's rape is seen by her fellow peasantry as a joke because it undermines her potential to achieve an improvement in class position. Sister Phibby's influence extends far and wide. We also see her walk the fifteen miles to the town of Jubilee to inform Malcolm and Priscilla Craig. Because Malcolm Craig's father and Jordan Plant's father were friends, the Craigs feel a special sympathy toward Bita. They too see Bita's rape as an obstacle to her potential rise in class position, although they view this as a tragic circumstance rather than a joke. Priscilla Craig in particular takes this as an opportunity for "taking Bita to train as an exhibit" (17). She wants to show that education in Christian moral doctrine can help a fallen peasant girl to get back on the road to success. The Craigs take her in at the mission and later send her to England for an education. In her recent description of the relations between class and popular culture in this society Carolyn Cooper explains that "upward social mobility in Jamaica requires the shedding of the old skin of early socialisation: mother tongue, mother culture, mother wit—the feminised discourse of voice, identity and native knowledge."[24] When Bita is sent abroad, "the peasants were stunned by the news and gossiped about nothing else" (29), and many are jealous they could not go abroad as she does. The Craigs thus convert Bita's early infamy into the occasion for instruction of the peasant class, and she is to become an example of redemption through moral instruction.

When Bita finally returns to Jamaica, she finds herself again the object of intense scrutiny and class conflict. In the opening scene we see her accompany the Coloured Choristers on the piano in a test of wills; the chorus varies the tempo to throw her off course, but she keeps up and wins their approval. As an officer of the mission, Bita is expected to stitch together the culture of the black peasants and the moral expectations of the white Christian faith. She must serve as both a model of exceptional virtue and as one of the folk. Her position makes her passage through public space somewhat awkward. On her first return to the public market in Jubilee we learn that Bita is not inclined to feel alienated from her people:

Many young natives had gone to the city or abroad for higher culture and had returned aloof from, if not actually despising, the
tribal life in which they were nurtured. But the pure joy that Bita
felt in the simple life of her girlhood was childlike and almost
unconscious. She could not reason and theorize why she felt that
way. It was just a surging free big feeling. (41)

Already we see her instinctively drawn to identify with her native people. Her shopping trip is described as an orgy, for we see her feel "an
impulse to touch and fondle a thousand times more than she wanted to
buy," and she revels in the crowd: "Bita mingled in the crowd, respon-
sive to the feeling, the colour, the smell, the swell and press of it. It gave
her the sensation of a reservoir of familiar kindred humanity into
which she had descended for baptism" (40). But her yearning to be
immersed in the crowd is contradicted by Mrs. Craig's desire that she
also stand apart from it as an example. When Bita reveals that she had
conversed with Hopping Dick, "an outstanding member of the un-
godly set" (39), she is reprimanded by Mrs. Craig and reminded that
members of the mission are to be "living examples of right conduct"
(45). The incident leaves Bita wondering about her future, worrying if
she can live up to Mrs. Craig's standards, and distractedly reading the
novels of Mrs. Humphrey Ward.

Emancipation and "Vulgar Amusements"

When Bita makes her first return to the village of Banana Bottom, we
see that she will eventually give in to the "surging free big feeling" that
hit her in the marketplace. Perhaps the first clue is that the visit coin-
cides with Emancipation Day, and Bita "anticipated with happiness the
freedom of going bandanna on a picnic day" (49). But Bita's liberating
indulgence goes beyond the sartorial: "she was overcome by a feeling
to capture and live again that moment of her barefooted girlhood" (59).
She will encounter difficulty in recapturing the moment, however, for
both Bita and the village are intimidated by each other—Bita because
she has been asked to perform for them, the village because "in their
eyes she was now a grand lady who had been to the high white folk's
country and was learned in their ways, just like one of them with only
the difference of pigmentation" (51). Bita does not seek to perform as a
lady for the village folk but to join them in their daily lives as one of

them. She had never been to one of the tea meetings, which are the "principal indigenous amusements of the peasantry," and when she hears the drum announcing one she is "suddenly seized with longing to go" (56). But tea meetings are denounced from the pulpit as "vulgar amusements," and she cannot go because of her position. She is destined to spend the next day handing out Euro-American children's literature as prizes for good conduct to the children of the village church.

Bita will have another chance, however, to go to a tea meeting. During the next day's picnic she meets Squire Gensir, an English folklorist who has taken up residence in the village area. "The peasants were his hobby" (71), and he has spent the last several years transcribing their folklore and songs. Bita complains that her position has prevented her from going to a tea meeting, but she is convinced to go with the squire, since "she thought it would make all the difference if she went like a spectator to a tea-meeting with . . . a person like Squire Gensir, who could do as he liked and yet command the respect of the highest and the lowest people" (74). Bita's education matches that of the squire, and they match each other in being exiles from their native cultures. They also share both an appreciation of and distance from the folk culture of the village; because he has not gone native, Bita is not expected to revert either. So Bita is able to go with him as a spectator to her native culture. But their experiences of the tea meeting are not the same. When Bita dares to join the dance, she gives in to her purported nature:

> Her body was warm and willing for that native group dancing. It came more natural to her than the waltzes and minuets, although she liked these too in a more artificial atmosphere.
> . . . And she danced forgetting herself, forgetting even Jubilee, dancing down the barrier between high breeding and common pleasures under her light stamping feet until she was one with the crowd. (84)

She discovers that she cannot be a mere spectator to the scene, and she wonders at Gensir's "merely cerebral" experience in comparison to hers: "Were [his] . . . nerves and body cells not touched as hers?" (85–86). Bita's forgetting on the dance floor is also her first remembering of her collective identity with her native folk.

Bita cannot commit an indiscretion without Sister Phibby Patroll spoiling the day. Sister Phibby has rushed to Jubilee as she did nine years previously to tell Priscilla Craig about Bita's attendance at the tea meeting. Mrs. Craig is tormented by the news:

> She had spent an afternoon in hell wrestling with the devil, who all black and flame-red with lifted tail kept dancing around and darting up to her to whisper satanisms in her ear:
> Bita was atavistic as was her race. A branch of the same root and the deceptive lovely flower would wither to seed a similar tree. (92)

Bita is completely absolved when she reveals Gensir had accompanied her to the tea meeting. But the Craigs take her interest as a warning and decide that she should get married as soon as possible. Once again, Bita's affiliation with her people has brought gossip and the charge of atavism.

Marriage Plot I: Class, Religiosity, Sexuality

Marriage will fix Bita's desires in a form acceptable to Mrs. Craig. Bita has known for some time that she is to be married to Herald Newton Day, a black theological student who is expected to take over the missionary when the Craigs retire, and Bita is to continue her work at the mission as his wife. It is as if their marriage is the true mission of the Craigs: "A cultured native couple succeeding to one of the finest missions in the colony. That in the minds of the Craigs would be the best tribute to their labour, the most fitting fulfillment to the pioneer purpose that lay behind the founding and building of Jubilee" (36). But Day is something of a phony, "full of self-satisfaction and, considering his youth, on too intimate terms with God" (97). Bita listens to him preach and realizes she cannot love him. She "longed to be free from the irritation of his presence" and fears that continued contact with him will drive her to break from the Craigs' plan for her entirely (110). When he praises her for being "like a pure-minded white lady," she can only reply, "I am myself" (100).

Fortunately for Bita, she is called back to Banana Bottom. Once again she has the opportunity to immerse herself in her past, this time quite literally. Taking a stroll along the Cane River, she comes upon the boys' bathing hole, where she watches five schoolboys bathe. Caught watching, she moves on to the girls' bathing hole, which evokes memories of many past swims: "All of her body was tingling sweet with affectionate feeling for the place" (117). Naked, she plunges into the water and exposes her breasts to the sun and feels ecstatic: "How delicious was the feeling of floating! To feel that one can suspend oneself upon a yawning depth and drift, drifting in perfect confidence without the slightest intruding thought of danger." The scene signals her safe immersion in her past, an immersion that contrasts sharply with the atavism Mrs. Craig imagines, while it also recalls her sense of being baptized in the crowd in the market. While in the water, her "thoughts flitted across her mind like cinema scenes," and these scenes are projected images of the world Mrs. Craig has introduced to her, including her college days, a trip to Germany with Mrs. Craig, and Herald Newton Day. As in her trip to the tea meeting, Bita is once again a spectator. But this time she views from within the safe, soothing waters of her girlhood swimming hole, where she shares memories with others of her village, and she views the world of the town and beyond. This time the cinematic apparatus distances her technologically from the world she recalls, just as earlier the folklorist had provided a way of mediating her distance from her people.

Squire Gensir's position as a folklorist provides Bita with a comparativist stance from which to review the religious practices of Christianity and Obeah. When Bita claims, during a visit to the squire's hut, that Obeah "is an awful crime," the squire replies: "Oh, it's just our civilization that makes it a crime. Obeah is only a form of primitive superstition. As Christianity is a form of civilized superstition" (124). This equivocal position is generally endorsed by the novel; each is understood as a superstition with a different political valence. So the squire complains that Bita ought to appreciate Obeah because it "is a part of your folklore, like your Anancy tales and your digging jammas. And your folklore is the spiritual link between you and your ancestral origin" (125). He chastises the missionaries for being "the wreck and ruin of folk art throughout the world" (126). Bita is presented with Obeah not as a question of faith but of aesthetics; through aesthetic appreciation she can recover her ancestral origin, and no spiritual conversion is required.

An extended side narrative seems to make the case that Obeah is a superstitious practice that will backfire on those who use it. Bita's friend Yoni Legge becomes jealous when Bita receives a letter from Tack Tally. Tack, Yoni's love interest, has written to apologize for stealing Bita's clothes while she was in the swimming hole. Yoni consults Wumba the Obeahman, who gives her a charm to protect her from Bita's evil in exchange for two months' salary. But, instead, Yoni falls victim to bad fortune: Sister Phibby finds her carrying on with Tack in the schoolhouse, her father has a heart attack when he hears of the tryst, and Tack hangs himself because he thinks he has killed Yoni's father. When Wumba discovers Tack's corpse, he immediately converts to Christianity. Bita remains unaffected by the charm, although of course she never intended evil in the first place. The episode is crowned by a sermon in which equivocation between Christian belief and Obeah is abjured, and the peasant congregation is urged to "throw the jungle out of your hearts and forget Africa" (156). The failure of the Obeah charm to protect Yoni from evil is here used as evidence that Obeah worship is instead an engagement with evil spirits, and Yoni's misfortune is taken to show that only worship of the Christian god will free one from evil.

This example of the futility of Obeah as a means to an end, and of its recuperation by Christian ideology as an example of why one should not stray from the worship of the Lord, is immediately counterpoised with Herald Newton Day's fall. In conversation over tea with Squire Gensir, Day advocates a policy of racial progress: "Life without progress is stagnation. Look at us Negroes, for example. The savage brutish state we were in both in Africa and in America before Civilization aroused us. We owe all we are today to progress" (171). Gensir replies merely that "progress is a grand fact" but does not believe in it. Day's position is undermined in the following scene, in which he is to deliver his valedictory sermon on the topic of personal purity. We see him confidently practicing his elocution, but, when the time for the sermon comes, he is nowhere to be found. He has "descended from the dizzy heights of holiness to the very bottom of the beast," and "the rumour ran through the region that Herald Newton had suddenly turned crazy and defiled himself with a nanny goat" (175). His absurd fall shows him up as a hypocrite and also compels the belief among the peasants that Obi has used Herald as an instrument to punish God. The scene thus shows how each religious system can convert the failings of its opponent into a justification of its own power. We also see a return to the notion of an equivocal balance between the two religious systems, such that each will be used when it seems the most efficacious route to some end, even when prior experience proves the route leads to futility.

Of course, Priscilla Craig has been shocked and dismayed over Day's fall, while Bita feels "as if a mysterious agent in nature had acted for her, but by a means so unusual, so terrible" (180). We see Herald's fall as the beginning of the end for Bita's stay at the mission in Jubilee. Her end is hastened in part because of Mrs. Craig's diminished trust in Bita and in Bita's interest in Hopping Dick. In one scene these two factors are conjoined. Mrs. Craig has a nightmare in which she is attacked by African masks, where she is "deprived of voice to shriek her utter terror among those bodiless barbaric faces circling and darting towards her and bobbing up and down with that mad grinning. . . . Suddenly she too was in motion and madly whirling round and round and round with the weird dancing masks" (199). In the meantime Bita has sneaked out of the mission to go to a dance with Hopping Dick. The conjunction suggests that Bita is becoming what Mrs. Craig's worst dreams portend. Indeed, when Bita admits an inclination to marry Hopping Dick if asked, Mrs. Craig concludes "that Bita at bottom was a nymphomaniac" (221). She telegrams Bita's family in Banana Bottom that Bita is ruining her reputation with Hopping Dick, and she goes home after Hopping Dick tells her he is not interested in marriage. As an experiment, Bita has failed.

Marriage Plot II: Autonomy and "Reverting to Type"

When Bita finally returns home to Banana Bottom, her father is pleased: "Her choosing of her own will to return there filled him with pride" (234). Many of the activities common to Banana Bottom recur upon her return. A phony religious revival led by an opportunistic white capitalist overwhelms the town during a severe drought, but his effort is undermined by a black woman who interrupts and provides what some call "the real old-time revival" (249). Here we see Bita once again give in to a frenzied collective dance:

> Bita seemed to be mesmerized by the common fetish spirit. It was a stranger, stronger thing than that of the Great Revival. Those bodies poised straight in religious ecstasy and dancing vertically

up and down, while others transformed themselves into curious whirling shapes, seemed filled with an ancient nearly-forgotten spirit, something ancestral recaptured in the emotional fervour, evoking in her memories of savage rites, tribal dancing with splendid swaying plumes, and the brandishing of the supple-jacks struck her symbolic of raised and clashing triumphant spears. (250)

Bita collapses in an ecstatic mesmeric trance in which she feels contact with her African lineage. This is the final scene in which she falls into a crowd ecstatically. Later, she recalls "a sensation of becoming a different person in a strange place" (253), and she appreciates Jubban's snatching her away from the circle dance. Jubban, her father's drayman, is to be her husband, and the remainder of the novel is devoted to proving the inevitability of this fact.

This inevitability is effected partially through the deaths of nearly all of the other characters. Crazy Bow returns briefly, attempts murder, and is returned to the madhouse, where he dies in a straitjacket. A hurricane blows in, and Bita's father, Jordan Plant, drowns with Malcolm Craig in the river. Priscilla Craig hears the news, has a stroke, and dies. Squire Gensir's spinster sister calls for him on her deathbed, and he returns to England, where he soon dies. McKay seems to be cleaning up the extraneous clutter of Bita's life so that she can live in simplicity with Jubban.

Jubban has been lurking around in the background as the perfect type of peasant demeanor. We often see him in picturesque settings, gently caring for an animal or carefully working the land. He has been Jordan Plant's favored assistant and is chosen to take over his farm after his death. Bita has her pick of suitors but picks Jubban even though she might have been expected to pick someone of higher class distinction. The narrator explains Bita's rationale:

Jubban was superior in one thing. He possessed a deep feeling for the land and he was a lucky-born cultivator. No one could do better than he in carrying on the work of the soil that had absorbed Jordan Plant's being and kept his heart's blood always warm. (291)

Her decision is disdained by those people in Jubilee who had expected her to progress in the class hierarchy. These people think she is "reverting to type," complaining that, "while girls with less education and chances were aspiring to ladylike living and trying to get away from their peasant origin, Bita had deliberately chosen to vegetate in the backwoods with a common drayman" (292).

But Bita's choice is not a reversion to type. Instead, she is demonstrating in her choice of Jubban authority over her sexual commitments. Her story began with the rape by Crazy Bow and the subsequent efforts of the Craigs to make her an example of Christian piety and the potential for achieving moral progress for her race. As an exemplar, Bita has witnessed her sexual intentions subjected to close scrutiny by the missionaries, the black professional class, and her village folk. Partially due to the tedium of being scrutinized and partially due to her oft-cited native instinct, she is drawn back home. And here she encounters, near the end of the novel, another rapist. She is walking through the savannah on the nearby plantation when the owner's son, Marse Arthur, tries to force himself on her. She fights him off until Jubban arrives and saves her. Whereas in Bita's early life a white woman intervened to save her from the purported sexual aggression of one of Bita's own people, now we see Bita saved from the more conventional rapist, Marse Arthur, "bastard near-white son of a wealthy country gentleman, enjoying all the local privileges of his birth and position" (264), by one of her fellow village folk, Jubban. Although we do not see her as fully self-sufficient—she must always be saved by someone else—we do see her reclaim her sense of her own sexual desires and value her body once again. Arthur has bitterly denounced the intrusion of Jubban on the scene of seduction and chides that she is "only a black gal" (262). As Bita later reflects on this insult, she views herself in the mirror, and her body achieves the lushness of the jungle:

> "Only a nigger gal!" She undressed and looked at her body in the long mirror of the old-fashioned wardrobe. She caressed her breasts like maturing pomegranates, her skin firm and smooth like the sheath of a blossoming banana, her luxuriant hair, close-curling like thick fibrous roots, gazed at her own warm-brown eyes, the infallible indicators of real human beauty. (266)

While this portrait of Bita would seem merely to exoticize her body, Bita's recent experience encourages her to frame this as a vision of an empowered self. Carolyn Cooper has recently explained how the contextual placement of "the vulgar discourses of the feminised native body"[25] suggest another reading:

> The emotive trope of blood and bone connotes what may be constructed as "racist" assumptions about biologically-determined culture, if the label is applied by the alienating Other. Assumed by the in-group, this figure of speech denotes a genealogy of ideas, a blood-line of beliefs and practices that are transmitted in the body, in oral discourse.[26]

Here we see her reclaim her body as an organic being, rather than as the site of moral scrutiny and racist insult. This organicism informs her final contentment, for she and Jubban have a child and work the land her father left for them.

The Folk as Alternative Modernity

That Bita's new family will work the land in the manner of peasants returns us to the economic argument of the novel. As we learned from Holt's account of the peasant appropriation of economic capital, choosing to work the land as a peasant allows Bita to occupy a relatively autonomous niche in a complex global economy. The novel made this clear in its early account of the coffee collective gone bad. In the concluding chapters the novel also reminds us of the local threats to the economic welfare of the Afro-Jamaican peasantry. In a late conversation at Squire Gensir's the relation of the emancipated slaves to imported Indian and Chinese workers is debated. Plantation owners brought in laborers from abroad who would work for less than the local Jamaican peasants in the post-emancipation era. The narrator argues against "the method of importing coolie labour" (240) and shows McKay's clear preference for the "hardy Negro peasantry" (238), who he claims are better workers. He also shows that the immigrant laborers are appreciated in some ways by the Jamaican public. The novel discourages the importation of workers in part because the practice puts Afro-Jamaican peasants out of work. And it also argues that these workers are gravely dependent on a large system of exchange that will not protect their livelihood. The end of the novel shows Banana Bottom subject to several years of drought, a hurricane, and floods, none of which augurs well for an agriculture-dependent economy. A shortage of food threatens most of the peasants, but not Jordan Plant, who, "as usual, had been a shrewd cultivator, never planting all of his best land with banana" (292). The narrator draws a moral: "The planters saw in the visitation of the elements a salutary lesson—for the peasant workers. For although the plantations had been ravaged, too, the planters had reserves of food and money that the peasants had not" (293). Most peasants became desperate because they relied too heavily on the novel's signature commodity, the banana, and had not diversified their planting enough to account for the vagaries of economic and natural disaster. Jordan Plant is thus held up as an exemplary peasant, and his daughter is to follow in his footsteps on the route to economic autonomy and political modernity.

Banana Bottom's narrative voice shuttles between melodramatic pathos and satirical jibes. The novel is strongly driven by the machinations of plot, and the narrator stays mostly on the surface of events to register the affective ideology of their consequences. Often the narrator registers pity, as when Bita is taunted by the folk ballad that "Crazy Bow was first"; at other times the narrator traces the plot development with sadistic satire, as when Herald Newton Day defiles himself with a nanny goat. In tracing the unfolding of the plot in this chapter, I have found it difficult not to be arch; the novel's constant engagement of purported inevitables, as when we repeatedly find that Bita is "a natural dancer" (192), demands a certain pathos, in that here Bita has been deprived of the opportunity to dance, while it also encourages in the reader a sadistic glee in seeing Bita succumb to her base nature. In this sense the novel encourages us to take the attitude of Sister Phibby Patroll, who takes pleasure in Bita's disgrace even as she intervenes to save her. But the narrative seems most sincere when it finds Bita returning to her folk roots sure of her own worth. As I have suggested, this is the place where the naturalistic drive of the novel is halted and she is inserted into the stable and ameliorative realm of the folk romance. Once Bita is returned to her roots, the narrative voice ceases to weigh in to register pathos for Bita's lost folk identity or to harshly disdain the characters who would prevent her from getting back to it or even to wryly suggest that Bita's return is inevitable. Indeed, here the narrative ceases to exist.

The novel's closure has rankled some critics who have viewed its utopianism as suspect. Like Gilkes, Lawrence, and other critics I have previously discussed, Hazel Carby lodges this complaint about the novel's romantic closure:

> Much of the argument of *Banana Bottom* emerges in the tension between attempts by missionaries to eradicate black cultural forms and the gentler forms of abuse present in white patronage of black culture. Against these forms of exploitation McKay reconstructs black culture as sustaining a whole way of life. But it is a way of life of the past, of his formative years, a place that the intellectual had to leave to become an intellectual and to which he does not return except in this Utopian moment.[27]

A consideration of the place of utopianism in Caribbean art, however, will help us to understand the political investments that motivate this novel's utopian conclusion. In his work on Afro-Caribbean narrative Patrick Taylor situates utopian, synchronic liberation within historical and narrative diachrony: "Liberating narrative . . . does not lose itself in an abstract universality, divorced from all temporality. Liberation is only meaningful as the realization of freedom in time, that is, as a lived universal."[28] McKay's "timeless" solution to the expediencies of contemporary political concerns is characteristic of many cultural projects in the region: in *The Repeating Island* Antonio Benítez-Rojo has described "the wish to reach the state of racial, social, and cultural non-violence" that undergirds "a utopian project of coexistence that made up for the fragmentary, unstable, and conflictual Antillean existence" in Caribbean cultural formations:[29]

> The cultural discourse of the Peoples of the Sea attempts, through real or symbolic sacrifice, to neutralize violence and to refer society to the transhistorical codes of Nature. . . . In this paradoxical space, in which one has the illusion of experiencing a totality, there appear to be no repressions or contradictions; there is no desire other than that of maintaining oneself within the limits of this zone for the longest possible time, in free orbit, beyond imprisonment or liberty.[30]

McKay's utopian fantasy, then, is best understood as motivated by the desire to resolve historical contradictions and constrictions in a speculative manner.

Such speculative resolution is hard-won, Simon Gikandi would argue: "An integrated discourse of self is surely the ultimate or possibly utopian desire of Caribbean writing, but it can only be reached after the negotiation of a historically engendered split between the self and its world, between this self and the language it uses."[31] Bita's story dramatizes this negotiation between self and world; McKay's own position as he created this drama reveals the impulses motivating this speculative resolution. Frequently described as a "double exile"[32] (from Harlem and Jamaica) writing from an ambivalent situation between home and abroad through which "the unity of identity and contradiction emerges with the greatest force,"[33] McKay was living in Tangier on an acre of land, growing potatoes, peas, carrots, and turnips for sustenance and struggling to write the novel that would restore him to financial stability.[34] McKay's garden provided greater sustenance than did the market on which *Banana Bottom* was sold: the Great Depression adversely affected the publishing industry, and the novel made no money.[35] So, while McKay's speculative return to Jamaica enacts a utopian fantasy, this fantasy is impelled by his lived experience in Tangier as both an internationally acclaimed novelist and a peasant. His situation ironically underscores the economic argument of the novel: in a volatile global marketplace, the development of peasant freeholds for subsistence farming will offer a relatively stable alternative for both the author and his heroine. It also recalls McKay's hopeful departure early in life for Tuskegee Institute, where he briefly studied agronomy. As we will see in the next chapter, Tuskegee's stress on individual discipline as a route to collective advancement for black Americans provided the impetus for other folk-centered aesthetic works in this era.

I have earlier noted the paradox of Bita's return to her folk identity: in liberating herself from the strictures of the civilizing efforts of the Craigs, Bita succumbs to her instinct. Her arrival back at Banana Bottom as emblematic earth mother seems simply to put her in her place. The novel would then seem to be an elaborate scheme to contain the political agency of Afro-Jamaican women. But, as I have suggested, Bita's affiliation with the peasant class has a political valence beyond that of a need for her to be true to herself; her affiliation bespeaks an

intransigence to the incursions of colonial rule as well as to the exigencies of a global commodity culture, and it thus allows her to create an
alternative modernity to the colonial modernity of the mission, whose
promise of autonomy through Christian civilization was so stultifying
for Bita. And here, perhaps, we see the stubborn attractiveness of an
aesthetics based in the folk. The appeal is not in mere nostalgia and a
sentimental recovery of lost origins but in the intractable logic of an
identity politics structured simultaneously by the promise of free
abstract self-expression and the solace of essentialism. Here, at the
unchanging historical horizon of the synchronic folk world, is both a
historical totality and, in the context of modern culture, a place from
which to argue.

Rural Modernity, Migration, and the Gender of Autonomy: The Novels of George Wylie Henderson

In Richard Wright's "Long Black Song" a white, traveling salesman from Chicago visits Sarah, a black sharecropper's wife in the rural South, to disastrous effect. The salesman wants to sell an instrument that combines a graphophone and clock in one box, but Sarah is not interested because, she says, "We git erlong widout time."[1] When the salesman demonstrates the graphophone for her, however, she swoons; the narrator describes her reaction as indicative of her commitment to a temporality structured around seasonal cycles: "She leaned her back against a post, trembling, feeling the rise and fall of days and nights, of summer and winter; surging, ebbing, leaping about her, beyond her, far out over the fields to where earth and sky lay folded in darkness."[2] Wright's opposition between the "timeless" rural woman and the mobile urban male is common to the literature of migration. In "Long Black Song" Sarah's timeless embodiment of seasonal cycles leaves her vulnerable to the sexual predation of the salesman. Her husband's murderous rage against the salesman leaves him with a simple choice: to migrate or to face a band of white avengers.[3]

As in Wright's story, much of the literature on African-American migration stresses men's mobility over women's rootedness. Sarah, like Claude McKay's Bita Plant, moves to the rhythms of seasonal change; both are examples of the "earth mother" who symbolically links maternity with agricultural production. In *Cane* many of the women are presented as being too fragile to make it in the city. The narrator of Toomer's "Fern," an African-American man from the North, considers bringing Fern back to the city with him, but he notes "the futility of mere change of place"; she is better off on the farm, he argues.[4] But, while the male migrant's mobility suggests his greater freedom, the literature on migration also frequently portrays the impetus for migration as flight from violence: Sarah's husband must choose between facing his avengers or fleeing his hard-won farm. For both the rooted woman and the wandering male, gender provides a logic of location in the Southern landscape. Thus, the earth mother has a cherished place on the farm, but she is also stuck there; similarly, the wandering migrant male is free to move about, but likely this is because he is fleeing violence or seeking work.

This chapter addresses the persistent pattern of gendered location in migration narratives that dramatize the achievement of individual autonomy for African Americans. Individual autonomy is a hallmark of political modernity, by which citizens understand their economic activity as a free exercise of their rights. In the context of agricultural modernization in the South, two opposed routes to individual autonomy opened up: a rural modernity in which subsistence farming would guarantee both economic and cultural endurance and an urban modernity in which migrants would discover refuge and plenitude in metropolitan centers. As I have suggested, the aspiration for rural modernity is typically linked to the figure of the woman, while migratory hopes were pinned on the mobile male. These incompatible stories suggest the persistence of the aspiration for autonomy in an era when economic modernization and chronic racial injustice were the decisive forces.

The Bildungsroman, Modernization, and Economic Autonomy

My investigation into this pattern of gendered autonomy focuses on two relatively forgotten novels by George Wylie Henderson. Although Henderson's novels have recently been reprinted through the Library of Alabama Classics series at the University of Alabama Press, they have received scant critical attention.[5] My interest in these books lies in their author's historical location and in his choice of form. Henderson was born in Warrior Stand, Alabama, in 1904, trained as a printer at

Tuskegee Institute from 1918 to 1922, and later moved to New York, where, after some struggles, he became an apprentice printer at the *New York Daily News*.[6] As we will see, much of Henderson's life story is woven into his books.[7] Moreover, his education at Booker T. Washington's Tuskegee, where African Americans were to learn to be self-reliant in order to advance the collective goals of the "race," provided the foundation for an ethos stressing individual autonomy as a route to political modernity. This ethos is underwritten by Henderson's choice of form: the generic structure of the Bildungsroman, the classic narrative of romantic self-discovery and individuation, is clearly reproduced in both of his novels. More specifically, the novels exhibit the features of what M. M. Bakhtin has called "the novel of human emergence," which he further categorizes by "the degree of assimilation of real historical time."[8]

Each of Henderson's two novels presents an African-American individual's search for autonomy under the pressures of modernization in the American South. His first novel, *Ollie Miss* (1935), is set in the shadow of Tuskegee and documents its heroine's discovery of "a farm of her own" where she can raise her child without the complications of a man's attentions.[9] This novel maintains the congruity of the folk world by grounding the heroine's autonomy in seasonal change; Ollie Miss labors in a fixed cycle that will sustain her livelihood and reproduce the folk world for her progeny. This novel typifies most of the novels Bakhtin discusses, in which "man emerged, developed, and changed within one epoch"; indeed, as we will see, this novel's focus on female development will encourage us to read this epoch as eternal.[10] Henderson's second novel, *Jule* (1946), traces the story of Ollie Miss's son as he comes "to be somebody."[11] His story begins on the farm and ends in New York, where he works his way up from dishwasher to apprentice printer with a union job; he returns to Alabama on the occasion of his mother's death to claim his bride and deliver her from a desiccated Southern landscape to the city, secure that he has become somebody after all. His story is characteristic of another type of the novel of emergence as Bakhtin defines it: "He is no longer within an epoch, but on the border between two epochs, at the transition point from one to the other."[12] The second novel suggests that the folk world portrayed in the first novel can no longer guarantee autonomy; *Jule* recognizes that in an era that saw the mechanization of farming in the South and the Great Migration of black Southerners from rural areas to urban centers, the best hope for autonomy lay in the emerging black proletariat.

Ollie Miss: Desiring Agent, Folk Emblem

In *Ollie Miss* the heroine becomes both emblem and agent of the per-petuation of an African-American folk community. Her role as an emblem is supported in part by the material presentation of the book: the novel achieves the look of a folk artifact primarily through a series of block prints by Lowell Leroy Balcolm. The image facing the first page (see fig. 5) presents a portrait of Ollie that is simple and direct; her profile is framed in a field that shows little motion. Other block prints retell parts of the novel by relating a scene to a caption from the text (see, e.g., fig. 6), reminiscent of medieval allegory. This allusion to a folk aesthetic is further reinforced by the visual motifs placed at the end of each chapter depicting items from everyday life in the rural South. Such images as a cabin, a three-legged skillet, a guitar, a mule, and a plow are presented without any motivated relation to the plot of the book and thus merely bring into view the implements of labor and of sustenance in a folk culture. But they also help to determine the way in which the book as printed object is received. The technology of the block print antedates the era of movable type and of the culture of lit-eracy more generally. Although the novel is itself a product of modern literary culture, Henderson has presented Ollie and her world as if they come from a folk world immune to the intrusion of modern life. This role is also supported by her eventual embodiment of the earth mother stereotype.[13]

Yet, while the book presents Ollie as an emblem, she is also, as I have said, presented as an agent in the perpetuation of folk life. The novel consequently tells the story of how she comes to choose her emblematic status. When *Ollie Miss* opens, we find the heroine in a rest-less state. It is dusk, and Ollie is about to depart on a journey through the swamp adjoining the farm where she works to visit her lover, Jule, whom she has not seen in eight weeks. Ollie's agitation concerns not only the imminent journey but also her feelings about her home on this farm. Ollie has been characterized by "an innocence that was as primi-tive and unpretentious as a child's" (*OM*, 2), and in the opening chap-ter her simplicity is related to a lack of devotion to one place. As we

Fig. 5. "Ollie." Block print by Lowell Leroy Balcolm. The figure faces the first page of the novel and has subsequently been used for the cover of the novel's reprinting in the Library of Alabama Classics series from the University of Alabama Press. George Wylie Henderson, *Ollie Miss*, xxii. (Reprinted by permission of Roslyn K. Allen.)

Fig. 6. "Ollie and Slaughter Returned to Their Plows and Contin-
ued until Noon." Block print by Lowell Leroy Balcolm. George
Wylie Henderson, *Ollie Miss*, 49. (Reprinted by permission of
Roslyn K. Allen.)

watch her make a nightly trip to the well, we wonder if her impulsive-
ness will take her away from this farm:

> Night after night, she came and let her bucket down into its [the
> well's] depth for what it could give. When it couldn't give any
> longer, she'd seek out another. Or, if she tired of what it had to

offer, she'd hit the trail for that which seemed the more appealing. Inside of her, she was simple enough. An impulse seized her and she moved. The mere knowledge of a picnic or a camp meeting . . . could set her blood pitching to a boiling heat. (*OM*, 3)

Tonight, however, she feels different: "something seemed to throb deep within her." This throbbing suggests that she is feeling a deeper commitment to something, but the object is not named. Instead, the narrative presents several scenes for which she feels some attachment. We see the cabin of Alex and Caroline, who employ her on their farm, and its hitching post—"her nearest approach to home!" (*OM*, 7)—and we observe the sense of security she enjoys here:

True, she'd forsake it [home] to frolic . . . , to inhale the smell of corn whisky on hot breaths, to dance to a nervous, half-crazed rhythm, strummed hot, like a blue flame, under a burning Alabama moon. But she'd come back, and Alex would let her stay.

We also see the work she does in a positive light—"She could plow. She could hoe and wield an ax."—and we see the farm populated by an inspiring lot: "from somewhere a voice would rise and split the dewy silence,—the field cry of a black soul to his ox!" (*OM*, 8). But, as she prepares to leave, Ollie looks at the four walls of her own cabin and finds the setting insufficient: "Dis is de only home I got, an' hit ain't enough—" (*OM*, 9). As the opening chapter closes, we sense that Ollie's restlessness will impel her to abandon her simple diffidence; her throbbing will settle into a deep attachment, perhaps to Jule.

But, before we witness Ollie's journey, Henderson provides us with eight chapters detailing Ollie's first arrival on the farm and the stir she makes there. Ollie has wandered onto the farm one spring evening, at dusk, looking for work and her first meal in two days. Ollie's past is murky at best: some say she's "one of those back-water women . . . sprung" from Black Bottom (*OM*, 11), while others say she comes from "down on the swamp" (*OM*, 12). The aura of mystery surrounding Ollie's origins engenders intense speculation, inspiring particularly strong reactions from two characters. Nan, a jealous and spiteful woman who is also the local gossip, takes an immediate antipathy to Ollie: she expects her to take off after her begged meal and accuses her of allowing "de mens to talk sweet talk to her." Nan encourages other women on the scene of Ollie's arrival to eye her with suspicion, if not disdain. But the men generally have a more favorable impression. Slaughter, Shell, and Willie view her with great interest: "From the first, they had watched her with a curious fascination" (*OM*, 18). For Slaughter, Ollie is particularly engaging; his "eyes were filled with consuming interest. . . . He felt helpless. His breathing became spasmodic and labored, and a strange warmth filled him." These extreme responses to Ollie are mollified by the avuncular Alex and his wife, who feed her and provide her with a tiny cabin; as she prepares for sleep there her first night, she ruminates on her recent independence from Jule and ponders over the undue attention given her upon her arrival.

Ollie continues to stand out even as she becomes part of the daily life of the farm. She has bragged that she can do anything on a farm, and apparently she works with more strength than the male hands. On her first day she "plowed row for row" with the men as they silently struggled to keep up to her pace (*OM*, 41). When she explains to her coworkers that "cussin' in front of 'omans is de same to me as cussin' in front of mens" (*OM*, 47), Shell wonders "whut kind of 'oman is dat?" (*OM*, 48). The others reply by wondering if she's a woman at all. Nan increases this speculation when she calls Ollie a "brazen heifer" for smoking a cigarette (*OM*, 59); the ladies of the farm smoke pipes and dip snuff. But, if Ollie does not compel respect from her female peers, she continues to compel Slaughter's "growing and vital fascination": "To him, the girl might have been a drug—a kind of obsession, cruel and consuming" (*OM*, 42). Ollie meets Slaughter's obsession with quiet diffidence—she "seemed scarcely conscious of the man at all" (*OM*, 43)—and she declines his advances. She has remained equally aloof after Nan's excoriation of her. Ollie's silence adds to her mystique and fans the flames of gossip.

About two weeks into her residence on the farm, Ollie elects to go to one of Lucy West's parties. Hearing the "swampy blues" (*OM*, 79), Ollie immediately joins in the dance, taking Little Willie as her partner. No longer quiet, here Ollie asserts her independence by making a spectacle of herself: "Old men and young swung their partners about to get a look at this girl, and ladies from Black Bottom craned their neck and dilated their black, snapping eyes at the boldness of this creature's hips" (*OM*, 80). Ollie's boldness compels several observers to try to rein her in: men fight over the chance to dance with her, and Lucy takes her aside to make the case that Ollie should settle down with Slaughter. But Ollie thinks there's no reason to fight over her: "Peoples fight ovah somethin' they owns, an' when they don't owns nuthin' they ain't got nuthin' to fight about" (*OM*, 85). Ollie's refusal to take on the status of property frustrates the community's attempt to contain her, while it also leads her to choose the young Willie over the reliable and marriageable Slaughter as dance partner and lover. When Willie returns to the men's cabin at dawn, after a night spent with Ollie in a bed of pine needles at stream's edge, Slaughter and Shell are both angry at Willie and surprised that Ollie would fall for him. Ollie continues to assert her independence from her new community, heedless of advice and apparently aimless in her choice of company.

But Ollie eventually settles into the routine of life on the farm. She does not do so by making a symbolic attachment (such as marriage) to a particular member of the community but, rather, by getting into the rhythm of agricultural work on the farm:

> Ollie, beginning her third week at Alex's, settled easily into the leisurely routine of hoeing and plowing. She went forth early when the dew was heavy and returned late when the dusk was thick. Work and sweat and the heat of day gave her little concern. She was born to work. . . . It was as simple as that, week in and week out. (*OM*, 111)

Although Nan takes her to task for "wallowin' around wid dem mens" at Lucy West's (*OM*, 118), Ollie does not let social scrutiny determine the pattern of her life. She follows the seasons "from sun to sun, from Monday morning to Saturday noon!" (*OM*, 109), and her own will, refusing profound attachment to anyone in her circle of acquaintances.

After the Plantation: Alabama Agriculture in the 1930s

Given the novel's discussion of the "leisurely routine" of work on the farm (*OM*, 111), it is worth pausing to consider how agricultural labor was organized in rural Alabama during the 1930s. The novel is set in Macon County, Alabama, home of Tuskegee Institute and the site for Charles S. Johnson's 1934 sociological study of six hundred black families, *Shadow of the Plantation*.[14] Johnson's study explicitly names romantic fiction in the plantation tradition as the descriptive genre his study is designed to demystify:

> The plantation as represented in tradition and popular fancy is so far removed from the existing institution as to be but slightly related to the character of the folk that it bred. In the romantic fiction, which has so largely supported the concept, it is a far-flung, comfortably self-contained agricultural unit, crested by a spacious white mansion with imposing colonnades supporting cool and spacious verandas, and surrounded in ample and flower-laden grounds. . . . There are long rows of white-washed Negro cabins; sleek, contented slaves, laughing and singing as they work; little pickaninnies capering with the abandonment of irresponsible fledglings in the clearings of the cabins or on the smoothly clipped lawns.[15]

In contrast to this view, which he notes is born of an inept comparison with feudalism,[16] Johnson takes the position that Southern cotton plantations were "based on a rigorous and dull routine, with strict diversification of labor" in which African Americans were completely dependent on the success of the landowners, who were in turn dependent upon a far-flung cash economy.[17] His corrective exercise in sociological realism reveals that the ideal of a "comfortably self-contained agricultural unit" was not to be achieved.[18] Johnson argues that, although the plantation system had withered away by the 1930s, "the present Negro population of these old plantation areas can best be understood by viewing it in the light of this plantation tradition, with its almost complete dependence upon the immediate landowner for guidance and control in virtually all those phases of life which are related to the moving world outside"; there was little change in society here since the plantation era, he claims.[19] But change, Johnson shows, would be inevitable: "The waste of the soil, the overproduction of cotton, the constant involvement of the credit system, have brought on an inevitable stagnation, both for planters and for the Negroes whose lives are linked with its ever declining fortunes."[20] Faced with stagnation and decline, black Southerners would leave rather than reform agricultural life: "A natural response to this has been the constant and determined movement away of both Negro and white populations to the city and its industries in so far as these industries could absorb them. . . . The romantic personalities of the past who dominated the plantation are rapidly passing."[21]

While Henderson's novel is not a plantation romance, it shares an optimism about the agrarian economy with those stories. In *Ollie Miss* Uncle Alex owns the farm; he hires on hands to work most of it and lets out the rest to sharecroppers (see, e.g., fig. 7). As Alex's avuncular title suggests, the farm's social setting is like that of a family. Although the novel suggests an ordinariness about Uncle Alex's farm, it would have been unusual to encounter a prosperous black landowner in the rural Alabama of the 1930s.[22] Moreover, given that Johnson's analysis of the depletion of the soil, the rise of migration patterns, and the difficulties of the credit system rings true with subsequent history, we can read Henderson's description of the leisurely routine of farm life as overly optimistic. Ollie Miss's achievement of a farm of her own would be singular indeed. Nevertheless, in the context of the literary contemplation of rural modernities the novel offers a speculative alternative to sharecropping and migration.

A Farm of Her Own: Sex, Labor, Reification

Before Ollie is to achieve a farm of her own, the novel must show her grapple with her unfixed desire. In July the growing cycle changes, and Ollie is able to leave the farm for a spell: we return to the opening scene of the novel and follow Ollie's departure to see Jule. Now she has "a definite mission" (*OM*, 131), and it takes her through the bottom in a rainstorm overnight. As she travels through the swamp, Ollie becomes immersed in the murky waters, and she forgets herself since "the only living thing she could think about now was Jule" (*OM*, 134). Her newly found sense of direction takes her to Jule's empty cabin, where she finds another woman's slip in the bed sheets. Upset, she goes to visit the neighboring cabin of Della, who once stole Jule's affections from Ollie Miss. She confirms that the slip belongs to a new woman in Jule's life, and Della and Ollie sit for a week watching for Jule's return, becoming "almost like sisters, with but a single, redeeming passion to mark their sisterhood" (*OM*, 148). Ollie must return to Alex's farm without seeing Jule, but she returns knowing that "the fact that she wanted to see Jule, made [her] . . . want to live" (*OM*, 153). The trip has

Fig. 7. "A Small Tenant Farm Producing Peanuts and Sweet
Potatoes in Southeastern Alabama, August 1938." Photograph
by Dorothea Lange. (Courtesy of the U.S. Farm Security Administration Collection, Prints and Photographs Division, Library of
Congress, LC-USF 34-18335-D.)

led her to abandon her aimlessness and to replace it with direction. She
has also experienced jealousy for Jule's new woman (she burned the
slip in the fireplace) and empathy with her former rival, Della. Ollie has
been changed by the trip, and these changes will affect how she makes
decisions throughout the rest of the novel.

We next encounter Ollie Miss attending the camp meeting two
months after her journey. Ollie is characteristically aloof as she makes
her way through the crowd, which has gathered from neighboring
communities for Gospel preaching, food and drink, and frolicking in
the woods.[23] In this scene Ollie seems aloof in a particularly directed
way; when she sees Willie, she declines his invitation to walk with him,
and she further rejects the opportunity to frolic in the way she had at

Lucy West's party. When she walks off alone down the road and encounters Jule, we see immediately where her energies are directed: she sees him, and "she caught at her lips with her teeth to keep them from trembling, and her body swayed back and forth on her feet, as though she were going to faint" (*OM*, 187). The usually self-possessed Ollie nearly falls apart. She begs him to break his promise to return that night to his new woman in Roba, and he complies and stays at Ollie's cabin. But Ollie senses danger in her emotional attachment to Jule: when she learns that Della has died, she tells Jule: "you done killed Della. . . . She couldn't want you an'—an' keep on livin' an' not hab you, like I could" (*OM*, 191–92). We finally see Ollie's answer to the "something [that] seemed to throb deep within her" presented in the first chapter (*OM*, 3), but it is an answer that is fraught with danger.

As it turns out, Ollie's sexual attachment to Jule results in a rupture of her control over her body. After Ollie wakes from her night with Jule, the narrator reveals the ambivalent news that "her body felt peacefully dead!":

> Her body used to feel things—used to live and breathe and respond to things. But now it only felt a little numb. . . . She could get up and leave her body there beside Jule until it ached and came alive again, if she wanted to. Then she could come back and repossess it, and Jule could go back to Roba yonder. (*OM*, 202)

In this assessment Ollie's desire has materialized into the form of her body, and she sees both her desire and her body transferred to Jule as property. For Ollie to repossess her body and its sentience, Jule must leave. But Ollie does not want to repossess her own body so much as she wants to possess Jule. Consequently, she becomes jealous when he leaves to return to Lena, the woman in Roba. Lena returns Ollie's jealousy. When Ollie attends the final night of the camp meeting, she is once again alienated from the crowd—"They kept marching and Ollie went on watching. She stared as though a barrier had been raised between her and them—as though they existed in another world apart from her, and she was no longer one among them" (*OM*, 217). But Ollie is drawn into the crowd when she discovers a fight between Lena and Jule, and she reveals herself as the source of Lena's jealousy. Ollie is badly stabbed by Lena, and she moves from a position of alienation from the crowd to that of its most intense interest. Lena has attempted to remove Ollie's body from the possibility of its possession by Jule, and the crowd eagerly consumes the spectacle.

But Ollie recovers, and in doing so she regains possession of her body. After her physical convalescence she makes two refusals that negate her standing in the economy of jealousy and possession she shared with Jule and Lena. First, she declines to implicate Lena in the stabbing when the sheriff presents her for identification. Then, she refuses Jule's offer of marriage. She explains her decision to Jule:

> Seem lak us was jes livin' because we wanted somethin'—jes because us craved somethin'—an' us jes went on livin' jes fer dat. Mebbe ef dere had been somethin' us could want an' not hab— somethin' us could work fer an' still want—mebbe hit mought hab been dif'ent. (*OM*, 272–73)

Ollie has concluded that sexual possession, once achieved, refuses to compel further desire; she needs to structure her life around something she "could work fer an' still want," a system of labor in which she will be perpetually motivated by need to keep living. Ollie is expecting Jule's baby, and she intends to find happiness working the land to care for it:

> Hit'll be somethin' to live an' work fer—somethin' to dream about whilst I is sweatin' wid de sun flat ag'in my back. When you kin work fer somethin', you kin be happy widout tryin' to 'splain hit to yo'self. (*OM*, 273)

When Ollie reclaims her body, she also returns to her love of work. In this sense she discovers an erotics of labor through which she can direct her energies and make the profound attachment promised in the opening chapter of the novel. If *Ollie Miss* is a love story, it is ultimately a story about its heroine's love of farm work.

"To Love Work for Its Own Sake": Ollie Miss and Booker T.

I suggested early on that *Ollie Miss* is set in the shadow of Tuskegee. Now that Ollie has fixed her desires on work, it is worth spelling out how Washington's school casts its shadow on Henderson's novel. Henderson was a 1922 graduate of Tuskegee and a "legacy" student as well (his father, pastor of Butler's AME Zion Church in Tuskegee, was an 1899 graduate).[24] His career at Tuskegee demonstrates a propensity for voicing the Washingtonian message: elected "Class Orator" in his senior year, Henderson had twice placed second in the school's annual Trinity Church Boston Oratorical Prize contest on the topics "Booker T. Washington, the Apostle of Industrial Education" in 1921 and the agricultural benefits of "Muscle Shoals and the South" in 1922.[25] The ideal of economic autonomy is central both to the narrative form Henderson chose and to the educational philosophy of Tuskegee Institute. The founder of Henderson's alma mater, Booker T. Washington, famously preached the doctrine of self-reliance and the "dignity of labour" such that his students "would be taught to see not only utility in labour, but beauty and dignity, would be taught, in fact, how to lift labour up from mere drudgery and toil, and would learn to love work for its own sake."[26] By training African Americans in agricultural and industrial techniques, Washington later argued, Tuskegee would prepare them for the vagaries of the job market:

> Tuskegee emphasizes industrial training for the Negro, not with the thought that the Negro should be confined to industrialism, the plow, or the hoe, but because the undeveloped material resources of the South offer at this time a field peculiarly advantageous to the worker skilled in agriculture and the industries, and here are found the Negro's most inviting opportunities for taking on the rudimentary elements that ultimately make for a permanently progressive civilization.[27]

For Washington "the race" would achieve progress through the hard work of self-reliant individuals; such individuals could work collectively to build black institutions like Tuskegee, providing a parallel institutional structure rather than integrating or otherwise challenging white institutions. As James Anderson's historical analysis makes clear, the Hampton-Tuskegee model of industrial education responded to the interests of Northern industrial philanthropists, who needed well-trained workers.[28] Washington's curriculum stressed the principle of self-reliance in both rural and urban settings, and this strategy proved relevant to the changes to occur thirty years later in Alabama. By Robin

Kelley's account the state lost 147,340 residents between 1935 and 1940, the highest net out-migration in the Southeast for that period.[29] As I have earlier suggested, this dramatic demographic transformation was attributable in part to the mechanization of farming and to the general change from sharecropping to wage farming as well as to the increased productivity of urban industry in the North and to the hopes of black Southerners for a better life.[30] In Henderson's novel, written following his own migration to New York, the principle of self-reliance survives migration. This survival attests both to the staying power of the Washingtonian promise and to the structural imperative of the Bildungsroman; indeed, the latter shapes the Washingtonian promise solely in terms of individual achievement, forgoing the substantial collective institution-building that Washington so aggressively pursued.

The Washingtonian promise and the expectations of form converge in the final scene of *Ollie Miss*. After Jule leaves Ollie, she goes to the cabin door and looks out onto the farm. What she sees and hears conveys the joy Ollie herself feels for farmwork:

> She could hear the hands, laughing and singing at the mill, while they ground sugar cane and stewed the juice to a thick, scalding syrup. Their voices came loud and strong with the drift of the wind, and went rushing over the fields and through the swamp, like winged music echoing through eternity. (*OM*, 274)

Ollie sees the collectivity of the folk on the farm as angels in heaven, working together in eternal bliss. We might expect, then, that in this final scene Ollie will overcome her alienation to the crowd and join them in the work of the farm. But, instead, the narrator tells us that Alex has promised her the ten acres around her cabin to sharecrop, and Ollie "had something to look forward to—a farm of her own. . . . [where] green things would live and grow that had been nurtured by the strength of her hands alone" (*OM*, 276). Although a sharecropper does not own her own farm, Ollie nevertheless comes to emblematize the mother who can support her child through her own labor. As she realizes that she has gained autonomy, "her body felt free and light and strangely at peace, and something within her soul seemed to sing to the rhythm that floated out from the mill." She has reclaimed her body and relieved her restlessness and plans to labor not as one of the hands on the farm but as one whose "hands alone" work in the perpetual collective rhythm of the other folk.

The Son's Migration: Gender and Revision in the Sequel

Henderson's first novel, *Ollie Miss*, presented a compelling drama of self-fulfillment in which the heroine achieves economic autonomy. By fulfilling the Washingtonian promise, Ollie Miss achieves political modernity in a rural setting. Some eleven years later Henderson would sit down to write a sequel to *Ollie Miss* that significantly revised her story and that situates the aspiration for modernity in her son's migration to the city.[31] Henderson's revisionary sequel changed both the setting by which self-fulfillment would be achieved and the gender of the main character. Henderson remained committed, however, to the ideal of autonomy and to its articulation through the Bildungsroman.

The logic of familial succession from mother to son provides the link between the two narratives. In *Ollie Miss* the heroine comes to form the center for a matriarchal line of succession, but in *Jule* this order is set aside as Ollie's son assumes the center of a set of patriarchal relations. Henderson's first novel presents the mother as a legitimate and nurturing center for rural African-American life. In his second novel the son develops and emerges into mimetic view with other men in the world of urban commerce, and women generally appear as obstacles to men's progress at worst and as domestic supplements to men at best: in *Ollie Miss* the heroine discovers that men hinder her work on the farm, while in *Jule* urban women are gold diggers who prevent the hero from advancing economically. In the urban setting black women come to embody a kind of illegitimacy as they form impediments to Jule's success.[32]

By writing a sequel, Henderson not only changed both the gender and the setting through which autonomy would be achieved; he also offered a revision of the aesthetic function of the folk developed in *Ollie Miss*. This revision primarily concerns the structural position of the folk with respect to narrative change. Whereas the first novel isolates the folk world and guarantees its perpetuity by having Ollie Miss calibrate labor with seasonal change to support the next generation, the second novel takes the folk world in Alabama as the point of departure for a young man's migration narrative. In *Jule* Henderson no longer dreams of a rural modernity through subsistence farming; the rural Alabama countryside, as Charles Johnson predicted, has dried up.

Jule is a boy's coming-of-age story, and in this novel (as in so many others) the boy comes of age by departing from dependency on his mother. Jule has grown up with his mother, Ollie Miss, on her farm. The narrator makes clear that both the farm and the mother, while crucial to the growth of young life, must eventually relinquish their progeny: "The earth was a woman. She conceived and gave birth. She suckled her young at her breast until they were full-grown. Then she relinquished them and slept silently until she was ready to conceive again" (*J*, 4). We witness Jule following Ollie Miss as she plows, dropping seeds in the furrow, and we see that this novel has recast Ollie's role on the farm. No longer living by the labor of her hands alone, Ollie now relies on her son to place the seed in the earth and promote new life. This symbolic division of labor is motivated here by the patriarchal logic that compels women to nurture the life that men purportedly create and name. And Henderson endorses this motivation by offering a major revision of Ollie's story. In the second chapter of *Jule* Ollie has a flashback to the night Big Jule "went away" (*J*, 12).[33] Readers of the first novel will recall that when Ollie refused Jule's proposal of marriage, Jule wandered off in a daze. In *Ollie Miss* the scene in which Ollie declares her independence is the dramatic conclusion to her quest for happiness and autonomy. But in the sequel Ollie remembers "clearly now, the way it was, as though it were only yesterday," and we are told that Ollie woke one night to find Big Jule readying for departure. He "feels like walkin' on new ground" and makes no promise to return. And here we see Ollie, who was so self-possessed in the first novel, desperately begging him to stay:

> She caught him and pinned him against the door, both arms locked about his waist. Big Jule stood there, his jaw lean and hard against the firelight, the cigarette butt dangling from his lips.
> "But I—I is gwine have a baby, Jule! I is—is . . ." (*J*, 13)

This announcement would have been old news to the Jule of the first novel. Readers of *Ollie Miss* will be surprised to watch Ollie humbly apologize to Jule and pledge to name her baby after him: "'Dat's de way it's got to be,' she told herself fiercely, " 'cause dat's de way it is! Big Jule is his pa!'" The doggedly independent Ollie of the first novel has been revised to accommodate a patriarchal pattern of development. She is now the mother who facilitates the succession of the name Jule from one generation to the next; where she had once been resolutely independent, she is now desperately acquiescent.

Henderson's revision of Ollie allows him to duplicate the pattern of gendered location I identified early in this chapter. This pattern arises in part out of actual migration patterns. Migration patterns by gender tend to suggest that more males than females migrated, although most measures of the trend focus on immigrants in urban centers rather than on out-migration sex ratios for rural communities. Louise Kennedy's study of the 1920s shows that Negro men predominated in industrial centers where the majority of the jobs were open to men rather than to women.[34] She also notes that in the South black women generally outnumbered black men. The trend intensified during the 1940s: migrants were twice as likely to be male as female in 1947, when there were ninety-three black men for every hundred black women in the South.[35] This empirical pattern is typically reproduced in the fiction on migration. In Henderson's hands the pattern is exaggerated by his commitment to the Bildungsroman, which is a novel of (male) development. In the case of *Ollie Miss* the heroine does not disrupt the ideology of the genre because it presents development as cyclical. In the case of a male-centered narrative like *Jule*, however, the story of the son's development is expected to unfold diachronically, and a mother is usually viewed as an obstacle to autonomy in such stories.

When *Jule* opens, it is clear that the time for Jule to depart from his mother's care is close at hand. We have learned that farming alone has not sustained Jule and his mother for the last twelve years; hunting, primarily for coons and possums, has been necessary to provide food. Ollie has trained Jule well, and tonight is Jule's first hunting adventure on his own, an adventure that serves as something of a rite of passage into manhood. Jule's independence as a twelve-year-old boy who hunts also provides the basis for a friendship with the only white boy in Hannon, Alabama, Rollo Cage. As the novel moves forward, we see the boys hunt and fish together, and through the friendship Jule forms a mimetic relation to his friend. When Jule's mother informs him that "Mr. Rollo is somebody," Jule replies that "I wants to be somebody too," specifically somebody "like" Mr. Rollo (*J*, 35). By mirroring Rollo,

Jule forms a homosocial bond through which he can imagine himself as a male equivalent to his friend.[36] Early on this bond centers on the mutual pleasures of "boyhood" and hunting. For Jule and Rollo male camaraderie transcends the color line; their friendship somehow blinds them to racial difference. As we will see, their ascendancy into adulthood will force them to recognize the workings of the color line in the rural South. But this early friendship will provide an important structure by which Jule will become "somebody" as an adult. The ability to hunt, we will see, proves a useful tool for Jule in leveling the class and race hierarchies in American culture.

In the rural Jim Crow South hunting offered a unique opportunity for interracial interaction. Black and white men hunted in the same woods, sometimes together. As hunters, black and white men alike shared common instruments and targets; hence, in a profoundly racist society, hunting allowed black men to imagine themselves in a position of equivalence with white men. At the very least both shared the same link on the food chain. But the shared interest in hunting also allowed for the formation of intimate male friendships. Critic John Loftis explains:

> In American literature . . . the hunt is a European and thus white tradition, and its heroic and mythic dimensions hardly seem available to black American writers—unless used ironically to underscore the gulf between the chivalrous white hero and the black field hand or urban outcast. But when deftly handled, this problematic theme becomes an artistic asset for the black writer: the hunt can embody the hero's maturation at the same time that its parodic implications dramatize the disparity between black and white possibilities of growth and development in American society.[37]

In the literature on migration the logic of the hunt informs the explanation for sudden departure. In such stories a stable relation between black and white males is destabilized, typically through a love conflict or an accidental shooting. The inevitable result is that the black man shifts positions from being a hunter to being the hunted: he is typically chased North by hounds or a lynch mob.[38]

In *Jule* the hero goes from being a boy hunter to being the object of the hunt through his accidental rupture of class and race hierarchies.

These hierarchies are present in *Jule* where they were not in *Ollie Miss*. In *Ollie Miss* Alex's farm was not troubled by class or caste divisions, and white Americans did not make their presence felt there. But in *Jule* these divisions provide a constant source of conflict. Caroline's sister, Kate, comes to visit from the city, where she cooks for "'quality' folk" (*J*, 36), and she registers constant disdain for country life and mores; on several occasions she insists on calling the new hands on the farm "de new niggers" (*J*, 37), despite the objections of Alex and Caroline. But the more dangerous division in Hannon occurs on the color line. When Jule is sixteen he falls in love with Bertha Mae, a black girl from the area.[39] Both Bertha Mae and Jule work on the farm of a white man, Boykin Keye. Bertha Mae keeps insisting to Jule that they elope, but she never explains her motivation; one evening she is on the verge of explaining the reason, when Boykin Keye shows up and declares, "So this is where you meet your nigger!" (*J*, 84). Bertha Mae has been inextricably involved with Boykin Keye, thus occasioning her wish for an elopement with Jule. Keye has used his racial privilege to prevent Bertha Mae from saying no to him, and he now perceives his black rival with murderous scorn.

It is not unusual for men's rivalry over a woman to turn to violence; here violence makes particularly salient the divisive force of race as it intersects with male homosociality. Boykin Keye cannot stand the possibility of being in a mimetic position with a man who is also black: "I ain't sharing no woman with a nigger!" he exclaims before attacking Jule (*J*, 84). When Jule successfully defends himself, knocking out Keye and disarming him, his victory provokes further scorn from whites in general, and he prepares to leave town in a hurry. The immediacy of the threat provokes many members of the community to recognize, apparently for the first time, that justice here is colored by racial difference. This recognition is not lost on Jule, who, in trying with some exasperation to explain the impetus for his departure to Rollo, suddenly perceives him as white:

> He swallowed hard and was silent. He looked at Rollo's face, at the tiny freckles that flecked his lids and wove a pattern across the bridge of his nose. He looked at Rollo's eyes, china-blue and vivid, at the mop of blond hair that fell over his eyes. Eyes he had seen a thousand times, without seeing them at all. Jule looked at Rollo as

though he were seeing him for the first time. Rollo was a white
boy. (*J*, 88)

Rollo too suddenly recognizes his privilege and almost as quickly
refuses it in an argument with his father: "If Boykin Keye is white, Dad,
I don't want to be white!" (*J*, 89). Rollo's tearful refusal is meant to be
one register of the loss to be suffered by Jule's departure. Ollie Miss,
though sad to see her son go, reformulates the departure as Jule's entry
into manhood. Echoing the impetus Jule's father gave for leaving her,
Ollie Miss tells her son he's "goin' to walk on new ground" and
reminds him, "You got to be somebody as long as you live" (*J*, 93). The
series of events leading to Jule's departure thus leaves him simultaneously with no choice but to leave and with the hope of attaining independence and success. Jule's migration is both a flight from personal
disaster and the opportunity to become somebody.

Flight and Agency in the Migrant's Narrative

Jule's flight is typical for stories about migration from the South to the
North. Such stories run counter to the recent trend toward rethinking
the historiography of migration. Revisionary histories of the Great
Migration have sought to portray black migrants as agents who made
careful assessments of their needs and desires and who developed
communication networks to enable the migration to the North. Joe
William Trotter's recent survey of the early sociological and historical
literature on the Great Migration has shown its tendency to portray
migrants as "irrational actors in a drama beyond their control."[40] In
these accounts "migration fever" would sweep over a small Southern
town, abetted by the infectious influence of the labor agent; in one
implausible account the lure of the North would require immediate
action:

> In the first communities visited by the representatives of northern
> capital, their offers created unprecedented commotion. Drivers
> and teamsters left their wagons standing in the street. Workers,
> returning home, scrambled aboard the trains for the North without
> notifying their employers or their families.[41]

Countering this tendency to portray black Southerners as the passive victims of the "push" and "pull" of economic circumstances, the new history shows us how black Southerners formed migration clubs, corresponded with friends and relatives about opportunities in urban centers, and read the *Chicago Defender* together. Thus, James Grossman's 1989 study, *Land of Hope: Chicago, Black Southerners, and the Great Migration*, emphasizes aspiration and agency to explain the phenomenon of migration. Grossman argues, for example, that, while "public values rested upon the assumption that blacks were by nature docile, dependent, and unambitious . . . the Great Migration represented a refusal by one-half million black southerners to cooperate" with the needs of Southern leaders.[42]

As I have suggested, literary treatments of migration have figured the Northern metropolis less as a "land of hope" and more as, to use Rudolph Fisher's phrase, "the city of refuge."[43] In Fisher's story by that name, published in *The New Negro*, Harlem tantalized King Solomon Gillis as a "land of plenty" from his perspective in rural North Carolina.[44] When Gillis shoots a white man and needs to escape lynching, he makes the journey North: the narrator tells us that "the shooting, therefore, simply catalyzed whatever sluggish mental reaction had been already directing King Solomon's fortunes toward Harlem. The land of plenty was more than that now: it was also the city of refuge."[45] Of course, in Fisher's satire Harlem offers neither plenitude nor refuge: Gillis is, according to one character, "so dumb he thinks ante-bellum's an old woman,"[46] and he is naively drawn into organized crime even though he aspires to be a policeman. What interests me most about "The City of Refuge" is the way in which it presents the shooting as a catalyst for migration. I am interested in this aspect of the story because it is so familiar: the rural black man takes up a gun and, quite by accident, shoots a white man. This circumstance engenders a manhunt in which the black man is chased across the countryside by a band of white men with aspirations for a lynching. The only hope for him, then, is flight to the city. Thus, while the historical reality may have been that the Great Migration arose out of black Southerners' interest in finding better work and a better life, the literary treatment of migration often portrays migrants as, to repeat Trotter's phrase, "irrational actors in a drama beyond their control."[47] Migration, this story tells us, arises out of an accidental rupture of race relations.

Like King Solomon Gillis and so many others, migration takes Jule to Harlem, and Henderson presents for us a Harlem with no real surprises: Jule witnesses the drinking, gambling, and violence so glamorized in the Harlem Renaissance period.[48] To all of this Jule remains mostly unaffected. He spends his time working in a restaurant, saving his money, and taking night classes at the YMCA to learn a trade. Jule's intention to be somebody is most endangered through his contact with women. In Alabama black women were not a threat to his goals but, rather, served as instruments to men's goals to create new life. Indeed, the first time Jule and Bertha Mae have sex, Bertha Mae is figured as a plow:

> The girl began to crawl. She crawled on her back, digging her heels into the sand. She squirmed over corn rows, inch by inch, her head plowing a furrow through the sand. Her breath was coming fast, hot against his throat. The boy could feel her body slipping. He gripped her and caught her body close. The girl clenched her teeth. (*J*, 73)

Jule eventually pins her against the hedgerow, and "he beat her body against the ground until it was still" (*J*, 74). The scene echoes earlier instances of Jule planting with his mother, while it also proves Bertha Mae quite literally to be a tool in Jule's hands. Such confidence is difficult to come by in the city, although modern women fare no better in Jule's Harlem. Here women have nothing to contribute to society except to expend capital, and most women do so wastefully and willfully. We first meet Anne and Maisie, two middle-aged women who drink copiously and cheat on their husbands. Both pretend to be "society gals" (*J*, 119), but Maisie's high-class party ends in a brawl. Anne has an affair with Jule and spends her husband's money buying gifts for him. Another woman, Lou, seems more wholesome, and Jule leaves Anne for her. But we witness Lou borrowing money from her uncle for the purpose of buying a gift for her mother, only to plan to buy new shoes with it. Lou's family thinks she spends her time trying to find a job, but she instead spends her time shuttling between two men, Jule and Jeff. We see her profiting from her efforts at Christmas, when she is showered with gifts from her men. But someone reveals Lou's deception to Jule, and he beats her because "he knew her for what she was: a slut that had been to finishing school, with the finishing part left out"

(*J*, 204). In the city, Jule believes, African-American women are gold diggers who illegitimately exploit men for their own selfish gains; Jule must learn to punish and repudiate such women, the novel argues, if he is to become somebody.

Jule's repudiation of urban women seems to be the first step he makes toward success. In this he is supported by other men. When Jule leaves Lou in disgust, he seeks refuge with a visit to Bob, a white friend who shares Jule's love for hunting:

> He climbed into the car and stepped on the starter. The motor roared. The motor sounded sweet. He turned into the river road and thought about Bob. Bob was like Rollo. Bob liked to hunt. Bob was nice. "I got to see Bob," he told himself. "Got to talk to Bob." (*J*, 206)

Jule associates Bob with his boyhood friend Rollo, and he retreats to boyish pursuits to seek comfort from his hurt. This strategy pays off for him: Bob's father owns a printing company, and Bob convinces his father and the local typographical union to take on Jule as their first black apprentice printer. Jule's friendship with Bob asserts the power of gender mimesis over racial difference. When Jule finally wins his apprentice card from a stubborn union leader, he goes out on the town to celebrate with a friend on the mutually agreed condition that there be "no gals" (*J*, 222). Free of the encumbrance of a devious woman, Jule has managed to break through a racist barrier in the workplace by forming bonds with other men.

Just as Jule has finally become somebody, he receives a telegram announcing the death of his mother. Jule returns to Hannon, Alabama, and finds a changed landscape: "He kept fixing things in his mind, the way they used to be, years ago. But they weren't the same any more. Everything looked strange and different, changed. Everything looked small. Tight and small" (*J*, 229). Hannon has shrunk in Jule's mind, while it has also become desiccated, "dead and brown, washed out," and Rollo agrees with Jule that "there's nothing here. Your ma wanted you to be somebody. You got to be somebody, Jule" (*J*, 232). The rural landscape is worn out now, and folk life seems to be dying along with Ollie Miss. But Jule saves one element to take home with him to New York: he brings Bertha Mae back, and together "they could hear singing, rising on the wind" (*J*, 234), the sound of spirituals they heard on their first night together in the cornfield. Jule returns to the city, where he has become somebody, with the voice of the folk transmuted through his country gal, Bertha Mae.

The entertainment of the ideal of individual autonomy for African Americans has an ambivalent effect in these novels. When we see Ollie achieve a farm of her own, we are allowed to speculate on the benefits of owning property and laboring for one's self. Likewise, when Jule breaks into the typographers' union, working for a decent wage seems to offer a new route for African Americans seeking autonomy in the industrial workplace. Both novels make the utopian gesture of expecting labor to pay off in self-fulfillment and political modernity. The utopianism of this gesture is undercut, however, when we come to understand that, for each of these successfully autonomous characters, autonomy is achieved by having a certain gender. Ollie was able to achieve her symbolic position as earth mother by stressing her relation to farming over and against her relations with men. Jule learned to repudiate urban women and form friendships with men in order to achieve economic autonomy; his marriage to Bertha Mae will provide him with a domestic supplement, placing her in the position of dependence upon him. Neither novel can imagine autonomy for both a man and a woman simultaneously.

Late in life Henderson was at work on a third novel, *Baby Lou and the Angel Bud*, that would join *Ollie Miss* and *Jule* in a trilogy concerning his Alabama folk.[49] The action of *Baby Lou* precedes *Ollie Miss* in time. It is set in Alabama and features the male children of Caroline and Alex, Lou and Bud. The novel includes an eighty-nine-year-old character, Damma, who is a former slave. This recognition of the slave past is accompanied by scenes of racial violence—the Ku Klux Klan makes an appearance, for example. In general, this novel draws broader contours of collective life among black characters and includes more scenes of black and white interaction than do Henderson's previous novels. The surviving typescript reveals an incomplete and unfocused narrative. Perhaps Henderson, who obviously felt great comfort working within the formal expectations of the Bildungsroman, could not complete a work with a dual focus on two brothers and great attention to collective life.

Both *Ollie Miss* and *Jule* refuse to consider the possibility that the folk, as collectivity, could offer another route to African-American empowerment. Each novel closes by depicting its lead character as an auditor to the African-American folk: Ollie appreciates the singing of the hands in the mill, while Jule hears "a big singing" of spirituals (*J*, 234). The primarily aesthetic function of the folk in these characters' lives forecloses the possibility that Ollie and Jule will form political strategies to achieve collective autonomy for African Americans. Each novel reinforces this foreclosure by presenting folk life as closed and distant. In *Ollie Miss*, as I have shown, this effect is achieved by the isolation of the narrative's domain. In *Jule* the African-American folk have passed with the hero's ascendancy into adulthood. Henderson's commitment to gendered autonomy, derived in part from his experience at Tuskegee and in part from his choice of form, leads him away from a consideration of collective action as a route to political modernity. As I have already indicated, Washington himself connected individual effort with collective institution building in a formula to create black political modernity in America; Henderson neglected the latter part of the formula. In the next chapter I will investigate how Richard Wright took up the question of collective action among African Americans in the early 1940s. His solutions will not derive from Washington's formula, of course; Wright will argue for a departure from the separateness of black culture toward a full integration of blacks into the proletarian public sphere.

6

The Folk, the Race, and Class Consciousness: Richard Wright's *12 Million Black Voices*

Most of the speculative alternatives to economic modernization we have considered have situated an individual's hope for political modernity in a particular landscape. Bita Plant's return home to *Banana Bottom* and Ollie Miss's achievement of a "farm of her own" placed these women's aspirations for self-sufficiency and free self-expression in the rural modernity of subsistence farming.[1] Many migration narratives situate the male migrant's aspiration "to be somebody," as *Jule* did, in the urban landscape.[2] In Richard Wright's *12 Million Black Voices* (1941) neither the rural nor the urban landscape promises democratic and economic freedom for African Americans: his narrative is accompanied by photographic images of rural and urban poverty, suggesting that neither place will necessarily nurture freedom for black Americans. While his history does not settle on a particular place in which black Americans are to achieve political modernity, he shares an interest with the other writers I've discussed in exploring the utility of the folk toward imagining a constructive politics for African America in the early twentieth century. Wright uses the folk to organize a narrative of collective development of the "race" in America. In Wright's history the fully developed African American will arrive in the "sphere of conscious history" due to the enabling recognition of proletarian class interests across the color line.[3] *12 Million Black Voices* will ultimately dispense with both the folk and the race as useful foundations for political

action, preferring instead to investigate the power of proletarian consciousness within the American nation.

Wright's advocacy of the development of class consciousness
among white and black American workers responds to the "Negro
Question" troubling most political thinkers on the Left in the 1920s and
1930s. The Negro Question concerned the degree to which black Americans as agents could be accommodated, both historically and practically, by a Marxian politics of proletarian agency. The question was
provoked in part by an analysis of labor relations during slavery, as
Paul Buhle's historical account makes clear:

> Why had Northern workers, and for that matter Southern workers,
> failed to support [slave rebellions] . . . energetically? Why had
> [slaves] . . . failed to win equal admission into the "nation"? In the
> old reductive Marxism, the last and critical question could not be
> asked because only classes were recognized as political agents; in
> the emerging Popular Front Marxism, by contrast, the positive
> embrace of Jeffersonian-Lincolnian traditions made any harsh
> answer impossibly painful.[4]

These questions, Buhle argues, provoked a turning away from the
orthodox position of "abstract internationalism" in the analysis of class
relations toward an analysis of the constitution of the working class
within specific national formations.[5] This shift in intellectual focus
coincided with more practical efforts to integrate labor unions and
party membership on the American Left. While there had been a long
history of white capitalists using black workers as strikebreakers,
Socialists, Communists, and Trotskyists all tried to organize black
workers and include them in the union structure during the 1930s.[6] As
Philip Foner notes in his history of black Americans' involvement in
American socialism, socialist leaders were asking themselves, "What
was the point of urging Negroes to be class- and not race-conscious, to
cease being scabs and join the unions of their trades, when they could
not enter?"[7] The answer to their question, as well as to the Negro Question in general, was to advocate a change in union policy toward Negro
membership. By answering the question, radical leaders sought in various ways to enable the full force of proletarian agency, both black and
white.

Much like the efforts of Left organizers to integrate unions,

Wright's literary response to the Negro Question is to acknowledge the history of race difference in America, and the ways in which it has divided the working class, so as to close the divide. When Wright wrote the text for *12 Million Black Voices*, in 1941, he was a member of the Communist Party and was in agreement with the Party's pacifist position concerning U.S. entrance into World War II. Although the Party's stance was motivated by its reading of the war as inspired by capitalist imperialism, Wright was motivated by a desire to prevent a repeat of the racial discrimination against black soldiers that had occurred during and after World War I. Until race discrimination at home was solved, Wright argued, blacks should not fight abroad. When the party changed its position and supported entrance into the war in 1941, Wright at first acquiesced; he wrote an introduction for a condensed version of *12 Million Black Voices* in which he spoke for "the American Negro" in support of the war effort, with a caveat: "we must also fight to preserve the kind of America where the struggle for the extension of democracy can be taken up with renewed vigor when our enemies are crushed."[8] But Wright also advocated continued progress on the Negro Question during the war, and, disappointed over the Party's unwillingness to press on toward a solution, he left the Party in 1942.[9] Thus, while the book seeks to cross the divide between blacks and whites through proletarian consciousness, this effort would be abandoned both by the Party and by Wright shortly after its publication.

His literary practice clearly draws upon the Marxist principles sketched out in his 1937 essay, "Blueprint for Negro Writing," particularly in his desire to present "a view of society as something becoming rather than as something fixed and admired" in order to "stand shoulder to shoulder with Negro workers in mood and outlook."[10] In that essay Wright also argues for an integration of black writers' works into both black and white social settings: "isolation exists *among* Negro writers as well as *between* Negro and white writers," he complains.[11] Wright states the central question of his essay: "Shall Negro writing be for the Negro masses, moulding the lives and consciousness of those masses toward new goals, or shall it continue begging the question of the Negroes' humanity?"[12] The argument of *12 Million Black Voices* supports Wright's clear preference to affirm the premise of the first question. But, as this analysis will show, the modes of address available in the form of the photo-documentary history do not offer much opportunity to mold the masses: the genre's principal audience is middle-class and presumably white. My study of Wright's text begins with a consideration of the argument of his historical narrative. This argument, which forms a homology with narratives of European national development, brings the African-American race into a position of equivalence with other Americans and thus allows Wright to make further claims about the efficacy of class politics within the national border. As I consider the formal setting in which Wright makes his argument, I discuss the narrative voice in *12 Million Black Voices* as well as the ways in which the photographs amplify Wright's claims about modernization. I close by considering Wright's position on the Negro Question in the years following *12 Million Black Voices*.

After the Middle Passage: African America as a "Separate Unity"

12 Million Black Voices emphasizes class affinity over racial identity in the narration of African-American history. Subtitled "A Folk History of the Negro in the United States," the book assimilates black history into a model of national development in which recognition of an "identity of interests" among poor blacks and whites will lead to "the death of our old folk lives" for blacks and the promise "to share in the upward march of American life" (144, 146). Wright's text is written under the influence of contemporary proletarian aesthetics: it employs Marxian analyses of the modes of production and class, and its narration through the first-person plural subject position projects a collectivist aesthetic. In this context the book's endorsement of America's promise of upward mobility would seem curious. Yet, as Barbara Foley's recent history of proletarian fiction makes clear, the book displays a more general shift in the function of the folk in Left politics of the time: she argues that "originally it was the *distinctiveness* of black folk culture— its intrinsically oppositional position relative to bourgeois cultural hegemony—that was heralded by radical critics seeking a usable black cultural tradition. By the late 1930s, however, this adversarial particularity was being inscribed in a nationalistic discourse that posited a synechdochic relation between black folk experience and that of the nation as a whole."[13] By emphasizing the working class's "identity of interests" across the color line (144), Wright imagines a community of equivalents within the national border. Wright's narrative analyzes the contingency of Negro identity and explores the position of the folk as inhabiting a developmental stage in the transition toward "the sphere of conscious history" (147). Thus, "A Folk History of the Negro in the United States" evacuates both *folk* and *Negro* as markers of transhistorical identity, while it insists upon an identity of class interests as forming the possibility for historical consciousness and national community.

Wright takes the long view in developing a genealogy of proletarian agency in the United States: his history begins with the Middle Passage. In his account enslaved Africans lost their cultural moorings during the transatlantic journey: "The trauma of leaving our African home, the suffering of the long middle passage, the thirst, the hunger, the horrors of the slave ship—all these hollowed us out, numbed us, stripped us, and left only physiological urges, the feelings of fear and fatigue" (15). Wright argues that captivity "reached down into the personalities of each one of us and destroyed the very images and symbols which had guided our minds and feelings in the effort to live." Much as Elaine Scarry has described the work of torture in *The Body in Pain* as it destroys language and obliterates the contents of consciousness of the tortured to confirm the power of the torturer, Wright's enslaved African loses linguistic and cultural antecedents and is brought into "new patterns of psychological reaction" and linguistic competence in English (41).[14] The newly arrived slave is a cultural tabula rasa whose raw and numbed body will be given a new consciousness with which to understand the images and symbols of life on American shores. Wright argues that the plantation owners shaped this new consciousness by separating slaves who shared linguistic and tribal origins; the owners thus eliminated difference among slaves, "welding us together into a separate unity with common characteristics of our own." In Wright's account the Middle Passage allows slavers to reshape Africans into a distinct category of person known as "the Negro."

Wright's account endorses a particular interpretation of the transformation effected through the Middle Passage, and it is worth spelling out here both the influences on it and the implications for this particular endorsement. His interpretation of the Middle Passage as a process that stripped Africans of their cultural antecedents reflected the dominant view in American social science at the time, and he acknowledges the influence of works by E. Franklin Frazier, Arthur Raper, and Louis Wirth in the foreword to the book.[15] But 1941 also occasioned the publication of *The Myth of the Negro Past,* in which Melville Herskovits critiqued the tabula rasa approach by tracing cultural retentions of Africanisms in African-American culture, thus demonstrating that the Negro did indeed have a past that antedated the Middle Passage.[16] The blank pages of Negro history could be filled with studies of various cultural retentions, Herskovits would argue. Although this scholarship may have been tempted to recreate one Negro past, recent scholarship has urged attention to the multiplicity of experiences deriving from the Middle Passage. Wolfgang Binder's recent survey of literature addressing the Middle Passage examines the empirical variation of memories about it.[17] Additionally, Kenneth Warren's recent analysis of "the difficulty of sustaining, from a new world perspective, the imaginative contemporaneity of Africa and the 'West' and of black elites and masses" cautions us that "the diaspora is a thought whose closure cannot be seen by any one individual nor imagined by any single text."[18] For Wright and the sociologists he endorses, amnesia is compelled through the Middle Passage; for Herskovits, Binder, and Warren, memory is a textual phenomenon that is inflected in different ways by individual consciousnesses. The latter approach, however, was only beginning to gain influence when Wright began his narrative.

By endorsing the tabula rasa approach, Wright is able to provide a descriptive narrative of how the Negro was constructed in America. As I have indicated, he argues that slavers melded African slaves into a separate unity by refusing to recognize the cultural antecedents that might have divided African from African. Wright's adoption of the tabula rasa theory allows him to describe the ways in which black and white difference was constructed both in the slave era and since. His description derives from his examination of how the slavers "spun tight ideological webs of their right to domination" as they participated in the post-Enlightenment creation of empire: "Daily these eager men slashed off the rotting trappings of feudal life, a life which for centuries had endowed man with a metaphysical worth, rank, use, and order; and, in its stead, they launched the foundations of a new dispensation to prove that man could step beyond the boundaries of ignorance and superstition and live by reason" (16). Enlightenment rationality freed slavers from feudal hierarchy; Wright makes one of the key critiques of the age of empire by demonstrating that slavers' newfound freedom was predicated upon the domination of non-Europeans.

Wright's narrative extends the critique of imperialism to the

American context by describing the plantation economy of colonial America as a new form of feudalism: "The gold of slave-grown cotton concentrated the political power of the Old South in the hands of a few Lords of the Land, and the poor whites decreased in number as we blacks increased" (16–17). While feudalism is arguably an inexact name for the organization of labor in the antebellum South, it provides Wright with a vocabulary by which he can name African Americans as a folk.[19] Wright's analysis of power in the Old South also addresses the ways in which poor whites have been pitted against blacks. The latter two constituencies are oppressed because the "Lords of the Land," as he calls them, maintain hegemony by "inciting us against one another" (17). Thus, racial difference is used to prevent recognition of an identity of interests among the poor.

Wright's historical project, we will remember, is to provide a genealogy of proletarian consciousness and the ways in which the full agency of the proletariat has been blocked in America by the problem of race difference. His narration of the Middle Passage and the construction of the Negro under slavery shows how Africans from disparate linguistic and tribal backgrounds were brought together into "a separate unity with common characteristics of our own" (41). The notion of a separate unity is repeated throughout *12 Million Black Voices*. For Wright the "unity" of the black community gives coherence to the project of narrating black history, even as the fact that it is separate suggests a process of differentiation in which poor whites and the Lords of the Land are actors in a shared history. Indeed, Wright is intent on demonstrating how the separate unity of the black community was developed through everyday contact with whites. He describes the "dual conduct" (41) with whites in which "we proceeded to build our language in inflections of voice, through tonal variety, by hurried speech, in honeyed drawls, by rolling our eyes, by flourishing our hands, by assigning to common, simple words new meanings, meanings which enabled us to speak of revolt in the actual presence of the Lords of the Land without their being aware!" (40). Through gesture and inflection, Wright argues, blacks developed a language of dissent by which they could voice their common resistance to white overseers without actually confronting them. This form of everyday resistance, as I have discussed earlier, allows blacks to develop a palpable sense of agency and community in a context in which both of these attributes are not acknowledged.[20]

The Form of the Argument

Before I address the ways in which Wright's text narrates the modernization of agriculture and the Great Migration, I want to discuss the ways in which the narrative voice of *12 Million Black Voices* amplifies Wright's claim about the separate unity of black life in America. I have already discussed the ways in which language and voice were important components of the construction of the Negro: under Wright's tabula rasa approach Africans lost their cultural moorings during the Middle Passage as well as their tribal languages. But, significantly, they were also assimilated into American culture through language. While blacks spoke English in the antebellum South, Wright has shown us how gesture and inflection can bend this language so that it marks the extent to which blacks had not been fully assimilated.

The book's narrative voice underwrites Wright's argument that the Negro remains unassimilated into the American collective voice. Wright's text speaks in the first-person plural, but the twelve million black voices subsumed under the collective pronoun remain distinct from the *we* that speaks in the preamble to America's constitution. Instead, the book addresses the reader as an outsider; it begins, "Each day when you see us black folk upon the dusty land of the farms or upon the hard pavement of the city streets, you usually take us for granted and think you know us, but our history is far stranger than you suspect, and we are not what we seem" (10). Wright invites the reader to examine the separate unity of black folk in America. While the book will ultimately conclude that "*we* are *you,* looking back at you from the dark mirror of our lives" (146), the narrative voice insists on a cleavage between white and black, between reader and narrator.

If black voices remain unassimilated into the American collective voice, Wright's narrative voice itself assimilates many different black voices into a unitary utterance.[21] Despite Wright's proviso that his book "intentionally does not include in its considerations those areas of Negro life which comprise the so-called 'talented tenth'" or the developing black middle class, in order "to simplify a depiction of a complex movement of a debased feudal folk toward a twentieth-century urbanization" (5), his narrative includes attention both to the black masses and elites. Indeed, Wright contrasts the "naive, peasant anger" he blames for the 1935 Harlem riots to the mixed-race radicalism of "disciplined, class-conscious groups" that banded together to focus attention

on the Scottsboro case (145), arguing that the latter was the more effective in advancing a progressive agenda. While Wright's collective voice
occasionally takes sides in debates internal to black politics, his voice
also collects disparate historical and geographical perspectives ranging
from slavery on Southern plantations to factory work in Chicago. The
narrator's voice projects a historical consciousness that is contemporaneous with three hundred years of black history. While this unity of
historical perspective is impossible to achieve through one individual's
point of view, Wright's positing of such a perspective allows his text to
present the separate unity of Negro life as an ongoing concern in American society.

    Just as the narrative voice assimilates multiple points of view into
a collective utterance, it also speaks through multiple modes of expression. John Reilly has argued that "12 Million Black Voices is simulated
oral utterance derived from the spontaneous arts that shape the ora-
tions of the preacher."[22] Reilly describes how the "preacher-narrator"
employs such devices as personification, allegory, and incantation in
service of "preaching the national text."[23] Wright's preacherly voice is
most evident at the beginning of chapter 3, which proclaims, "Our time
has come!" (92), as it narrates the exodus to the North during the Great
Migration. But the sermon form and its speaker are not the only modes
of expression incorporated into Wright's narrative voice: Wright's
voice cites a number of modes of expression through simulation of the
sermon, pedantic historical narrative, and documentary voice-over
narration.[24] The book amplifies the speaker's voice by juxtaposing its
claims with photographs and captions. In the first chapter, for example,
Wright's text describes "America's paternalistic code toward her black
maid, her black industrial worker, her black stevedore, her black
dancer, her black waiter, her black sharecropper" (18). This list is illus-
trated by Edwin Rosskam's photo-text, in which each type of worker is
displayed through a separate photograph accompanied by a caption.
At other times the captions link a series of images into a narrative pro-
gression. One series begins with the caption "Our lives are walled with
cotton" and shows a landscape with fields and shacks bisected by a dirt
road (50); it continues with a picture of a solitary farmer plowing (fig.
8) and the caption "We plow and plant cotton" (51). The next captions
state that "We chop cotton" and "We pick cotton" (52–53); each is
accompanied by images of small groups of workers performing those
tasks. The narrative concludes with a juxtaposition of images of death:

on the left we read, "When Queen Cotton dies . . ." and see a worn, abandoned plow resting like a skeleton on a dried-up field (54); on the right the question continues: "how many of us will die with her?" (55). The final image is of a crude grave under a mound of dirt. The captions create narrative continuity among the images, which in this series came from four different states and as many photographers.

While there are a number of modes of verbal expression enunciated through Wright's narrative voice, the most direct generic antecedent for the book is the photo-documentary book, in which photographic images are framed by an explanatory narrative and captions.[25] Maren Stange's history of social documentary photography in America, *Symbols of Ideal Life*, argues that the explanatory narratives in these texts tend to de-radicalize images of poverty.[26] Wright's voicing of the separate unity of Negro life provides readers with the opportunity to learn about another "half" of American society. His address to the reader as "you" duplicates a rhetorical strategy employed by many contemporary photo-documentary histories written in the 1930s and 1940s in conjunction with photographers associated with the Farm Security Administration.[27] The title of *You Have Seen Their Faces*, a joint project between novelist Erskine Caldwell and photographer Margaret Bourke-White, suggests the structure of a narrative that allows the shocked reader to witness the horrors of rural poverty.[28] Stange has argued that the Farm Security Administration designed the photographic project as the public relations component of its plan to modernize rural agriculture. She explains how the photographs carried out this mandate:

> The subjects of FSA photographs were presented to their mass audiences shorn of social and cultural vigor and interest, not only by framing and composition but also by text, caption, and graphic arrangements that made of local particularities, collectivities, and attachments simultaneously examples of outmoded "social emotions" and nostalgic evocations of a receding popular life . . . [I]t was exactly their hopeless maneuverability, their enforced lack of attachment, that made such rural people the ideal "symbols of ideal life" that it was finally the purpose of FSA photography to create. Having nothing to lose, they were unthreatened by change—they were an exemplary constituency for reform.[29]

Fig. 8. "Plowing Cotton, Georgia." Photograph by Dorothea Lange. Richard Wright, *12 Million Black Voices,* 51. (Courtesy of the U.S. Farm Security Administration Collection, Prints and Photographs Division, Library of Congress, LC-USF 34–17965.)

By viewing FSA images of vulnerable sharecroppers and the like, readers were encouraged to support government programs to modernize agriculture. The archive itself, as has been noted by recent scholarship, was considerably ambiguous and diverse with respect to the images available for framing; the framers settled on images of poverty to get their message across.[30] The narrative frames of photo-documentary books situated the reader, "you," as a sympathetic, sentimental witness to the ravages of poverty and as a middle-class reader who might be able to do something about it.

Wright's book duplicates this narrative structure by addressing its reader as "you." Additionally, his book also frames photographs selected with Edwin Rosskam from the Farm Security Administration files.[31] But to what extent does Wright's book act as publicity for the reforms sought by the Farm Security Administration's documentary aesthetic? Some readers saw the book as offering resistance to government policy, leading the FBI to make the case for sedition charges against Wright.[32] But the book equivocates on the issue of government reforms when it addresses the modernization of agricultural practices. Early on, farm machinery appears as a predatory threat on the Southern landscape: "There began to crawl across the landscape lumbering machines that magically threatened to turn millions of our black fingers idle" (25). Frequently, Wright's narrator speaks resignedly of the inexorable force of modernization: "How can we win this race with death when our thin blood is set against the potency of gasoline, when our weak flesh is pitted against the strength of steel, when our loose muscles must vie with the power of tractors?" (49). This expression of resignation to industrial farming resists the spirit of modernization because of its human consequences for black farmhands, while it also accepts modernization as inevitable; he does not propose an alternative solution except for migration. In sum, Wright's book complains about the consequences of the mechanization of farm labor but is resigned to such changes. Wright's folk are powerless to move against modernization; they can simply move on.

After the Great Migration: The Priority of Class Affinity

In preparing to narrate the Great Migration, Wright's text provides pictures of a barren and depopulated Southern landscape. "Vast changes engulf our lives," the narrator intones, and the book presents two facing pictures to illustrate the changes in the landscape (78). One is a photograph of a spare wooden shack atop a barren hillside (see fig. 9). The text accompanying this image describes the ravages of deforestation, erosion, soil depletion, and flooding; this place can no longer produce agricultural wealth. Juxtaposed with this picture of the depopulated homestead is a rather more fecund agricultural landscape (see fig. 10). But the second photograph shows five tractors moving in a line across the field, and Wright's text tells of the "tread as of doom . . . of the thundering tractors and cotton-picking machines that more and more render our labor useless" (79). The remainder of the paragraph on this

Fig. 9. "Eroded Land, Alabama." Photograph by Arthur
Rothstein. Richard Wright, *12 Million Black Voices*, 78. (Courtesy
of the U.S. Farm Security Administration Collection, Prints
and Photographs Division, Library of Congress, LC-USF
34–25430-D.)

page describes migrant farmworkers desperately moving from state to
state as they follow the picking cycle. Wright's narrative presents the
rural South as a place in which one can no longer establish roots, both
in the literal sense of growing one's own crops and in the sense of staying in one place to labor and raise a family.

Again, Wright's folk can simply move on; they are passive victims
of historical change. And yet Wright attempts to describe their willing-
ness to move on as indicative of an aspiration for autonomy: "Our drifting is the expression of our hope" (86). This hope allows black Southerners to form an aspiration for an alternative to the modernized South:
migration to the North. Like many recent commentators on the Great
Migration, Wright seeks to emphasize the aspirations of migrants by
portraying them as agents of historical change.[33] But Wright's text will
not imagine the North as the site of a sufficient alternative modernity.

Fig. 10. "Tractors in Cotton Field, Mississippi." Photograph by
Marion Post. Richard Wright, *12 Million Black Voices*, 79. (Courtesy of the U.S. Farm Security Administration Collection, Prints
and Photographs Division, Library of Congress, LC-USF
34–54739.)

In chapter 3, "Death on the City Pavements," Wright portrays many
urban scenes in which poverty is as desperate as it was in the rural
South. Wright blames racism and the Bosses of the Buildings, who
occupy the structural position of the Lords of the Land in his description of the South, for urban poverty. But he also blames "our naive folk
minds" for the difficulties of black Americans in the city (120). Wright
describes recent migrants as an "utterly unprepared folk" who
"needed the ritual and guidance of institutions to hold our atomized
lives together in lines of purpose" (93). The text thus presents migrants
as helpless, naive victims in need of guidance and reform. This is clear
in the tension between the caption and the image for Russell Lee's
"Street Scene under the El" (fig. 11). The image shows four children
dwarfed by the towering staircase to the El tracks. Although the children do not appear to be in great distress (and, indeed, one smiles

Fig. 11. "Street Scene under the El." Photograph by Russell Lee.
Richard Wright, *12 Million Black Voices*, 139. (Courtesy of the
U.S. Farm Security Administration Collection, Prints and Pho-
tographs Division, Library of Congress, LC-USF 34–38601.)

broadly), the caption reads, "The streets claim our children" (139); here
is an example of when the ambiguity of the photographic archive is not
fully contained by the frame of the photo-documentary history.

Migrants will be enabled to achieve political agency by their expo-
sure to other workers in the city, Wright argues. In his narrative political modernity will arise when African Americans recognize an "identity of interests" with other members of the industrial proletariat (144).
Wright attributes the ascendancy of black Americans into the "sphere
of conscious history" to the interaction of unemployed black and white
laborers during the Depression (147): "we encountered for the first time
in our lives the full effect of those forces that tended to reshape our folk
consciousness, and a few of us stepped forth and accepted within the
confines of our personalities the death of our old folk lives, an acceptance of a death that enabled us to cross class and racial lines, a death

that made us free" (144). Wright situates effective political agency in "class-conscious groups" formed across the color line, while he disparages the "naive, peasant anger" of "inarticulate black men and women" who caused extensive damage in the 1935 Harlem riot (145). Wright's answer to the Negro Question is to require black men and women to evacuate the folk as a form of consciousness and to enter into the sphere of conscious history. By rejecting the cultural traces of living as a separate unity in America, black men and women are to come together with other members of the working class to address their common concerns. Urban life will enable recent migrants to understand history and to break with their folk past.

Wright's advocacy of a break with the folk past is not without its contradictions. Given his earlier interest in the ways in which gesture and inflection in black language created a discourse with which to voice dissent, his later dismissal of "our old folk lives" as indicative of a pre-political consciousness rings hollow (144). Moreover, despite his proviso in the foreword to the book that he would neglect the talented tenth, his formulation of an alternative politics is oddly Du Boisian: it relies upon a coterie of like-minded, class-conscious intellectuals to formulate appropriate political strategies.[34] His formulation also blends easily into a nationalist vision of the American melting pot, in which blacks have caught up with European immigrants and poor whites and, through raised consciousness, can now expect "the right to share in the upward march of American life" (146).

These contradictions also pertain to the Left agenda for addressing the Negro Question during the time when Wright composed the text for *12 Million Black Voices*. In short, by attending to the history of race relations in America, radicals hoped to integrate labor unions and thereby foster proletarian political agency. While this plan enabled many blacks to participate in the proletarian public sphere, such gains were insubstantial without concomitant attention to widespread racial discrimination in American society. This answer to the Negro Question asked blacks to suppress their race consciousness when race presented a daily obstacle to the "upward march" of the Negro.

The contradictions in a solution to the Negro Question based in class consciousness caught up with Wright shortly after the publication of *12 Million Black Voices*. Wright's departure from the Communist Party was precipitated by his disappointment in the Party's unwillingness to press for racial equality during World War II. Consequently,

Wright began to fix his political energies on the Negro rather than on the proletariat. In 1945, in his preface to St. Clair Drake's and Horace Cayton's *Black Metropolis*, a sociological study of Chicago's black belt, Wright signals his departure from a politics centered on class:

> The political Left often gyrates and squirms to make the Negro problem fit rigidly into a class-war frame of reference, when the roots of that problem lie in American culture as a whole; it tries to anchor the Negro problem to a patriotism of global time and space, which robs the problem of its reality and urgency, of its concreteness and tragedy.[35]

One can read in these lines the basis for a critique of *12 Million Black Voices* and of the 1930s Left's response to the Negro Question. While Wright's book acknowledges the "urgency" and "tragedy" of black poverty, his narrative "gyrates and squirms" to relate the problem to a need for proletarian class consciousness across the color line.

12 Million Black Voices's schematic history of black America uses the essentialist narrative of the development of a race from a folk to bring African Americans into a position of equivalence with whites and immigrant groups. In the course of doing so, the book demonstrates the historical contingency of the Negro and it begs that the folk be left behind so that a class-conscious politics could be developed to counter the ravages of modernization. While the book performs a service for those who would like to see the Negro race as a historical construct rather than as an essence, the book seems to move too quickly to dismiss the folk as naive and unconscious in its reformulation of politics around class consciousness. This move is underwritten in part by the generic inheritance of the photo-documentary history, which frames pictures of impoverished rural and urban citizens as passive victims of inevitable change—the perfect candidates for sentimental bourgeois reform activity. The conjuncture between Wright's advocacy for working-class solidarity and the book's inheritance of a form constitutive of a middle-class consciousness contributes to the mix of radical and nationalist strains of argument in *12 Million Black Voices*.

7

Conclusion: Local Histories and World Historical Narrative

I began this book by discussing the problems with the situation of the folk in vernacular criticism. Vernacular criticism had posited the folk as the unmediated origin of African-American cultural expression; by identifying the unique formal attributes of African-American folk expression, the vernacular critics have tried to define, across time, an African-American literary tradition. Critics of vernacular criticism, working from the lessons of post-structuralism, have sought a recognition of the contingency of the discursive constitution of the folk, both in literary criticism and in the social text of African America. My task has been to work that recognition into a historicist critical practice. By attending to the economic, demographic, and formal contexts giving rise to the discourse on the folk, I have sought to understand the ways in which various aesthetic appropriations of the folk mediate historical change. Key to my analysis has been a focus on the concept of modernity, both in its universalizing valence and in its local manifestations. Reading critically through what Dipesh Chakrabarty has called the "transition narrative" of development, I have discovered a variety of local modernities that disrupt the world historical pretensions of the European narrative of national development.[1]

Indeed, if Jean and John Comaroff are right to note that the age of empire has produced not one global modernity but, rather, "many modernities," then my work in these pages has also demonstrated that there are "many folks" in African-American literary discourse.[2] Jean Toomer's folk was chiefly a spectral presence that provided the soundtrack for a vision of the Georgia landscape in the midst of great change: as Toomer ambivalently presented the countryside as both a peasant utopia and as a worn-out and unproductive agricultural wasteland, his folk sang spirituals in the background. In Zora Neale Hurston's Polk County, Florida, however, the folk—or at least those who found some utility in folklore—were not Toomer's choir intoning the "everlasting song" of a bygone era; in Polk County migrant workers in a lumber camp used folklore to articulate resistance to their bosses and to create a sense of community.[3] Claude McKay, too, saw the presentist utility of the logic of the folk for African peoples in the industrial age. His heroine's romantic self-fulfillment through recovery of her folk identity did not so much recreate a utopian past as it offered an alternative to colonial cultural ideology and an opportunity to escape the exigencies of the global commodities market through subsistence farming. George Wylie Henderson's heroine Ollie Miss also discovered an alternative modernity through subsistence farming; Henderson's vision was different from McKay's, however, in that it was strongly inflected by the individualist ethos of Booker T. Washington—indeed, it is this ethos, rather than a particular mode of production, that constitutes modernity for Henderson. This contrasts sharply with Richard Wright's understanding of modernity. Wright, perhaps the writer to take most seriously the world historical dimensions of folk discourse, emphasized the collective aspect of African-American folk identity, even as he sought to narrate the dissolution of that identity into a race-neutral class consciousness. Each of these narrative engagements with the folk has shaped it in quite different ways and, in turn, has proffered distinctive visions of modernity in African America.

These findings unsettle the notion of a literary tradition centered on a solitary folk origin. They do so simply by noting that what exactly constituted the folk had not been consensually established during this period, if ever. This is so, to be sure, because metropolitan writers had different political and aesthetic investments in the idea of folk culture. It is also so because these writers addressed quite different locations in their stories of African-American life. My readings in the preceding chapters have taken me deep into research on Greene and Hancock Counties, Georgia; Polk County, Florida; Jamaica; Tuskegee, Alabama; Harlem; and Chicago. While the universalizing aspect of folk discourse would tend to make each place the same, or at least place it somewhere on the immanent trajectory of economic and cultural development into modernity, I have sought to read each instance of folk-centered narration as an intrication of such universalizing tropes as *folk* and *modernity* within particular locations of historical contingency. These local variations, I believe, often reformulate the notions of the folk and the modern into something quite other than one might expect.

Indeed, reading critically against the transition narrative of development has led me to create a critical vocabulary that is often counterintuitive. The term *rural modernity*, for example, is oxymoronic to most readers; it is meant to show how the economic arrangement of subsistence farming responds to expectations for modern citizenship. By assuming that the rural is always premodern, archaic, or nostalgic, we give assent to the supposedly intrinsic logic of developmental narrative, thereby missing the possibility that modern logics can be (and have been) revised to fit rural landscapes. My guess is that this kind of critical analysis will be a useful model not only for future studies in African-American culture but also for work in post-colonial studies and investigations of other nonmetropolitan cultural settings.

As I point toward more global implications for my argument and methods, however, I want to return to the question of African-American exceptionalism. One of the persistent worries about the deconstruction of black difference is that it leaves African Americans without a crucial tool—the coherence of shared identity—around which to build a politics.[4] On the other hand, critics of the identity politics of vernacular criticism have pointed out the way in which it elides internal dissent within black political discourse.[5] It is supremely ironic, however, that the terms of this debate, from the Washington–Du Bois era to the present day, have been so exercised with defining black difference around the Eurocentric narrative of the development of a folk into modernity. Ironic, that is, because one the chief distinctions between the history of African Americans and other peoples now defined as modern is, broadly speaking, their forced migration during the slave trade and, more recently, the vast internal migration of black Americans from the South to the North. What is exceptional about the experience of African peoples in the Americas, then, is not that they created a literary tradition out of an oral, folk tradition (for, if we are to believe the stories of European cultural development, what people did not?). The broad contours of African-American history—enslavement, the Middle Passage, emancipation, and migration—provide a grand historical schematic that profoundly disrupts and reshapes the transition narrative provided by the European Enlightenment. The story, then, of the African-American engagement with folk discourse is not one of building up a unitary tradition; it is, rather, a story of retrofitting Eurocentric notions of cultural development with the particularity of African-American experiences and locations.

I end this book with hope that I have moved the study of African-American literature through an important impasse. By placing several mediations of the folk within their formal and historical contingencies, I have sought to decenter the trope and to display the plurality of political investments made through it. These plural responses disrupt the universalizing discourse on modernity and the folk, both in African-American cultural expressions and modern cultures in general. They suggest that we rethink what we mean by the folk in other contexts. And they confirm the cognitive value of literature, as mediation, to enable us to speculate about our pasts, our futures, what might have been, and what could yet be.

Notes

1. Langston Hughes, *The Big Sea* (1940; rpt., New York: Hill and Wang, 1993), 228.
2. Alain Locke, ed., *The New Negro* (1925; rpt., New York: Atheneum, 1968), 15–16. For investigations into the periodicity of the New Negro and the Harlem (or Negro) Renaissance, see Henry Louis Gates Jr., "The Face and Voice of Blackness," in *Modernism, Gender, and Culture: A Cultural Studies Approach*, ed. by Lisa Rado (New York and London: Garland, 1997), 161–72; James A. Miller, "African-American Writing of the 1930s: A Prologue," in *Radical Revisions: Rereading 1930s Culture*, ed. Bill Mullen and Sherry Lee Linkon (Urbana and Chicago: University of Illinois Press, 1996), 78–90; Eric J. Sundquist, *To Wake the Nations: Race in the Making of American Literature* (Cambridge and London: Harvard University Press, 1993), 334–47.
3. Locke, *New Negro*, 4, 7. The logic of Locke's attribution of leadership to the masses is not so generous as it first appears. As John Brown Childs has argued, "The intellectuals needed the energy of the people—but the people needed the intellectuals for a fundamental kind of guidance" (73). See John Brown Childs, "Afro-American Intellectuals and the People's Culture," *Theory and Society* 13 (1984): 69–90.
4. Throughout this study, when I use the term *folk*, I mean to signify that the term, rather than a particular empirical group, forms the object of inquiry here.
5. W. E. B. Du Bois, *The Souls of Black Folk* (1903; rpt., New York and Scarsborough, Ontario: New American Library, 1969), 51–52.
6. Ibid., 136.
7. Booker T. Washington, *Up from Slavery* (1901), in *Three Negro Classics*, ed. John Hope Franklin (New York: Avon, 1965), 67.
8. Ibid., 77.
9. Du Bois, *Souls of Black Folk*, 51. For a discussion of Washington's attempts to staunch migration, see James R. Grossman, *Land of Hope: Chicago, Black Southerners, and the Great Migration* (Chicago and London: University of Chicago Press, 1989), 38–65.
10. For example, folklorist Arthur Huff Fauset advocated the collection of African-American folklore to advance the argument that it "rivals in amount as well as in quality

that of any people on the face of the globe" and, through its similarity with other folk traditions, "prove[s] the common ancestry of man, both with regard to his mental and cultural inheritance." See Arthur Huff Fauset, "American Negro Folk Literature," in Locke, *New Negro*, 238, 242.

11. Benedict Anderson, *Imagined Communities: Reflections on the Origin and Spread of Nationalism* (1983; rpt., London and New York: Verso, 1987), 37.

12. Jean and John Comaroff, introduction to *Modernity and Its Malcontents: Ritual and Power in Postcolonial Africa*, ed. by Jean Comaroff and John Comaroff (Chicago and London: University of Chicago Press, 1993), xi.

13. See Bernard W. Bell, *The Afro-American Novel and Its Tradition* (Amherst: University of Massachusetts Press, 1987); and Robert Bone, *The Negro Novel in America*, rev. ed. (New Haven: Yale University Press, 1965), esp. 51–107. See also Robert Bone, *Down Home: Origins of the Afro-American Short Story* (1975; rpt., New York: Columbia University Press, 1988); and Nathan Huggins, *Harlem Renaissance* (New York: Oxford University Press, 1971).

14. Diana Fuss, *Essentially Speaking: Feminism, Nature, and Difference* (New York: Routledge, 1989), 90.

15. Ibid., 92.

16. Houston Baker Jr., *Modernism and the Harlem Renaissance* (Chicago: University of Chicago Press, 1987), 68.

17. Ibid., 63–64.

18. Ibid., 66.

19. Ibid., 86.

20. Ibid., 92.

21. Ibid., 100.

22. Ibid.

23. Henry Louis Gates Jr., "Canon-Formation, Literary History, and the Afro-American Tradition: From the Seen to the Told," in *Afro-American Literary Study in the 1990s*, ed. Houston Baker Jr. and Patricia Redmond (Chicago and London: University of Chicago Press, 1989), 38.

24. Barbara E. Johnson, "Response," in Baker and Redmond, *Afro-American Literary Study*, 42.

25. Ibid.

26. Kenneth W. Warren, *Black and White Strangers: Race and American Literary Realism* (Chicago and London: University of Chicago Press, 1993), 139.

27. Fuss, *Essentially Speaking*, 92.

28. Ibid.

29. bell hooks, "Essentialism and Experience," *American Literary History* 3, no. 1 (spring 1991): 172–73. The essay is a review of Fuss's book.

30. Hazel V. Carby, "Ideologies of Black Folk: The Historical Novel of Slavery," in *Slavery and the Literary Imagination*, ed. Deborah E. McDowell and Arnold Rampersad (Baltimore and London: Johns Hopkins University Press, 1989), 126–27. Also see the final chapter of her book *Reconstructing Womanhood: The Emergence of the Afro-American Woman Novelist* (New York and Oxford: Oxford University Press, 1987), 163–75.

31. Ibid., 127.

32. Ibid., 140.

33. Hazel V. Carby, "The Politics of Fiction, Anthropology, and the Folk: Zora Neale Hurston," in *New Essays on* Their Eyes Were Watching God, ed. Michael Awkward (Cambridge: Cambridge University Press, 1990), 77. I take up this essay more fully in chapter 3.
34. Carby, "Ideologies of Black Folk," 140.
35. Robin D. G. Kelley, "Notes on Deconstructing 'The Folk,'" *American Historical Review* 97, no. 5 (December 1992): 1402.
36. Paul de Man provides a useful exposition of the concept of modernity. In "Literary History and Literary Modernity" he examines "the necessary experience of any present as a *passing* experience that makes the past irrevocable and unforgettable, because it is inseparable from any present or future": "Modernity exists in the form of a desire to wipe out whatever came earlier, in the hope of reaching at last a point that could be called a true present, a point of origin that marks a new departure. This combined interplay of deliberate forgetting with an action that is also a new origin reaches the full power of the idea of modernity." See Paul de Man, *Blindness and Insight: Essays in the Rhetoric of Contemporary Criticism*, 2d. rev. ed. (Minneapolis: University of Minnesota Press, 1983), 148–49.
37. Perry Anderson, "Modernity and Revolution," in *Marxism and the Interpretation of Culture*, ed. Cary Nelson and Lawrence Grossberg (Urbana and Chicago: University of Illinois Press, 1988), 318. Anderson's essay is an extended appreciation and critique of Marshall Berman's *All That Is Solid Melts into Air* (New York: Simon and Schuster, 1983). I take up neither the full force of that critique nor the remainder of Anderson's speculations about socialist revolution here. For a relevant discussion of Berman, Anderson, and modernity in black culture, see Paul Gilroy, *The Black Atlantic: Modernity and Double Consciousness* (Cambridge: Harvard University Press, 1993), 46–50.
38. Dipesh Chakrabarty, "Postcoloniality and the Artifice of History: Who Speaks for 'Indian' Pasts?" *Representations*, no. 37 (winter 1992): 20–21. Central texts concerning the post-colonial critique of modernity and peasant studies include: Ranajit Guha and Gayatri Chakravorty Spivak, eds., *Selected Subaltern Studies* (New York and Oxford: Oxford University Press, 1988); James C. Scott, *Weapons of the Weak: Everyday Forms of Peasant Resistance* (New Haven and London: Yale University Press, 1985); and Gayatri Chakravorty Spivak, "Can the Subaltern Speak?" in Nelson and Grossberg, *Marxism and the Interpretation of Culture*, 271–313.

   Robin Kelley has recently sought to develop an understanding of the internal politics of the black community in the Jim Crow South by employing the insights of these scholars of South Asia. See Robin D. G. Kelley, "'We Are Not What We Seem': Rethinking Black Working-Class Opposition in the Jim Crow South," *Journal of American History* 80, no. 1 (June 1993): 75–112; this article forms the basis for an expanded and revised version presented in his recent book: see Robin D. G. Kelley, *Race Rebels: Culture, Politics, and the Black Working Class* (1994; rpt., New York: Free, 1996), chaps. 1–3.
39. That the promise of citizenship is not equally fulfilled for all individuals in all places is, of course, one of the chief stories of the modern era and of recent critical theory. For a particularly relevant feminist approach to this problem, see Rita Felski, *The Gender of Modernity* (Cambridge and London: Harvard University Press, 1995).
40. Chakrabarty, "Postcoloniality and the Artifice of History," 8.

41. Ibid., 4.

42. Ibid., 23.

43. Jean Comaroff and John Comaroff, *Modernity and Its Malcontents*, xi.

44. Ibid.

45. Ibid., xiv.

46. Gilroy, *Black Atlantic*, 19.

47. For a critique of the argument for African-American exceptionalism and an account of its origins in American Studies, see Kenneth W. Warren, "Delimiting America: The Legacy of Du Bois," *American Literary History* 1, no. 1 (spring 1989): 172–89.

48. Sterling A. Brown, *Southern Road* (New York: Harcourt Brace, 1932), 8, ll. 3–4. Further references are cited parenthetically in the text.

49. Vera M. Kutzinski, "The Distant Closeness of Dancing Doubles: Sterling Brown and William Carlos Williams," *Black American Literature Forum* 16, no. 1 (spring 1982): 21.

50. Alain Locke, "Sterling Brown: The New Negro Folk-Poet," in *Negro: An Anthology*, ed. Nancy Cunard (1934; abridged ed. New York: Frederick Ungar, 1970), 88–92.

51. See in particular Joanne V. Gabbin, *Sterling Brown: Building the Black Aesthetic Tradition* (1985; rpt., Charlottesvile and London: University Press of Virginia, 1994); Stephen E. Henderson, "The Heavy Blues of Sterling Brown: A Study of Craft and Tradition," *Black American Literature Forum* 14, no. 1 (spring 1980): 32–44; Charles Rowell, "Sterling A. Brown and the Afro-American Folk Tradition," in *The Harlem Renaissance Re-examined*, ed. Victor A. Kramer (New York: AMS, 1987), 315–37.

52. See in particular Hartmut Grandel, "The Role of Music in the Self-Reflexive Poetry of the Harlem Renaissance," in *Poetics in the Poem: Critical Essays on American Self-Reflexive Poetry*, ed. Dorothy Z. Baker (New York: Peter Lang, 1997), 119–31; Gary Smith, "The Literary Ballads of Sterling A. Brown," *College Language Association Journal* 32, no. 4 (June 1989): 393–409.

53. Kimberly W. Benston, "Sterling Brown's After-Song: 'When de Saints Go Ma'ching Home' and the Performances of Afro-American Voice," *Callaloo* 5, nos. 1–2 (1982): 42.

54. Robert B. Stepto, "Sterling A. Brown: Outsider in the Harlem Renaissance?" in *The Harlem Renaissance: Revaluations*, ed. Amritjit Singh, William S. Shiver, and Stanley Brodwin (New York and London: Garland, 1989), 77.

55. Langston Hughes, "The Negro Artist and the Racial Mountain," rpt. ed., *Langston Hughes Review* 4, no. 1 (1985): 2.

56. Arnold Rampersad, *The Life of Langston Hughes*, vol. 1: 1902–1941, *I, Too, Sing America* (New York and Oxford: Oxford University Press, 1986), 66. For studies of Hughes's engagement with the form and substance of the blues, see David Chinitz, "Literacy and Authenticity: The Blues Poems of Langston Hughes," *Callaloo* 19, no. 1 (1996): 177–92; Steven C. Tracy, *Langston Hughes and the Blues* (Urbana and Chicago: University of Illinois Press, 1988); and Steven C. Tracy, "To the Tune of Those Weary Blues," in *Langston Hughes: Critical Perspectives Past and Present*, ed. Henry Louis Gates Jr. and K. A. Appiah (New York: Amistad, 1993), 69–93.

57. Langston Hughes, *Selected Poems of Langston Hughes* (1959; New York: Vintage, 1974), 279.

58. Langston Hughes, *The Collected Poems of Langston Hughes*, ed. Arnold Rampersad (New York: Knopf, 1994), 27.

59. Langston Hughes, *Fields of Wonder* (New York: Knopf, 1947), 99.

60. Hughes, *Collected Poems*, 212.
61. Ibid.
62. Hughes, *Selected Poems*, 292.
63. Ibid., 291.
64. Ibid., 297.
65. On the topic of Hughes's elusiveness, see Karen Jackson Ford, "Making Poetry Pay: The Commodification of Langston Hughes," in *Marketing Modernisms: Self-Promotion, Canonization, Rereading,* ed. Kevin J. H. Dettmar and Stephen Watt (Ann Arbor: University of Michigan Press, 1996), 275–96.
66. Similarly, Lawrence Buell has argued that "American pastoral representation cannot be linked to a single ideological position" (14). American pastoralism, he argues, has been "conceived as a dream both hostile to the standing order of civilization (decadent Europe, later hypercivilizing America) yet at the same time a model for the civilization in the process of being built" (20); he concludes by calling for a recognition of the multivalence of pastoral ideology, including its relation to a post-colonial context. See Lawrence Buell, "American Pastoral Ideology Reappraised," *American Literary History* 1, no. 1 (spring 1989): 1–29.
67. For a critique of tradition-centered literary histories in a cross-cultural context, see Gillian Bottomley, *From Another Place: Migration and the Politics of Culture* (Cambridge: Cambridge University Press, 1992).
68. In formulating an understanding of speculative, alternative modernities in literature, I found Loren Kruger's discussion of what she calls the "virtual public sphere" in popular theater to be a useful model. See Loren Kruger, "Placing 'New Africans' in the 'Old' South Africa: Drama, Modernity, and Racial Identities in Johannesburg, circa 1935," *Modernism/Modernity* 1, no. 2 (April 1994): 113–31; Loren Kruger, *The National Stage: Theatre and Cultural Legitimation in England, France, and America* (Chicago and London: University of Chicago Press, 1992), 3–29.
69. Anderson, "Modernity and Revolution," 318.
70. Fredric Jameson, *The Political Unconscious: Narrative as a Socially Symbolic Act* (Ithaca: Cornell University Press, 1981), 76; Hayden White, *The Content of the Form: Narrative Discourse and Historical Representation* (Baltimore and London: Johns Hopkins University Press, 1987).
71. Myra Jehlen, "History beside the Fact: What We Learn from *A True and Exact History of Barbadoes,*" in *The Politics of Research,* ed. E. Ann Kaplan and George Levine (New Brunswick, N.J.: Rutgers University Press), 138.

Chapter 2

1. See *The Wayward and the Seeking: A Collection of Writings by Jean Toomer,* ed. Darwin T. Turner (Washington, D.C.: Howard University Press, 1980), 123.
2. *A Jean Toomer Reader: Selected Unpublished Writings,* ed. Frederik L. Rusch (New York and Oxford: Oxford University Press, 1993), 24.
3. Jean Toomer, *Cane,* ed. Darwin T. Turner (1923; rpt., New York: Norton, 1988), 14. All further references are to this edition and are cited parenthetically in the text.
4. In describing the folk in *Cane* as spectral, I take inspiration from Vera Kutzinski, who

has written: "The text's purportedly sensual lyricism, much like the 'radiant beauty' of the southern landscape, has to it an eerie, nightmarish quality that unsettles its readers (or at least this reader) more than it communicates an abiding sense of 'spiritual fusion' and 'harmony.'" See Vera M. Kutzinski, "Unseasonal Flowers: Nature and History in Plácido and Jean Toomer," *Yale Journal of Criticism* 3, no. 2 (1990): 166.

Nicholas Lemann's discussion of "nearly spectral sharecropper cabins" in post-migration Mississippi suggests the pervasiveness of this association; see Nicholas Lemann, *The Promised Land: The Great Black Migration and How It Changed America* (New York: Alfred A. Knopf, 1991), 50.

5. The details of this trip have been frequently recounted in the critical literature on Toomer; see in particular Cynthia Earl Kerman and Richard Eldridge, *The Lives of Jean Toomer: A Hunger for Wholeness* (Baton Rouge and London: Louisiana State University Press, 1987), 79–116. It is possible, however, that some parts of the second section of *Cane* were written prior to his trip to Sparta; see George B. Hutchinson, "Jean Toomer and the 'New Negroes' of Washington," *American Literature* 63, no. 4 (December 1991): 683–92.

6. Jack Temple Kirby, *Rural Worlds Lost: The American South, 1920–1960* (Baton Rouge: Louisiana State University Press, 1987), 31.

7. Ibid., 119.

8. Forrest Shivers, *The Land Between: A History of Hancock County, Georgia, to 1940* (Spartanburg, S.C.: Reprint Company, 1990), 288.

9. See Arthur F. Raper, *Preface to Peasantry: A Tale of Two Black Belt Counties* (Chapel Hill: University of North Carolina Press, 1936), 184, table 41.

10. See Alan Golding, "Jean Toomer's *Cane*: The Search for Identity through Form," *Arizona Quarterly* 39, no. 3 (autumn 1983): 197–214. Major attempts to articulate the identity through form argument include John M. Reilly, "The Search for Black Redemption: Jean Toomer's *Cane*," *Studies in the Novel* 2 (1970): 312–24; Patricia Watkins, "Is There a Unifying Theme in *Cane?*" *College Language Association Journal* 15 (1971–72): 303–5; Bernard W. Bell, "Portrait of the Artist as High Priest of Soul: Jean Toomer's *Cane*," *Black World* 23, no. 11 (September 1974): 4–19, 92–97; Odette C. Martin, "*Cane*: Method and Myth," *Obsidian* 2, no. 1 (1976): 5–20; Howard Faulkner, "The Buried Life: Jean Toomer's *Cane*," *Studies in Black Literature* 7, no. 1 (winter 1976): 1–5. See also the various positions elaborated in Therman O'Daniel, ed., *Jean Toomer: A Critical Evaluation* (Washington, D.C.: Howard University Press, 1988).

Although not explicitly engaged in the identity through form argument, Laura Doyle reconciles the contradictory messages in Toomer's text by asserting that Toomer "critiques his own aesthetic practice" through "self-consciousness and self-exposure" (102); the effect is to uphold the argument that a unifying consciousness motivates the meanings in *Cane:* see Laura Doyle, *Bordering on the Body: The Racial Matrix of Modern Fiction and Culture* (New York and Oxford: Oxford University Press, 1994), 81–109.

11. Nellie Y. McKay, *Jean Toomer, Artist: A Study of His Literary Life and Work, 1894–1936* (Chapel Hill and London: University of North Carolina Press, 1984), 46.

12. Bernard W. Bell, *The Afro-American Novel and Its Tradition* (Amherst: University of Massachusetts Press, 1987), 97. A *Künstlerroman* is a novel of development in which the hero is an artist, and it is the defining subgenre of the Bildungsroman (e.g.,

Goethe's *Wilhelm Meister* or Joyce's *A Portrait of the Artist as a Young Man*). While *Cane* engages the figure of the male artist enjoying a *Wanderjahr* in the rural South, it does not insist upon totality and closure in the same way as its generic antecedents have—or, indeed, as critics like Bell and McKay have insisted.

13. McKay, *Jean Toomer, Artist*, 108.

14. Bell, *Afro-American Novel and Its Tradition*, 97–98.

15. Bernard Bell is not the only critic to schematize the book in this way. See, among many others, William K. Spofford, "The Unity of Part One of Jean Toomer's *Cane*," *Markham Review* 3 (1972): 58–60; Clyde Taylor, "The Second Coming of Jean Toomer," *Obsidian* 1 (winter 1975): 37–57; Robert Jones, "Jean Toomer as Poet: A Phenomenology of the Spirit," *Black American Literature Forum* 21, no. 3 (fall 1987): 253–73, and the more elaborate schematic provided in his book *Jean Toomer and the Prison-House of Thought* (Amherst: University of Massachusetts Press, 1993); Jeanne Kerblat-Houghton, "Mythes ruraux et urbains dans *Cane* de Jean Toomer (1894–1967)," in Groupe de Recherche et d'Études Nord-Américaines, *Mythes ruraux et urbains dans la culture Américaine* (Provence: Université de Provence Service des Publications, 1990), 67–77.

16. Michael North's recent description of the book would seem to endorse my view: in contrast to the understanding of the book as a circle, "it would be more accurate to say that there is a constant shuttling back and forth between literary forms such as lyric in a simple state and complex variations on them or mixtures of them." See Michael North, *The Dialect of Modernism: Race, Language, and Twentieth-Century Literature* (New York and Oxford: Oxford University Press, 1994), 167. Another reading emphasizing the collage of genres in *Cane* is provided in Linda Wagner-Martin, "Toomer's *Cane* as Narrative Sequence," in *Modern American Short Story Sequences: Composite Fictions and Fictive Communities*, ed. J. Gerald Kennedy (Cambridge, New York, and Melbourne: Cambridge University Press, 1995), 19–34.

Another way to read history back into *Cane* is through extensive research of the text's historical references: Barbara Foley's recent work demonstrates that "once one recognizes Toomer's veiled historical allusions, it becomes difficult, if not impossible, to read *Cane* as an abstractly lyrical representation of Southern life" (754); see Barbara Foley, "Jean Toomer's Sparta," *American Literature* 67, no. 4 (December 1995): 747–75.

17. Toomer's text contrasts with Lawrence Levine's expectation that, "although it happened neither suddenly nor completely, the sacred world view so central to black slaves was to be shattered in the twentieth century"; rather than show the shattering of a stable worldview, Toomer's text entertains the possibility of an alternative modernity. See Lawrence W. Levine, *Black Culture and Black Consciousness: Afro-American Folk Thought from Slavery to Freedom* (New York: Oxford University Press, 1977), 158.

18. Raper, *Preface to Peasantry*, 3.

19. Ibid., 87.

20. Shivers, *Land Between*, 291.

21. Edward E. Lewis, *The Mobility of the Negro: A Study in the American Labor Supply* (New York: Columbia University Press, 1931), 112.

22. Shivers, *Land Between*, 211.

23. Elizabeth Wiley Smith, *The History of Hancock County, Georgia,* vol. 1 (Washington, Ga.: Wilkes, 1974), 123–24.
24. Barbara Foley, "'In the Land of Cotton': Economics and Violence in Jean Toomer's *Cane," African American Review* 32, no. 2 (1998): 183. Foley provides an account of Toomer's "somewhat shallow" economic analysis in *Cane* that is both compatible with the one I've provided here and more extensive (187).
25. Raper, *Preface to Peasantry,* 406.
26. Ibid.
27. For a compatible reading of this poem, see Walter Benn Michaels, *Our America: Nativism, Modernism, Pluralism* (Durham and London: Duke University Press, 1995), 61.
28. This practice is discussed in chapters 4 and 5, in relation to Claude McKay's *Banana Bottom* and George Wylie Henderson's *Ollie Miss,* respectively.
29. Most migration narratives feature male protagonists, while folk narratives tend to center on women: see my discussion of this pattern in chapter 5.
30. Migration patterns by gender tend to suggest that more males than females migrated, although most measures of the trend focus on immigrants in urban centers rather than on out-migration sex ratios. Louise Kennedy's study of the 1920s shows that Negro men predominated in industrial centers where the majority of the jobs were open to men; she also notes that in the South black women generally outnumbered black men. See Louise Venable Kennedy, *The Negro Peasant Turns Cityward* (1930; rpt., New York: AMS, 1968), 140–42. Another study notes that, in states with a decrease in rural black population, the decrease in males is greater than the decrease in females: see Dean Dutcher, *The Negro in Modern Industrial Society: An Analysis of Changes in the Occupations of Negro Workers, 1910–1920* (Lancaster, Pa.: Dean Dutcher, 1930), 24.

   Most commentators concur with Kennedy's reading of the sex ratio. Florette Henri notes that Kennedy's conclusion contradicts census figures, which show more black women than black men in urban areas. Henri believes that the government under-counted black males, however; she gives Kennedy's study greater credence. See Florette Henri, *Black Migration: Movement North, 1900–1920* (Garden City, N.Y.: Anchor Press / Doubleday, 1975), 95–96. Recent works in this area by Darlene Clark Hine and Carole Marks provide portraits of black women's roles in the Great Migra-tion, while they also point up the need for more research in the field. See Darlene Clark Hine, "Black Migration to the Urban Midwest: The Gender Dimension, 1915–1945," in *The Great Migration in Historical Perspective: New Dimensions of Race, Class, and Gender,* ed. Joe William Trotter Jr. (Bloomington and Indianapolis: Indiana University Press, 1991), 127–46; and Carole Marks, *Farewell—We're Good and Gone: The Great Black Migration* (Bloomington and Indianapolis: Indiana University Press, 1989), 45–48.

   It is important to remember, however, that migration rates by gender were com-plexly aggregated within families, just as they were also related to economic and other institutional factors. Cf. Elizabeth Clark-Lewis, *Living In, Living Out: African American Domestics in Washington, D.C., 1910–1940* (Washington, D.C., and London: Smithsonian Institution Press, 1994), 51–66; and Earl Lewis, "Afro-American Adap-tive Strategies: The Visiting Habits of Kith and Kin among Black Norfolkians during the First Great Migration," *Journal of Family History* 12, no. 4 (1987): 407–20.

31. For a general discussion of "the ways in which migrants creatively use the commercial media to build communities around shared aesthetics of place and to mediate place as well" in Washington, D.C., and elsewhere (39), see Brett Williams, "The South in the City," *Journal of Popular Culture* 16, no. 3 (winter 1982): 30–41.

32. In order to describe the complex organization of labor, gender, and reproduction in beehives, entomologists have borrowed bits and pieces from various taxonomies of political systems, frequently to bizarre effect. Consider the following from one children's encyclopedia from the period:

> [Bees] live in a republic where the citizens do all the governing without voting, where the many kings are powerless, and the one much cherished queen works as hard as any of her subjects, and longer. Honey-bees are perfect socialists; they labor without competition or personal reward, and they have everything in common. They are divided into castes, as workers, queens, and drones, but these castes exist for the benefit of all, not for their own private advantage.

See "Bee" in *Compton's Pictured Encyclopedia and Fact Index*, 15 vols., 24th rev. ed. (1922; rpt., Chicago: F. E. Compton, 1945), 2:73.

33. As Barbara Foley has recently argued, Kabnis's fear had a concrete referent: lynching was on the rise in 1921. See Foley, "'In the Land of Cotton,'" 192. Foley's contention is that Toomer's strongest historical engagement with the scene in Sparta arose through his representation of racial violence, which many historians have correlated to the depressed economy, although she notes that Toomer does not make this connection himself.

    Farah Griffin's recent discussions of *Cane* also stress the immediacy of racial violence (instead of emphasizing the notion of mythic pastoralism) in Toomer's Georgia. See Farah Jasmine Griffin, *"Who Set You Flowin'?": The African-American Migration Narrative* (New York and Oxford: Oxford University Press, 1995).

34. In this sense I concur with Barbara Foley's assertion that "Toomer's class politics were as contradictory as his racial politics." See Foley, "Jean Toomer's Washington and the Politics of Class: From 'Blue Veins' to Seventh-Street Rebels," *Modern Fiction Studies* 42, no. 2 (summer 1996): 313.

Chapter 3

1. Robin D. G. Kelley, "'We Are Not What We Seem': Rethinking Black Working-Class Opposition in the Jim Crow South," *Journal of American History* 80, no. 1 (June 1993): 76.

2. Kelley, "'We Are Not What We Seem,'" 77. The term *hidden transcript* is borrowed from James C. Scott, *Domination and the Arts of Resistance: Hidden Transcripts* (New Haven: Yale University Press, 1990). Other major influences include Michel de Certeau, *The Practice of Everyday Life*, trans. Steven F. Rendall (Berkeley: University of California Press, 1984); and Eugene D. Genovese, *Roll, Jordan, Roll: The World the Slaves Made* (1972; rpt., New York: Vintage Books, 1976).

3. Kelley, "'We Are Not What We Seem,'" 76.

4. Quoted in ibid., 75.

5. Robert E. Hemenway, *Zora Neale Hurston: A Literary Biography* (Urbana and Chicago: University of Illinois Press, 1977), 167.

6. Cheryl A. Wall, "*Mules and Men* and Women: Zora Neale Hurston's Strategies of Narration and Visions of Female Empowerment," *Black American Literature Forum* 23, no. 4 (winter 1989): 661. See her more extensive treatment of Hurston (particularly on the issue of the narrative frame): Cheryl A. Wall, *Women of the Harlem Renaissance* (Bloomington and Indianapolis: Indiana University Press, 1995), chap. 4.

7. Priscilla Wald, "Becoming 'Colored': The Self-Authorized Language of Difference in Zora Neale Hurston," *American Literary History* 2, no. 1 (spring 1990): 79.

8. In this vein, see also Adrianne R. Andrews, "Of *Mules and Men* and Men and Women: The Ritual of Talking B[l]ack," in *Language, Rhythm, and Sound: Black Popular Cultures into the Twenty-First Century*, ed. Joseph K. Adjaye and Adrianne R. Andrews (Pittsburgh: University of Pittsburgh Press, 1997), 109–20; and Mary Katherine Wainwright, "Subversive Female Folk Tellers in *Mules and Men*," in *Zora in Florida*, ed. Steve Glassman and Kathryn Lee Seidel (Orlando: University of Central Florida Press, 1991), 62–75.

   One reader who sees the feminist message as subversive, but not submerged, is Pearlie Peters, in "Women and Assertive Voice in Hurston's Fiction and Folklore," *Literary Griot* 4, nos. 1–2 (spring–fall 1992): 100–110.

9. Barbara Johnson, "Thresholds of Difference: Structures of Address in Zora Neale Hurston," in *"Race," Writing, and Difference*, ed. Henry Louis Gates Jr. (Chicago and London: University of Chicago Press, 1986), 318.

10. Ibid., 328. For important critiques of her approach, see Elizabeth Abel, "Black Writing, White Reading: Race and the Politics of Feminist Interpretation," *Critical Inquiry* 19, no. 3 (spring 1993): 470–98; Susan Lurie, *Unsettled Subjects: Restoring Feminist Politics to Poststructuralist Critique* (Durham and London: Duke University Press, 1997), 30–43; and Tzvetan Todorov, "'Race,' Writing, and Culture," in Gates, *"Race," Writing, and Difference*, 370–80.

11. One feminist study, however, reads Hurston's ethnography as replicating the structure of "containment" in the camp: "The story is a unit whose function is not to transform anyone's thoughts about his or her working conditions" (44); my argument here strongly contradicts this observation. See Susan Willis, *Specifying: Black Women Writing the American Experience* (Madison and London: University of Wisconsin Press, 1987).

12. See, for example, Miriam DeCosta Willis, "Folklore and the Creative Artist: Lydia Cabrera and Zora Neale Hurston," *College Language Association Journal* 27, no. 1 (September 1983): 81–90.

13. Sandra Dolby-Stahl, "Literary Objectives: Hurston's Use of Personal Narrative in *Mules and Men*," *Western Folklore* 51 (January 1992): 52. Dolby-Stahl refers to James Clifford and George E. Marcus, eds., *Writing Culture: The Poetics and Politics of Ethnography* (Berkeley: University of California Press, 1986).

14. See in particular D. A. Boxwell, "'Sis Cat' as Ethnographer: Self-Presentation and Self-Inscription in Zora Neale Hurston's *Mules and Men*," *African American Review* 26, no. 4 (winter 1992): 605–17; John Dorst, "Reading *Mules and Men*: Toward the Death of the Ethnographer," *Cultural Anthropology* 2 (1987): 305–18; Deborah Gordon, "The Politics of Ethnographic Authority: Race and Writing in the Ethnography of Margaret Mead and Zora Neale Hurston," in *Modernist Anthropology: From Fieldwork to Text*, ed. Marc Manganaro (Princeton: Princeton University Press, 1990), 146–62;

Anthony R. Hale, "Framing the Folk: Zora Neale Hurston, John Millington Synge, and the Politics of Aesthetic Ethnography," *Comparatist* 20 (1996): 50–61; Beth Harrison, "Zora Neale Hurston and Mary Austin: A Case Study in Ethnography, Literary Modernism, and Contemporary Ethnic Fiction," *MELUS* 21, no. 2 (summer 1996): 89–106; Graciela Hernández, "Multiple Subjectivities and Strategic Positionality: Zora Neale Hurston's Experimental Ethnographies," in *Women Writing Culture,* ed. Ruth Behar and Deborah A. Gordon (Berkeley, Los Angeles, and London: University of California Press, 1995), 148–65; bell hooks, *Yearning: Race, Gender, and Cultural Politics* (Boston: South End, 1990), chap. 14; Rosan Augusta Jordan, "Not into Cold Space: Zora Neale Hurston and J. Frank Dobie as Holistic Folklorists," *Southern Folklore* 49 (1992): 109–31; and Benigno Sánchez-Eppler, "Telling Anthropology: Zora Neale Hurston and Gilberto Freyre Disciplined in Their Field-Home-Work," *American Literary History* 4, no. 3 (fall 1992): 464–88.

15. Since I first drafted this chapter, other scholars have begun to explore the question of everyday resistance in Hurston's book. See, in particular, Susan Meisenhelder, "Conflict and Resistance in Zora Neale Hurston's *Mules and Men," Journal of American Folklore* 109 (summer 1996): 267–88.

16. Hazel V. Carby, "The Politics of Fiction, Anthropology, and the Folk: Zora Neale Hurston," in *New Essays on* Their Eyes Were Watching God, ed. Michael Awkward (Cambridge: Cambridge University Press, 1990), 77. But cf. Mikell, who claims that "the historical framework is implicit rather than explicit in *Mules and Men*" (33): Gwendolyn Mikell, "The Anthropological Imagination of Zora Neale Hurston," *Western Journal of Black Studies* 7, no. 1 (1983): 27–35.

17. Michele Wallace offers another critique of the feminist mystification of Hurston; see Wallace, *Invisibility Blues: From Pop to Theory* (London and New York: Verso, 1990), chap. 20.

18. Carby, "The Politics of Fiction, Anthropology, and the Folk," 80. Hernández concurs with my reading of Carby; see Hernández, "Multiple Subjectivities." We might also note, as Laura Reed-Morrisson has, that Carby ignores the influence of Franz Boas's relativist intervention into race-centered anthropological method on Hurston's work. See Laura Reed-Morrisson, " 'Money and Fun and Foolishness': Rethinking Work and Play in *Mules and Men* and *Their Eyes Were Watching God*," Typescript, University of Chicago, 1994.

19. Polk County, Florida, Publicity Department, *Polk County, Florida* (Bartow, Fla.: Polk County Publicity Department, [1928?]), 3.

20. Ibid.

21. Ibid., 3, 6.

22. Ibid., 17.

23. Zora Neale Hurston, *Mules and Men* (1935; rpt., New York: Harper Perennial, 1990), 59. All further references are cited parenthetically in the text.

24. Charlotte Todes, *Labor and Lumber* (New York: International, 1931), 83. Todes's study is aimed toward urging unionization of the workers. For another study in this vein, see Industrial Workers of the World, 3d. ed., *The Lumber Industry and Its Workers* (Chicago: Industrial Workers of the World, [1922?]). Despite segregation, the IWW included Negro timber workers in its ranks; see the discussion of the IWW and the Brotherhood of Timber Workers in Sterling D. Spero and Abram L. Harris, *The Black*

Worker: The Negro and the Labor Movement (1931; rpt., New York: Atheneum, 1968), 331–32.

In contrast, the U.S. government provides a portrait of the cypress industry from the perspective of the commodity and its uses; see W. LeRoy Neubrech, *American Southern Cypress* (Washington, D.C.: United States Government Printing Office, 1939). For a historical perspective from the standpoint of the capitalist manager, see Archer H. Mayor, *Southern Timberman: The Legacy of William Buchanan* (Athens: University of Georgia Press, 1988).

25. Todes, *Labor and Lumber*, 83–84.
26. This problem is also discussed in Lynda Marion Hill, *Social Rituals and the Verbal Art of Zora Neale Hurston* (Washington, D.C.: Howard University Press, 1996), 74–75.
27. Genovese, *Roll, Jordan, Roll*, 621.
28. Vladimir Propp, "The Nature of Folklore" (1946), in *Theory and History of Folklore*, ed. Anatoly Liberman, trans. Ariadna Y. Martin and Richard P. Martin (Minneapolis: University of Minnesota Press, 1984), 4, 11.
29. Zora Neale Hurston, "How It Feels to Be Colored Me," *World Tomorrow* 11 (May 1928): 215–16.
30. Hemenway, *Zora Neale Hurston*, 298.
31. Zora Neale Hurston and Dorothy Waring, *Polk County: A Comedy of Negro Life on a Sawmill, with Authentic Negro Music, in Three Acts* (1944), Typescript, New York Public Library, 1-4-4. For a more extensive discussion of *Polk County*, see John Lowe, "From Mule Bones to Funny Bones: The Plays of Zora Neale Hurston," *Southern Quarterly* 33, nos. 2–3 (winter–spring 1995): 65–78.
32. Carby, "Politics of Fiction, Anthropology, and the Folk," 80.
33. Kelley, "'We Are Not What We Seem,'" 78.

Chapter 4

1. Claude McKay, *A Long Way from Home* (1937; rpt., New York: Arno Press and the New York Times, 1969), 300, 186.
2. In a chapter called "The Backward Glance" Renu Juneja makes a similar argument about the place of folk culture in recent works by George Lamming and Paule Marshall; see Renu Juneja, *Caribbean Transactions: West Indian Culture in Literature* (London and Basingstoke: Macmillan Caribbean, 1996), 50–86.
3. I follow Fredric Jameson in describing the *folk* as an ideologeme; see Jameson, *The Political Unconscious: Narrative as a Socially Symbolic Act* (Ithaca: Cornell University Press, 1981), 87.
4. Bernard W. Bell defines *Banana Bottom* as a folk romance; see Bell, *The Afro-American Novel and Its Tradition* (Amherst: University of Massachusetts Press, 1987), 112–19.
5. Richard Priebe has discussed the novel as naturalistic. See Richard Priebe, "The Search for Community in the Novels of Claude McKay," *Studies in Black Literature* 3, no. 2 (summer 1972): 22–30.
6. Kenneth Ramchand, "Claude McKay and *Banana Bottom*," *Southern Review* (Australia) 4 (1970): 54, 66.

7. George E. Kent, "The Soulful Way of Claude McKay," *Black World* 20 (November 1970): 49. See also Kent's later article in which he situates the novel within the Harlem Renaissance tradition because of "its emphasis on racial definition, without stress upon economics" (222), although he concludes that it is not "a searching analysis of the problem of identity" (233): Kent, "Claude McKay's *Banana Bottom* Reappraised," *College Language Association Journal* 18 (December 1974): 222–34.

8. Michael Gilkes, *The West Indian Novel* (Boston: Twayne Publishers, 1981), 14.

9. Ibid.

10. Ibid.

11. Leota S. Lawrence, "Three West Indian Heroines: An Analysis," *College Language Association Journal* 21 (1977): 242. For another unhappy reading of the novel, see Stephen H. Bronz, *Roots of Negro Racial Consciousness* (New York: Libra Publishers, 1964), 86.

12. Lawrence, "Three West Indian Heroines," 250. Geta LeSeur echoes Lawrence (perhaps too literally) when she writes that "anyone familiar with the West Indian culture would agree that McKay's Bita is a romanticized version of West Indian womanhood"; see LeSeur, *Ten Is the Age of Darkness: The Black Bildungsroman* (Columbia and London: University of Missouri Press, 1995), 192. Elaine Campbell praises McKay's characterization, however: "McKay appropriately created a female protagonist who, to his great credit, serves as much more than a sort of archetypal mother figure"; see Campbell, "Two West Indian Heroines: Bita Plant and Fola Piggott," *Caribbean Quarterly* 29, no. 2 (June 1983): 25. For further analyses of Bita's characterization and the problem of typology, see Melvin B. Rahming, *The Evolution of the West Indian's Image in the Afro-American Novel* (Millwood, N.Y., New York, and London: Associated Faculty, 1986), 126–34; and Michael B. Stoff, "Claude McKay and the Cult of Primitivism," in *The Harlem Renaissance Remembered*, ed. Arna Bontemps (New York: Dodd, Mead, 1972), 126–46.

13. George Lamming, "The Peasant Roots of the West Indian Novel," in *Critics on Caribbean Literature*, ed. Edward Baugh (New York: St. Martin's Press, 1978), 25. The essay is excerpted from Lamming's *The Pleasures of Exile* (London: Michael Joseph, 1960).

   Banana Bottom is often taken to be a predecessor to the later post-colonial novel in the West Indies (see in particular Kenneth Ramchand, *The West Indian Novel and Its Background*, 2d ed. [London: Heinemann, 1983]). Although the novel was written in Tangier and published in the United States for the American market, it was later taken as a touchstone for writers in the West Indies bent on producing an indigenous literature. It consequently has been placed in at least two lineages, West Indian and African American. See P. S. Chauhan, "Rereading Claude McKay," *College Language Association Journal* 34 (September 1990): 68–80. Eckhard Breitinger discusses the difficulty of placing McKay in any strictly national tradition; see Breitinger, "In Search of an Audience, in Search of the Self: Exile as a Condition for the Works of Claude McKay," in *The Commonwealth Writer Overseas: Themes of Exile and Expatriation*, ed. Alastair Niven (Brussells: Librairie Marcel Didier, 1976), 175–84. Also see Michael North's recent discussion of McKay's dialect poetry and the issue of exile as they pertain to *Banana Bottom*: North, *The Dialect of Modernism: Race, Language, and Twentieth-Century Literature* (New York and Oxford: Oxford University Press, 1994), 100–123.

For a biographical account of the production and reception of the novel, see Wayne F. Cooper, *Claude McKay: Rebel Sojourner in the Harlem Renaissance* (1987; rpt., New York: Schocken Books, 1990). See also James R. Giles, *Claude McKay* (Boston: Twayne, 1976); and Tyrone Tillery, *Claude McKay: A Black Poet's Struggle for Identity* (Amherst: University of Massachusetts Press, 1992).

14. Lamming, "Peasant Roots of the West Indian Novel," 26.

15. Gordon Rohlehr, "The Folk in Caribbean Literature," in Baugh, *Critics on Caribbean Literature*, 28.

16. Ibid., 30. The term *folk-urban continuum* was first developed by Robert Redfield and the Chicago School of Sociology. For a useful bibliography of Redfield's works (and work influenced by it) as well as a trenchant critique of the concept of the folk-urban continuum, see Sidney W. Mintz, "The Folk-Urban Continuum and the Rural Proletarian Community," *American Journal of Sociology* 59, no. 2 (September 1953): 136–43.

17. Thomas C. Holt, *The Problem of Freedom: Race, Labor, and Politics in Jamaica and Britain, 1832–1938* (Baltimore and London: Johns Hopkins University Press, 1992), 146–47.

18. Ibid., 175.

19. Sidney W. Mintz, "The Caribbean as a Socio-Cultural Area," *Cahiers d'Histoire Mondiale* 9, no. 4 (fall 1966): 931–32. See also Sidney W. Mintz, "From Plantations to Peasantries in the Caribbean," in *Caribbean Contours*, ed. Sidney W. Mintz and Sally Price (Baltimore and London: Johns Hopkins University Press, 1985), 127–53; and Mintz, "Folk-Urban Continuum."

20. Claude McKay, *Gingertown* (1932; rpt., Salem, N.H.: Ayer, 1991), 186.

21. Selwyn R. Cudjoe, *Resistance and Caribbean Literature* (Chicago, Athens, Ohio, and London: Ohio University Press, 1980). Similarly, H. Nigel Thomas examines the "counterhegemonic thrust" of the novel (379); see Thomas, "Claude McKay's *Banana Bottom*: A Black Response to Late Nineteenth and Early Twentieth Century White Discourse on the Meaning of Black Reality," in *Nationalism vs. Internationalism: (Inter)National Dimensions of Literatures in English*, ed. Wolfgang Zach and Ken L. Goodwin (Tübingen: Stauffenburg Verlag, 1996), 379–88. For more on the topic of resistance in this region, see Thomas Bremer and Ulrich Fleischmann, eds., *Alternative Cultures in the Caribbean: First International Conference of the Society of Caribbean Research, Berlin, 1988* (Frankfurt am Main: Vervuert Verlag, 1993).

22. Claude McKay, *Banana Bottom* (1933; rpt., New York: Harcourt Brace Jovanovich, 1961), 11. All further references are cited parenthetically in the text. H. Nigel Thomas notes the homology between Bita's story and the Pygmalion myth; see Thomas, "Claude McKay's *Banana Bottom*," 381.

23. McKay's "experimental" stance toward rape has rankled many feminist readers; I do not mean to endorse his stance here, but I do mean to explore the implications of it for understanding the development of the novel. Geta LeSeur's caveat is worth repeating: "Because of the setting and era of this story, the idea of rape is not developed. Although this is the first time that this issue is addressed in a West Indian novel, what its treatment indicates about the culture and about the place of women in that culture is bothersome for contemporary readers." See LeSeur, *Ten Is the Age of Darkness*, 153.

Also cf. Eve Kosofsky Sedgwick, *Between Men: English Literature and Male Homosocial Desire* (New York: Columbia University Press, 1985), 8–11; Sedgwick discusses the ways in which the cultural meanings of rape circulate in the story of Scarlett O'Hara even when her attack by a black thief in *Gone with the Wind* did not include sexual assault.

24. Carolyn Cooper, *Noises in the Blood: Orality, Gender, and the "Vulgar" Body of Jamaican Popular Culture* (1993; rpt., Durham: Duke University Press, 1995), 2–3.

25. Cooper, *Noises in the Blood,* 198.

26. Ibid., 4. For more on the question of women's roles and agencies in Caribbean literary discourse, see Carole Boyce Davies and Elaine Savory Fido, eds., *Out of the Kumbla: Caribbean Women and Literature* (Trenton, N.J.: Africa World, 1990).

27. Hazel V. Carby, "The Politics of Fiction, Anthropology, and the Folk: Zora Neale Hurston," in *New Essays on* Their Eyes Were Watching God, ed. Michael Awkward (Cambridge: Cambridge University Press, 1990), 78–79.

28. Patrick Taylor, *The Narrative of Liberation: Perspectives on Afro-Caribbean Literature, Popular Culture, and Politics* (Ithaca and London: Cornell University Press, 1989), 3. Caribbean modernists like Wilson Harris, Alejo Carpentier, and Edouard Glissant have been understood to rupture totalizing historical utopianism, however; for example, Barbara J. Webb argues that, "rather than the symmetrical, transparent totalities that have for so long dominated cultural and literary discourse, Harris (like Carpentier and Glissant) proposes the asymmetrical, complex interrelations of the cross-cultural imagination"; see Webb, *Myth and History in Caribbean Fiction: Alejo Carpentier, Wilson Harris, and Edouard Glissant* (Amherst: University of Massachusetts Press, 1992), 25.

In his theoretical writings Glissant argues that "writing seems linked to the transcendental notion of the individual, which today is threatened by and giving way to a cross-cultural process"; see Glissant, *Caribbean Discourse: Selected Essays,* trans. and with an intro. by J. Michael Dash (Charlottesville: University Press of Virginia, 1989), 126.

29. Antonio Benítez-Rojo, *The Repeating Island: The Caribbean and the Postmodern Perspective,* trans. James E. Maraniss (Durham and London: Duke University Press, 1992), 53.

30. Ibid., 17. Although Benítez-Rojo is careful to avoid the assumption that, as Cooper has put it, "the West Indies is a chain of indistinguishable islands" (*Noises in the Blood,* 188), his rhetoric often modulates into the kind of universalizing discourse quoted here.

31. Simon Gikandi, *Writing in Limbo: Modernism and Caribbean Literature* (Ithaca and London: Cornell University Press, 1992), 18.

32. Irma Watkins-Owens, *Blood Relations: Caribbean Immigrants and the Harlem Community, 1900–1930* (Bloomington and Indianapolis: Indiana University Press, 1996), 156.

33. Franklin Knight, "Discussion," in *Process of Unity in Caribbean Society: Ideologies and Literature,* ed. Ileana Rodríguez and Marc Zimmerman (Minneapolis: Institute for the Study of Ideologies and Literatures, 1983), 116.

34. Similarly, Jan Carew claims that "the Caribbean writer by going abroad is in fact . . . searching for an end to exile"; see Carew, *Fulcrums of Change* (Trenton, N.J.: Africa World, 1988), 91.

35. Cooper, *Claude McKay,* 274–75, 281.

Chapter 5

1. Richard Wright, *Uncle Tom's Children* (1938), reprinted in *Richard Wright: Early Works*, ed. Arnold Rampersad (New York: Library of America, 1991), 333.

2. Ibid., 335.

3. Werner Sollors concludes that this choice indicates that Wright "refrains from idyllicizing the rural world and uses the contrast to sketch the grim alternative the protagonists face of either dying or escaping traumatized" (123). See his extensive discussion of the story in Werner Sollors, "Modernization as Adultery: Richard Wright, Zora Neale Hurston, and American Culture of the 1930s and 1940s," *Hebrew University Studies in Literature and the Arts* 18 (1990): 109–55.

4. Jean Toomer, *Cane*, ed. Darwin T. Turner (1923; rpt., New York: Norton, 1988), 17.

5. Two articles in the "images of women" tradition address Henderson's *Ollie Miss* by comparison with other black female characters. See Lonnell E. Johnson, "The Defiant Black Heroine: Ollie Miss and Janie Mae—Two Portraits from the 30's," *Zora Neale Hurston Forum* 4, no. 2 (spring 1990): 41–46; and Patricia Kane and Doris Y. Wilkinson, "Survival Strategies: Black Women in *Ollie Miss* and *Cotton Comes to Harlem*," *Critique: Studies in Modern Fiction* 16, no. 1 (1974): 101–9.

Robert Bone pairs Henderson with Hurston in his discussion of authors who explore "aspects of the racial past"; see Bone, *The Negro Novel in America*, rev. ed. (New Haven: Yale University Press, 1965), 123–26.

6. For the most complete biography of Henderson, see Emmanuel S. Nelson's entry in *Dictionary of Literary Biography*, vol. 51, s.v. "George Wylie Henderson."

7. His earlier short fiction takes up similar autobiographical references (see Edythe Robertson, "Young Bronx Printer Strides toward Fame," *New York Amsterdam News*, 31 August 1932, 2). He published nine short stories during 1932 and 1933 in the *New York Daily News* as part of the paper's "Daily Story from Real Life" series. He later became a regular contributor of fiction for *Redbook* magazine. For a complete record of his short fiction publications, see David G. Nicholls, "George Wylie Henderson: A Primary and Secondary Bibliography," *Bulletin of Bibliography* 54, no. 4 (December 1997): 335–38.

8. M. M. Bakhtin, "The *Bildungsroman* and Its Significance in the History of Realism (Toward a Historical Typology of the Novel)" (1936–38), in *Speech Genres and Other Essays*, ed. Caryl Emerson and Michael Holquist, trans. Vern W. McGee (Austin: University of Texas Press, 1986), 21.

9. George Wylie Henderson, *Ollie Miss* (1935; rpt., Tuscaloosa and London: University of Alabama Press, 1988), 276. All further references are cited parenthetically in the text with the abbreviation *OM*.

The novel was originally printed by Stokes in New York in 1935, at which time an edition was also printed in England by Secker. The Library of Alabama Classics version appears to be a direct reprint of the original plates, with the addition of an introduction by Blyden Jackson.

10. Bakhtin, "*Bildungsroman*," 23.

11. George Wylie Henderson, *Jule* (1946; rpt., Tuscaloosa and London: University of Alabama Press, 1989), 232. All further references are cited parenthetically in the text with the abbreviation *J*.

12. Bakhtin, "*Bildungsroman*," 23.

13. One contemporary reviewer noted Henderson's appropriation of the stereotype: "Ollie Miss is a universal figure; and there are some of us who are apt to find these universal figures, with their woolly heads among the stars and their splay feet planted firmly on mother earth, just as tedious as any sophisticated *femme fatale*. . . . Mother-love and land-hunger are at once satisfied"; see Peter Quennell, review of *Ollie Miss*, by George Wylie Henderson, *New Statesman and Nation* 9, 1 June 1935, 829. Most reviews (and there were many) were positive, however; for a complete listing of the reviews, see Nicholls, "George Wylie Henderson."

14. The introduction to the Alabama edition of the novel makes this connection. See Blyden Jackson, introduction to Henderson, *Ollie Miss*, xvi.

15. Charles S. Johnson, *Shadow of the Plantation* (1934; rpt., Chicago: University of Chicago Press, 1979), 1. For a compatible critique of the comparison to feudalism, see Susan Willis, *Specifying: Black Women Writing the American Experience* (Madison and London: University of Wisconsin Press, 1987), 4–5.

16. The comparison, however, is frequently asserted; see, for example, the chapter on "The Flight from Feudal America" in E. Franklin Frazier, *The Negro Family in the United States* (1939; rpt., rev. and abridged ed., New York: Dryden Press, 1951), 225–44.

17. Johnson, *Shadow of the Plantation*, 2.

18. Ibid., 1.

19. Ibid., 3.

20. Ibid., 104.

21. Ibid., 212.

22. Cf. Leo McGee and Robert Boone, eds., *The Black Rural Landowner—Endangered Species: Social, Political, and Economic Implications* (Westport, Conn., and London: Greenwood Press, 1979).

23. For a discussion of the recreational value of the frolics in communities such as Ollie's, see Johnson, *Shadow of the Plantation*, 181–83.

24. *Tuskegee Student*, 13 May 1916, 5.

25. The prizes were awarded to students who "write and deliver the best essays on subjects assigned for the competition," a selection of over twenty topics each year addressing issues in agriculture, labor, education, politics, and African-American history; see *Fortieth Annual Catalog* (Tuskegee, Ala.: Tuskegee Normal and Industrial Institute, 1920–21), 149; *Forty-first Annual Catalog* (Tuskegee, Ala.: Tuskegee Normal and Industrial Institute, 1921–22), 147.

26. Booker T. Washington, *Up from Slavery* (1901), in *Three Negro Classics*, ed. John Hope Franklin (New York: Avon Books, 1965), 67, 108.

27. Booker T. Washington, ed., *Tuskegee and Its People: Their Ideals and Achievements* (1905; rpt., Freeport, N.Y.: Books for Libraries, 1971), 10–11.

28. See James D. Anderson, *The Education of Blacks in the South, 1860–1935* (Chapel Hill and London: University of North Carolina Press, 1988), 79–109.

29. Robin D. G. Kelley, *Hammer and Hoe: Alabama Communists during the Great Depression* (Chapel Hill and London: University of North Carolina Press, 1990), 174–75.

30. For an analysis of such hopes and of the mixed results of migration, see James R. Grossman, *Land of Hope: Chicago, Black Southerners, and the Great Migration* (Chicago and London: University of Chicago Press, 1989).

31. *Ollie Miss* is itself a revision of a 1932 story, "'Thy Name Is Woman.'" In this story a woman named "Daughter" appears on Alex's farm and asks for food and work; she is taken away by the sheriff when it is revealed that she murdered the father of her baby, who declined to marry her and support the child. See George W. Henderson, "'Thy Name Is Woman,'" *New York Daily News*, 15 July 1932, 29.

32. Cf. Hortense J. Spillers, "Mama's Baby, Papa's Maybe: An American Grammar Book," *Diacritics* 17, no. 2 (summer 1987): 65–81.

33. The character named Jule in *Ollie Miss* is referred to as Big Jule in *Jule* to avoid confusion with the son by the same name. Like Jule, Henderson shared names with his father, the Reverend George W. Henderson.

34. Louise Venable Kennedy, *The Negro Peasant Turns Cityward* (1930; rpt., New York: AMS, 1968), 140–42.

35. Daniel M. Johnson and Rex R. Campbell, *Black Migration in America: A Social Demographic History* (Durham: Duke University Press, 1981), 105. Also see *Sixteenth Census of the United States: 1940: Population: Internal Migration 1935 to 1940: Color and Sex of Migrants* (Washington, D.C.: United States Government Printing Office, 1943), esp. table 1.

36. The classic elaboration of the theory of "male homosocial desire" is Eve Kosofsky Sedgwick, *Between Men: English Literature and Male Homosocial Desire* (New York: Columbia University Press, 1985). Also, cf. Spillers, "Mama's Baby, Papa's Maybe," 80; she argues that the figure of the illegitimately empowered African-American woman has emerged "because legal enslavement removed the African-American male not so much from sight as from *mimetic* view as a partner in the prevailing social fiction of the Father's name, the Father's law."

37. John E. Loftis, "Domestic Prey: Richard Wright's Parody of the Hunt Tradition in 'The Man Who Was Almost a Man,'" *Studies in Short Fiction* 23, no. 4 (fall 1986): 437.

38. Lawrence R. Rodgers has codified *Jule* as a "communal migrant" novel (132), a refinement of the "fugitive migrant novel" (97), in which the "general emphasis shifts from the fugitive's theme of flight to one of quest" (132); see Rodgers, *Canaan Bound: The Afro-American Great Migration Novel* (Urbana and Chicago: University of Illinois Press, 1997). For a thematic discussion of the narrative of flight, see Phyllis Rauch Klotman, *Another Man Gone: The Black Runner in Contemporary Afro-American Literature* (Port Washington, N.Y., and London: Kennikat, 1977).

39. This character seems to be based on a personage from Henderson's days at Tuskegee: in the Tuskegee yearbook's chart listing characteristics of each member of the class of 1922, the entry for Henderson's "pastime" is "Wooing Bertha." (*Carver* [Tuskegee, Ala.: Senior Class, Tuskegee Normal and Industrial Institute, 1922]).

40. Joe William Trotter Jr., "Introduction: Black Migration in Historical Perspective," in *The Great Migration in Historical Perspective: New Dimensions of Race, Class, and Gender*, ed. Trotter (Bloomington and Indianapolis: Indiana University Press, 1991), 7.

41. Emmet J. Scott, *Negro Migration during the War* (1920; rpt., New York: Arno, 1969), quoted in Trotter, "Introduction," 7.

42. Grossman, *Land of Hope*, 38–39.

43. Contemporary historians have begun to place more emphasis on racial violence as an impetus for migration. See Stewart E. Tolnay and E. M. Beck, "Black Flight: Lethal

Violence and the Great Migration, 1900–1930," *Social Science History* 14, no. 3 (fall 1990): 347–70.

44. Rudolph Fisher, "The City of Refuge," in *The New Negro*, ed. Alain Locke (1925; rpt., New York: Atheneum, 1968), 58. Given the sacred orientation of the "City of Refuge" in spirituals and blues lyrics, Fisher's title provokes an ironic comparison between Harlem and heaven; see the discussion in Farah Jasmine Griffin, *"Who Set You Flowin'?": The African-American Migration Narrative* (New York and Oxford: Oxford University Press, 1995), 63.

45. Fisher, "City of Refuge," 58.

46. Ibid., 60.

47. Trotter, "Introduction," 7.

48. For a wide-ranging discussion of the representation of the city in African-American literature, see Charles Scruggs, *Sweet Home: Invisible Cities in the Afro-American Novel* (Baltimore and London: Johns Hopkins University Press, 1993).

49. George Wylie Henderson, "Baby Lou and the Angel Bud" (typescript, n.d.), Collection of Roslyn Kirkland Allen.

Chapter 6

1. George Wylie Henderson, *Ollie Miss* (1935; rpt., Tuscaloosa and London: University of Alabama Press, 1988), 276.

2. George Wylie Henderson, *Jule* (1946; rpt., Tuscaloosa and London: University of Alabama Press, 1989), 232.

3. Richard Wright, *12 Million Black Voices*, photo direction by Edwin Rosskam (New York: Viking, 1941), 147. All further references are cited parenthetically in the body of the text.

4. Paul Buhle, *Marxism in the United States: Remapping the History of the American Left* (London: Verso, 1987), 168.

5. Ibid., 169.

6. Howard Zinn, *A People's History of the United States* (New York: Harper and Row, 1980), 396.

7. Philip S. Foner, *American Socialism and Black Americans: From the Age of Jackson to World War II* (Westport, Conn., and London: Greenwood Press, 1977), 345.

8. Richard Wright, "12 Million Black Voices," *Coronet* 11 (April 1942): 78. See the discussion in Michel Fabre, *The Unfinished Quest of Richard Wright*, trans. Isabel Barzun, 2d ed. (Urbana and Chicago: University of Illinois Press, 1993), 227; for further details of this moment in Wright's life, see 207–31. See also Yoshinobu Hakutani, *Richard Wright and Racial Discourse* (Columbia and London: University of Missouri Press, 1996), 101–13.

9. See also Wright's account of his membership in and departure from the Communist Party: Richard Wright, "I Tried to Be a Communist," pts. 1–8, *Atlantic Monthly* (August 1944): 61–70; pts. 9–13, *Atlantic Monthly* (September 1944): 48–56.

10. Richard Wright, "Blueprint for Negro Writing" (1937), in *Richard Wright Reader*, ed. Ellen Wright and Michel Fabre (New York: Harper and Row, 1978), 39.

11. Ibid., 48.

12. Ibid., 40.

13. Barbara Foley, *Radical Representations: Politics and Form in U.S. Proletarian Fiction, 1929–1941* (Durham and London: Duke University Press, 1993), 192. Foley briefly discusses Wright's text in this section of the book, subtitled "Black Culture: Folk or Proletarian?"

14. Elaine Scarry, *The Body in Pain: The Making and Unmaking of the World* (New York and Oxford: Oxford University Press, 1985).

15. The key works include: E. Franklin Frazier, *The Negro Family in the United States* (1939; rpt., rev. and abridged ed., New York: Dryden, 1951); Arthur F. Raper and Ira De A. Reid, *Sharecroppers All* (Chapel Hill: University of North Carolina Press, 1941); Louis Wirth, "Urbanism as a Way of Life," *American Journal of Sociology* 44, no. 1 (July 1938): 1–24.

   For more on the intellectual history of Wright's involvement with the Chicago School of Sociology, see Robert Bone, "Richard Wright and the Chicago Renaissance," *Callaloo* 9, no. 3 (summer 1986): 446–68; and Carla Cappetti, *Writing Chicago: Modernism, Ethnography, and the Novel* (New York: Columbia University Press, 1993).

16. Melville J. Herskovits, *The Myth of the Negro Past* (1941; rpt., Boston: Beacon Press, 1958). For a provocative critique of Herskovits's approach, see Walter Benn Michaels, "Race into Culture: A Critical Genealogy of Cultural Identity," *Critical Inquiry* 18, no. 4 (summer 1992): 655–85.

17. Wolfgang Binder, "Uses of Memory: The Middle Passage in African American Literature," in *Slavery in the Americas,* ed. Binder (Würzburg: Königshausen and Neumann, 1993), 539–64. For a treatment of the theme that includes the Caribbean context, see Wilson Harris, "Oedipus and the Middle Passage," in *Crisis and Creativity in the New Literatures in English,* ed. Geoffrey V. Davis and Hena Maes-Jelinek (Amsterdam and Atlanta: Rodopi, 1990), 9–21.

18. Kenneth W. Warren, "Appeals for (Mis)recognition: Theorizing the Diaspora," in *Cultures of United States Imperialism,* ed. Amy Kaplan and Donald Pease (Durham: Duke University Press, 1993), 393, 405. For a compatible analysis of "African-American culture as a complex multiple synthesis of pre-migration and post-migration factors" (23), see Ingrid T. Monson, "Forced Migration, Asymmetrical Power Relations and African-American Music: Reformulation of Cultural Meaning and Musical Form," *World of Music* 32, no. 3 (1990): 22–45.

19. Charles Johnson has argued against portraying the plantation of the South as a form of feudalism. See my discussion of Johnson in chapter 5; and Charles S. Johnson, *Shadow of the Plantation* (1934; rpt., Chicago: University of Chicago Press, 1979).

20. See chapter 3. Robin Kelley discusses *12 Million Black Voices* as displaying the "hidden transcript" of black working-class resistance in the Jim Crow South in an article whose title is derived from Wright's work. See Kelley, "'We Are Not What We Seem': Rethinking Black Working-Class Opposition in the Jim Crow South," *Journal of American History* 80, no. 1 (June 1993): 76.

21. William Stott has complained that "Wright's use of the first person plural conflates the present with the past so that all American Negroes of all time are made to share his opinions"; see Stott, *Documentary Expression and Thirties America* (New York: Oxford University Press, 1973), 235.

22. John M. Reilly, "Richard Wright Preaches the Nation: *12 Million Black Voices*," *Black American Literature Forum* 16, no. 3 (fall 1982): 117. Reilly has also addressed this text in an earlier essay; see Reilly, "The Reconstruction of Genre as Entry into Conscious History," *Black American Literature Forum* 13, no. 1 (spring 1979): 3–6.

23. Reilly, "Richard Wright Preaches the Nation," 118, 117.

24. For a discussion of the ways in which Wright's narrative voice resembles voice-over narration in documentary film, see Jack B. Moore, "The Voice in *12 Million Black Voices*," *Mississippi Quarterly* 42, no. 4 (fall 1989): 415–24.

   Wright himself composed the book on a dictaphone over a three-day period. See Kenneth Kinnamon and Michel Fabre, eds., *Conversations with Richard Wright* (Jackson: University Press of Mississippi, 1993), 47.

25. This context is discussed in John Rogers Puckett, *Five Photo-Textual Documentaries from the Great Depression* (Ann Arbor: UMI Research, 1984), chap. 5.

26. Maren Stange, *Symbols of Ideal Life: Social Documentary Photography in America, 1890–1950* (Cambridge: Cambridge University Press, 1989), xv. An early example of the genre, Jacob Riis's *How the Other Half Lives* (1890), encouraged a middle-class audience to view police mug shots, charity records, and Riis's own photographs of urban poverty as entertainment: "Simultaneously titilating his audience with photographic versions of conventional urban subjects and exhorting them to take up tenement reform as a basis for class solidarity, Riis affirmed middle-class privilege, associating the images he showed with both entertainment and ideology." See Stange, *Symbols of Ideal Life*, xv.

   Riis framed his photographs in public lectures as well as a book. For the book, see Jacob A. Riis, *How the Other Half Lives: Studies among the Tenements of New York* (1890; rpt., Cambridge: Belknap Press of Harvard University Press, 1970).

27. On the tension between aestheticism and social utility in early-twentieth-century photography, see Alan Trachtenberg, *Reading American Photographs: Images as History: Mathew Brady to Walker Evans* (New York: Hill and Wang, 1989), esp. chap. 4, "Camera Work / Social Work." On the institutional framing of photography as an art, see Christopher Phillips, "The Judgment Seat of Photography," *October*, no. 22 (fall 1982): 27–63.

28. Erskine Caldwell and Margaret Bourke-White, *You Have Seen Their Faces* (New York: Modern Age Books, [1937]). Other important works of this genre contemporaneous with Wright's include James Agee and Walker Evans, *Let Us Now Praise Famous Men* (1941; rpt., Boston: Houghton Mifflin, 1988), although Agee's narrative in many ways resists the documentary aesthetic; and Herman Clarence Nixon, *Forty Acres and Steel Mules* (Chapel Hill: University of North Carolina Press, 1938).

29. Stange, *Symbols of Ideal Life*, 129–30.

30. See in particular Lawrence W. Levine, "The Historian and the Icon: Photography and the History of the American People in the 1930s and 1940s"; and Alan Trachtenberg, "From Image to Story: Reading the File," in *Documenting America, 1935–1943*, ed. Carl Fleischhauer and Beverly W. Brannan (Berkeley, Los Angeles, and London: University of California Press, 1988), 15–42, 43–73.

31. For Wright's account of the selection process, see "Readers and Writers" (radio interview with Edwin Seaver, December 23, 1941), in Kinnamon and Fabre, *Conversations with Richard Wright*, 43–44.

32. Such charges were never brought, although Wright continued to be watched because of his ties to the Communist Party. For a discussion of this episode in Wright's life, see Addison Gayle, *Richard Wright: Ordeal of a Native Son* (Garden City, N.Y.: Anchor Press / Doubleday, 1980), 146–48, 152–53.

33. See the essays in Joe William Trotter Jr., ed., *The Great Migration in Historical Perspective: New Dimensions of Race, Class, and Gender* (Bloomington and Indianapolis: Indiana University Press, 1991); and James R. Grossman, *Land of Hope: Chicago, Black Southerners, and the Great Migration* (Chicago and London: University of Chicago Press, 1989).

34. For a discussion of Wright's political-economic vocabulary in relation to those of Du Bois, Marx, and Lenin, see Jack B. Moore, "The View from the Broom Closet of the Regency Hyatt: Richard Wright as a Southern Writer," in *Literature at the Barricades,* ed. Ralph F. Bogardus and Fred Hobson (University: University of Alabama Press, 1982), 140–41.

35. Richard Wright, introduction to *Black Metropolis: A Study of Negro Life in a Northern City,* by St. Clair Drake and Horace R. Cayton (New York: Harcourt, Brace, 1945), xxix.

Chapter 7

1. Dipesh Chakrabarty, "Postcoloniality and the Artifice of History: Who Speaks for 'Indian' Pasts?" *Representations,* no. 37 (winter 1992): 4.

2. Jean and John Comaroff, introduction to *Modernity and Its Malcontents: Ritual and Power in Postcolonial Africa,* ed. by Jean Comaroff and John Comaroff (Chicago and London: University of Chicago Press, 1993), xi.

3. Jean Toomer, *Cane,* ed. Darwin T. Turner (1923; rpt., New York: Norton, 1988), 14.

4. See bell hooks, "Essentialism and Experience," *American Literary History* 3, no. 1 (spring 1991): 171–83.

5. See Kenneth W. Warren, *Black and White Strangers: Race and American Literary Realism* (Chicago and London: University of Chicago Press, 1993), 131–43.

Select Bibliography

Abel, Elizabeth. "Black Writing, White Reading: Race and the Politics of Feminist Inter-
   pretation." *Critical Inquiry* 19, no. 3 (spring 1993): 470–98.
Agee, James, and Walker Evans. *Let Us Now Praise Famous Men.* 1941. Reprint. Boston:
   Houghton Mifflin, 1988.
Anderson, Benedict. *Imagined Communities: Reflections on the Origin and Spread of National-
   ism.* 1983. Reprint. London and New York: Verso, 1987.
Anderson, James D. *The Education of Blacks in the South, 1860–1935.* Chapel Hill and Lon-
   don: University of North Carolina Press, 1988.
Anderson, Perry. "Modernity and Revolution." In *Marxism and the Interpretation of Cul-
   ture,* edited by Cary Nelson and Lawrence Grossberg. Urbana and Chicago: Uni-
   versity of Illinois Press, 1988.
Andrews, Adrianne R. "Of *Mules and Men* and Men and Women: The Ritual of Talking
   B[l]ack." In *Language, Rhythm, and Sound: Black Popular Cultures into the Twenty-First
   Century,* edited by Joseph K. Adjaye and Adrianne R. Andrews. Pittsburgh: Uni-
   versity of Pittsburgh Press, 1997.
Baker, Houston, Jr. *Modernism and the Harlem Renaissance.* Chicago: University of Chicago
   Press, 1987.
Baker, Howard. "Some Notes on New Fiction." *Southern Review* 1 (1935): 178–91.
Bakhtin, M. M. *Speech Genres and Other Late Essays.* Edited by Caryl Emerson and Michael
   Holquist. Translated by Vern W. McGee. Austin: University of Texas Press, 1986.
Bell, Bernard W. *The Afro-American Novel and Its Tradition.* Amherst: University of Massa-
   chusetts Press, 1987.
———. "Portrait of the Artist as High Priest of Soul: Jean Toomer's *Cane.*" *Black World* 23,
   no. 11 (September 1974): 4–19, 92–97.
Benítez-Rojo, Antonio. *The Repeating Island: The Caribbean and the Postmodern Perspective.*
   Translated by James E. Maraniss. Durham and London: Duke University Press,
   1992.
Benston, Kimberly W. "Sterling Brown's After-Song: 'When de Saints Go Ma'ching
   Home' and the Performance of Afro-American Voice." *Callaloo* 5, nos. 1–2 (1982):
   33–42.

Berman, Marshall. *All That Is Solid Melts into Air*. New York: Simon and Schuster, 1983.

Binder, Wolfgang. "Uses of Memory: The Middle Passage in African American Litera-ture." In *Slavery in the Americas*, edited by Wolfgang Binder. Würzburg: Königs-hausen and Neumann, 1993.

Bone, Robert. *Down Home: Origins of the Afro-American Short Story*. 1975. Reprint. New York: Columbia University Press, 1988.

———. *The Negro Novel in America*. Rev. ed. New Haven: Yale University Press, 1965.

———. "Richard Wright and the Chicago Renaissance." *Callaloo* 9, no. 3 (summer 1986): 446–68.

Bottomley, Gillian. *From Another Place: Migration and the Politics of Culture*. Cambridge: Cambridge University Press, 1992.

Boxwell, D. A. "'Sis Cat' as Ethnographer: Self-Presentation and Self-Inscription in Zora Neale Hurston's *Mules and Men*." *African American Review* 26, no. 4 (winter 1992): 605–17.

Breitinger, Eckhard. "In Search of an Audience, In Search of the Self: Exile as a Condition for the Works of Claude McKay." In *The Commonwealth Writer Overseas: Themes of Exile and Expatriation*, edited by Alastair Niven. Brussells: Librairie Marcel Didier, 1976.

Bremer, Thomas, and Ulrich Fleischmann, eds. *Alternative Cultures in the Caribbean: First International Conference of the Society of Caribbean Research, Berlin, 1988*. Frankfurt am Main: Vervuert Verlag, 1993.

Bronz, Stephen H. *Roots of Negro Racial Consciousness*. New York: Libra, 1964.

Brown, Sterling A. *Southern Road*. New York: Harcourt, Brace, 1932.

Buell, Lawrence. "American Pastoral Ideology Reappraised." *American Literary History* 1, no. 1 (spring 1989): 1–29.

Buhle, Paul. *Marxism in the United States: Remapping the History of the American Left*. Lon-don: Verso, 1987.

Caldwell, Erskine, and Margaret Bourke-White. *You Have Seen Their Faces*. New York: Modern Age, [1937].

Campbell, Elaine. "Two West Indian Heroines: Bita Plant and Fola Piggott." *Caribbean Quarterly* 29, no. 2 (June 1983): 22–29.

Cappetti, Carla. *Writing Chicago: Modernism, Ethnography, and the Novel*. New York: Columbia University Press, 1993.

Carby, Hazel V. "Ideologies of Black Folk: The Historical Novel of Slavery." In *Slavery and the Literary Imagination*, edited by Deborah E. McDowell and Arnold Ramper-sad. Baltimore and London: Johns Hopkins University Press, 1989.

———. "The Politics of Fiction, Anthropology, and the Folk: Zora Neale Hurston." In *New Essays on* Their Eyes Were Watching God, edited by Michael Awkward. Cam-bridge: Cambridge University Press, 1990.

———. *Reconstructing Womanhood: The Emergence of the Afro-American Woman Novelist*. New York and Oxford: Oxford University Press, 1987.

Carew, Jan. *Fulcrums of Change*. Trenton, N.J.: Africa World, 1988.

Chakrabarty, Dipesh. "Postcoloniality and the Artifice of History: Who Speaks for 'Indian' Pasts?" *Representations*, no. 37 (winter 1992): 1–26.

Chauhan, P. S. "Rereading Claude McKay." *College Language Association Journal* 34 (Sep-tember 1990): 68–80.

Childs, John Brown. "Afro-American Intellectuals and the People's Culture." *Theory and Society* 13 (1984): 69–90.

Chinitz, David. "Literacy and Authenticity: The Blues Poems of Langston Hughes." *Callaloo* 19, no. 1 (1996): 177–92.

Clark-Lewis, Elizabeth. *Living In, Living Out: African American Domestics in Washington, D.C., 1910–1940.* Washington, D.C., and London: Smithsonian Institution Press, 1994.

Clifford, James, and George E. Marcus, eds. *Writing Culture: The Poetics and Politics of Ethnography.* Berkeley: University of California Press, 1986.

Comaroff, Jean, and John Comaroff, eds. *Modernity and Its Malcontents: Ritual and Power in Postcolonial Africa.* Chicago and London: University of Chicago Press, 1993.

Cooper, Carolyn. *Noises in the Blood: Orality, Gender, and the "Vulgar" Body of Jamaican Popular Culture.* 1993. Reprint. Durham: Duke University Press, 1995.

Cooper, Wayne F. *Claude McKay: Rebel Sojourner in the Harlem Renaissance.* 1987. Reprint. New York: Schocken, 1990.

Cudjoe, Selwyn R. *Resistance and Caribbean Literature.* Chicago, Athens, Ohio, and London: Ohio University Press, 1980.

Davies, Carole Boyce, and Elaine Savory Fido, eds. *Out of the Kumbla: Caribbean Women and Literature.* Trenton, N.J.: Africa World, 1990.

de Certeau, Michel. *The Practice of Everyday Life.* Translated by Steven F. Rendall. Berkeley: University of California Press, 1984.

de Man, Paul. *Blindness and Insight: Essays in the Rhetoric of Contemporary Criticism,* 2d rev. ed. Minneapolis: University of Minnesota Press, 1983.

Dolby-Stahl, Sandra. "Literary Objectives: Hurston's Use of Personal Narrative in *Mules and Men.*" *Western Folklore* 51 (January 1992): 51–63.

Dorst, John. "Reading *Mules and Men:* Toward the Death of the Ethnographer." *Cultural Anthropology* 2 (1987): 305–18.

Doyle, Laura. *Bordering on the Body: The Racial Matrix of Modern Fiction and Culture.* New York and Oxford: Oxford University Press, 1994.

Du Bois, W. E. B. "The Conservation of Races." In *A W. E. B. Du Bois Reader,* edited by Andrew Paschal. New York: Macmillan, 1971.

———. *The Souls of Black Folk.* 1903. Reprint. New York and Scarsborough, Ontario: New American Library, 1969.

Dutcher, Dean. *The Negro in Modern Industrial Society: An Analysis of Changes in the Occupations of Negro Workers, 1910–1920.* Lancaster, Pa.: Dean Dutcher, 1930.

Fabre, Michel. *The Unfinished Quest of Richard Wright.* Translated by Isabel Barzun, 2d ed. Urbana and Chicago: University of Illinois Press, 1993.

Faulkner, Howard. "The Buried Life: Jean Toomer's *Cane.*" *Studies in Black Literature* 7, no. 1 (winter 1976): 1–5.

Fauset, Arthur Huff. "American Negro Folk Literature." In *The New Negro,* edited by Alain Locke. 1925. Reprint. New York: Atheneum, 1968.

Felski, Rita. *The Gender of Modernity.* Cambridge and London: Harvard University Press, 1995.

Fisher, Rudolph. "The City of Refuge." In *The New Negro,* edited by Alain Locke. 1925. Reprint. New York: Atheneum, 1968.

Foley, Barbara. "'In the Land of Cotton': Economics and Violence in Jean Toomer's *Cane*." *African American Review* 32, no. 2 (1998): 181–98.

———. "Jean Toomer's Sparta." *American Literature* 67, no. 4 (December 1995): 747–76.

———. "Jean Toomer's Washington and the Politics of Class: From 'Blue Veins' to Seventh-Street Rebels." *Modern Fiction Studies* 42, no. 2 (summer 1996): 289–321.

———. *Radical Representations: Politics and Form in U. S. Proletarian Fiction, 1929–1941.* Durham and London: Duke University Press, 1993.

Foner, Philip S. *American Socialism and Black Americans: From the Age of Jackson to World War II.* Westport, Conn., and London: Greenwood Press, 1977.

Ford, Karen Jackson. "Making Poetry Pay: The Commodification of Langston Hughes." In *Marketing Modernisms: Self-Promotion, Canonization, Rereading,* edited by Kevin J. H. Dettmar and Stephen Watt. Ann Arbor: University of Michigan Press, 1996.

Frazier, E. Franklin. *The Negro Family in the United States.* 1939. Rev. and abridged ed. New York: Dryden Press, 1951.

Fuss, Diana. *Essentially Speaking: Feminism, Nature, and Difference.* New York: Routledge, 1989.

Gabbin, Joanne V. *Sterling Brown: Building the Black Aesthetic Traditon.* 1985. Reprint. Charlottesville and London: University Press of Virginia, 1994.

Gates, Henry Louis, Jr. "Canon-Formation, Literary History, and the Afro-American Tradition: From the Seen to the Told." In *Afro-American Literary Study in the 1990s,* edited by Houston Baker Jr. and Patricia Redmond. Chicago: University of Chicago Press, 1989.

———. "The Face and Voice of Blackness." In *Modernism, Gender, and Culture: A Cultural Studies Approach,* edited by Lisa Rado. New York and London: Garland, 1997.

Gayle, Addison. *Richard Wright: Ordeal of a Native Son.* Garden City, N.Y.: Anchor Press / Doubleday, 1980.

Genovese, Eugene D. *Roll, Jordan, Roll: The World the Slaves Made.* 1972. Reprint. New York: Vintage Books, 1976.

Gikandi, Simon. *Writing in Limbo: Modernism and Caribbean Literature.* Ithaca and London: Cornell University Press, 1992.

Giles, James R. *Claude McKay.* Boston: Twayne, 1976.

Gilkes, Michael. *The West Indian Novel.* Boston: Twayne, 1981.

Gilroy, Paul. *The Black Atlantic: Modernity and Double Consciousness.* Cambridge: Harvard University Press, 1993.

Glissant, Edouard. *Caribbean Discourse: Selected Essays.* Translated and with an introduction by J. Michael Dash. Charlottesville: University Press of Virginia, 1989.

Golding, Alan. "Jean Toomer's *Cane*: The Search for Identity through Form." *Arizona Quarterly* 39, no. 3 (autumn 1983): 197–214.

Gordon, Deborah. "The Politics of Ethnographic Authority: Race and Writing in the Ethnography of Margaret Mead and Zora Neale Hurston." In *Modernist Anthropology: From Fieldwork to Text,* edited by Marc Manganaro. Princeton: Princeton University Press, 1990.

Grandel, Hartmut. "The Role of Music in the Self-Reflexive Poetry of the Harlem Renaissance." In *Poetics in the Poem: Critical Essays on American Self-Reflexive Poetry,* edited by Dorothy Z. Baker. New York: Peter Lang, 1997.

Griffin, Farah Jasmine. *"Who Set You Flowin'?": The African-American Migration Narrative.* New York and Oxford: Oxford University Press, 1995.

Grossman, James R. *Land of Hope: Chicago, Black Southerners, and the Great Migration.* Chicago and London: University of Chicago Press, 1989.

Guha, Ranajit, and Gayatri Chakravorty Spivak, eds. *Selected Subaltern Studies.* New York and Oxford: Oxford University Press, 1988.

Hakutani, Yoshinobu. *Richard Wright and Racial Discourse.* Columbia and London: University of Missouri Press, 1996.

Hale, Anthony R. "Framing the Folk: Zora Neale Hurston, John Millington Synge, and the Politics of Aesthetic Ethnography." *Comparatist* 20 (1996): 50–61.

Harris, Wilson. "Oedipus and the Middle Passage." In *Crisis and Creativity in the New Literatures in English,* edited by Geoffrey V. Davis and Hena Maes-Jelinek. Amsterdam and Atlanta: Rodopi, 1990.

Harrison, Beth. "Zora Neale Hurston and Mary Austin: A Case Study in Ethnography, Literary Modernism, and Contemporary Ethnic Fiction." *MELUS* 21, no. 2 (summer 1996): 89–106.

Hemenway, Robert E. *Zora Neale Hurston: A Literary Biography.* Urbana and Chicago: University of Illinois Press, 1977.

Henderson, George Wylie. "Baby Lou and the Angel Bud." Typescript, n.d. Collection of Roslyn Kirkland Allen.

———. *Jule.* 1946. Reprint. Tuscaloosa and London: University of Alabama Press, 1989.

———. *Ollie Miss.* 1935. Reprint. Tuscaloosa and London: University of Alabama Press, 1988.

———. "'Thy Name Is Woman.'" *New York Daily News,* 15 July 1932, 29.

Henderson, Stephen E. "The Heavy Blues of Sterling Brown: A Study of Craft and Tradition." *Black American Literature Forum* 14, no. 1 (spring 1980): 32–44.

Henri, Florette. *Black Migration: Movement North, 1900–1920.* Garden City, N.Y.: Anchor Press / Doubleday, 1975.

Hernández, Graciela. "Multiple Subjectivities and Strategic Positionality: Zora Neale Hurston's Experimental Ethnographies." In *Women Writing Culture,* edited by Ruth Behar and Deborah A. Gordon. Berkeley, Los Angeles, and London: University of California Press, 1995.

Herskovits, Melville J. *The Myth of the Negro Past.* 1941. Reprint. Boston: Beacon, 1958.

Hill, Lynda Marion. *Social Rituals and the Verbal Art of Zora Neale Hurston.* Washington, D.C.: Howard University Press, 1996.

Hine, Darlene Clark. "Black Migration to the Urban Midwest: The Gender Dimension, 1915–1945." In *The Great Migration in Historical Perspective: New Dimensions of Race, Class, and Gender,* edited by Joe William Trotter Jr. Bloomington and Indianapolis: Indiana University Press, 1991.

Holt, Thomas C. *The Problem of Freedom: Race, Labor, and Politics in Jamaica and Britain, 1832–1938.* Baltimore and London: Johns Hopkins University Press, 1992.

hooks, bell. "Essentialism and Experience." *American Literary History* 3, no. 1 (spring 1991): 171–83.

———. *Yearning: Race, Gender, and Cultural Politics.* Boston: South End, 1990.

Huggins, Nathan. *Harlem Renaissance.* New York: Oxford University Press, 1971.

Hughes, Langston. *The Big Sea.* 1940. Reprint. New York: Hill and Wang, 1993.

——. *The Collected Poems of Langston Hughes*, edited by Arnold Rampersad. New York: Knopf, 1994.

——. *Fields of Wonder*. New York: Knopf, 1947.

——. "The Negro Artist and the Racial Mountain." 1926. Reprint. *Langston Hughes Review* 4, no. 1 (1985): 1–4.

——. *Selected Poems of Langston Hughes*. 1959. Reprint. New York: Vintage, 1974.

Hurston, Zora Neale. "How It Feels to Be Colored Me." *World Tomorrow* 11 (May 1928): 215–16.

——. *Mules and Men*. 1935. Reprint. New York: Harper Perennial, 1990.

Hurston, Zora Neale, and Dorothy Waring. *Polk County: A Comedy of Negro Life on a Sawmill, with Authentic Negro Music, in Three Acts*. Typescript, New York Public Library, 1944.

Hutchinson, George B. "Jean Toomer and the 'New Negroes' of Washington." *American Literature* 63, no. 4 (December 1991): 683–92.

Industrial Workers of the World. *The Lumber Industry and Its Workers*. 3d ed. Chicago: Industrial Workers of the World, [1922?].

Jameson, Fredric. *The Political Unconscious: Narrative as a Socially Symbolic Act*. Ithaca: Cornell University Press, 1981.

Jehlen, Myra. "History beside the Fact: What We Learn from *A True and Exact History of Barbadoes*." In *The Politics of Research*, edited by E. Ann Kaplan and George Levine. New Brunswick, N.J.: Rutgers University Press, 1997.

Johnson, Barbara E. "Response." In *Afro-American Literary Study in the 1990s*, edited by Houston Baker Jr. and Patricia Redmond. Chicago: University of Chicago Press, 1989.

——. "Thresholds of Difference: Structures of Address in Zora Neale Hurston." In *"Race," Writing, and Difference*, edited by Henry Louis Gates Jr. Chicago and London: University of Chicago Press, 1986.

Johnson, Charles S. *Shadow of the Plantation*. 1934. Reprint. Chicago: University of Chicago Press, 1979.

Johnson, Daniel M., and Rex R. Campbell. *Black Migration in America: A Social Demographic History*. Durham: Duke University Press, 1981.

Johnson, Lonnell E. "The Defiant Black Heroine: Ollie Miss and Janie Mae—Two Portraits from the 30's." *Zora Neale Hurston Forum* 4, no. 2 (spring 1990): 41–46.

Jones, Robert. *Jean Toomer and the Prison-House of Thought*. Amherst: University of Massachusetts Press, 1993.

——. "Jean Toomer as Poet: A Phenomenology of the Spirit." *Black American Literature Forum* 21, no. 3 (fall 1987): 253–73.

Jordan, Rosan Augusta. "Not into Cold Space: Zora Neale Hurston and J. Frank Dobie as Holistic Folklorists." *Southern Folklore* 49 (1992): 109–31.

Juneja, Renu. *Caribbean Transactions: West Indian Culture in Literature*. London and Basingstoke: Macmillan Caribbean, 1996.

Kane, Patricia, and Doris Y. Wilkinson. "Survival Strategies: Black Women in *Ollie Miss* and *Cotton Comes to Harlem*." *Critique: Studies in Modern Fiction* 16, no. 1 (1974): 101–9.

Kelley, Robin D. G. *Hammer and Hoe: Alabama Communists during the Great Depression*. Chapel Hill and London: University of North Carolina Press, 1990.

———. "Notes on Deconstructing 'The Folk.'" *American Historical Review* 97, no. 5 (December 1992): 1400–1408.

———. *Race Rebels: Culture, Politics, and the Black Working Class.* 1994. Reprint. New York: Free, 1996.

———. "'We Are Not What We Seem': Rethinking Black Working-Class Opposition in the Jim Crow South." *Journal of American History* 80, no. 1 (June 1993): 75–112.

Kennedy, Louise Venable. *The Negro Peasant Turns Cityward.* 1930. Reprint. New York: AMS, 1968.

Kent, George E. "Claude McKay's *Banana Bottom* Reappraised." *College Language Association Journal* 18 (December 1974): 222–34.

———. "The Soulful Way of Claude McKay." *Black World* 20 (November 1970): 37–51.

Kerblat-Houghton, Jeanne. "Mythes ruraux et urbains dans *Cane* de Jean Toomer (1894–1967)." In *Mythes ruraux et urbains dans la culture Américaine,* edited by Groupe de Recherche et d'Études Nord-Américaines. Provence: Université de Provence Service des Publications, 1990.

Kerman, Cynthia Earl, and Richard Eldridge. *The Lives of Jean Toomer: A Hunger for Wholeness.* Baton Rouge and London: Louisiana State University Press, 1987.

Kinnamon, Kenneth, and Michel Fabre, eds. *Conversations with Richard Wright.* Jackson: University Press of Mississippi, 1993.

Kirby, Jack Temple. *Rural Worlds Lost: The American South, 1920–1960.* Baton Rouge: Louisiana State University Press, 1987.

Klotman, Phyllis Rauch. *Another Man Gone: The Black Runner in Contemporary Afro-American Literature.* Port Washington, N.Y., and London: Kennikat, 1977.

Knight, Franklin. "Discussion." In *Process of Unity in Caribbean Society: Ideologies and Literature,* edited by Ileana Rodríguez and Marc Zimmerman. Minneapolis: Institute for the Study of Ideologies and Literatures, 1983.

Kruger, Loren. *The National Stage: Theatre and Cultural Legitimation in England, France, and America.* Chicago and London: University of Chicago Press, 1992.

———. "Placing 'New Africans' in the 'Old' South Africa: Drama, Modernity, and Racial Identities in Johannesburg, circa 1935." *Modernism/Modernity* 1, no. 2 (April 1994): 113–31.

Kutzinski, Vera M. "The Distant Closeness of Dancing Doubles: Sterling Brown and William Carlos Williams." *Black American Literature Forum* 16, no. 1 (spring 1982): 32–44.

———. "Unseasonal Flowers: Nature and History in Plácido and Jean Toomer." *Yale Journal of Criticism* 3, no. 2 (1990): 153–79.

Lamming, George. "The Peasant Roots of the West Indian Novel." In *Critics on Caribbean Literature,* edited by Edward Baugh. New York: St. Martin's, 1978.

———. *The Pleasures of Exile.* London: Michael Joseph, 1960.

Lawrence, Leota S. "Three West Indian Heroines: An Analysis." *College Language Association Journal* 21 (1977): 238–50.

Lemann, Nicholas. *The Promised Land: The Great Migration and How It Changed America.* New York: Alfred A. Knopf, 1991.

LeSeur, Geta. *Ten Is the Age of Darkness: The Black Bildungsroman.* Columbia and London: University of Missouri Press, 1995.

Levine, Lawrence W. *Black Culture and Black Consciousness: Afro-American Folk Thought from Slavery to Freedom.* New York: Oxford University Press, 1977.

———. "The Historian and the Icon: Photography and the History of the American People in the 1930s and 1940s." In *Documenting America, 1935–1943,* edited by Carl Fleischhauer and Beverly W. Brannan. Berkeley, Los Angeles, and London: University of California Press, 1988.

Lewis, Earl. "Afro-American Adaptive Strategies: The Visiting Habits of Kith and Kin among Black Norfolkians during the First Great Migration." *Journal of Family History* 12, no. 4 (1987): 407–20.

Lewis, Edward E. *The Mobility of the Negro: A Study in the American Labor Supply.* New York: Columbia University Press, 1931.

Locke, Alain, ed. *The New Negro.* 1925. Reprint. New York: Atheneum, 1968.

———. "Sterling Brown: The New Negro Folk-Poet." In *Negro: An Anthology,* edited by Nancy Cunard. Abridged ed. New York: Frederick Ungar, 1970.

Loftis, John E. "Domestic Prey: Richard Wright's Parody of the Hunt Tradition in 'The Man Who Was Almost a Man.'" *Studies in Short Fiction* 23, no. 4 (fall 1986): 437–42.

Lowe, John. "From Mule Bones to Funny Bones: The Plays of Zora Neale Hurston." *Southern Quarterly* 33, nos. 2–3 (winter–spring 1995): 65–78.

Lurie, Susan. *Unsettled Subjects: Restoring Feminist Politics to Poststructuralist Critique.* Durham and London: Duke University Press, 1997.

Marks, Carole. *Farewell—We're Good and Gone: The Great Black Migration.* Bloomington and Indianapolis: Indiana University Press, 1989.

Martin, Odette C. "*Cane:* Method and Myth." *Obsidian* 2, no. 1 (1976): 5–20.

Mayor, Archer H. *Southern Timberman: The Legacy of William Buchanan.* Athens: University of Georgia Press, 1988.

McGee, Leo, and Robert Boone, eds. *The Black Rural Landowner—Endangered Species: Social, Political, and Economic Implications.* Westport, Conn., and London: Greenwood Press, 1979.

McKay, Claude. *A Long Way from Home.* 1937. Reprint. New York: Arno Press and the New York Times, 1969.

———. *Banana Bottom.* 1933. Reprint. New York: Harcourt Brace Jovanovich, 1961.

———. *Gingertown.* 1932. Reprint. Salem, N.H.: Ayer, 1991.

McKay, Nellie Y. *Jean Toomer, Artist: A Study of His Literary Life and Work, 1894–1936.* Chapel Hill and London: University of North Carolina Press, 1984.

Meisenhelder, Susan. "Conflict and Resistance in Zora Neale Hurston's *Mules and Men.*" *Journal of American Folklore* 109 (summer 1996): 267–88.

Michaels, Walter Benn. *Our America: Modernism, Nativism, Pluralism.* Durham and London: Duke University Press, 1995.

———. "Race into Culture: A Critical Genealogy of Cultural Identity." *Critical Inquiry* 18, no. 4 (summer 1992): 655–85.

Mikell, Gwendolyn. "The Anthropological Imagination of Zora Neale Hurston." *Western Journal of Black Studies* 7, no. 1 (1983): 27–35.

Miller, James A. "African-American Writing of the 1930s: A Prologue." In *Radical Revisions: Rereading 1930s Culture,* edited by Bill Mullen and Sherry Lee Linkon. Urbana and Chicago: University of Illinois Press, 1996.

Mintz, Sidney W. "The Caribbean as a Socio-Cultural Area." *Cahiers d'Histoire Mondiale* 9, no. 4 (fall 1966): 912–37.

———. "The Folk-Urban Continuum and the Rural Proletarian Community." *American Journal of Sociology* 59, no. 2 (September 1953): 136–43.

———. "From Plantations to Peasantries in the Caribbean." In *Caribbean Contours*, edited by Sidney W. Mintz and Sally Price. Baltimore and London: Johns Hopkins University Press, 1985.

Monson, Ingrid T. "Forced Migration, Asymmetrical Power Relations and African-American Music: Reformulation of Cultural Meaning and Musical Form." *World of Music* 32, no. 3 (1990): 22–45.

Moore, Jack B. "The View from the Broom Closet of the Regency Hyatt: Richard Wright as a Southern Writer." In *Literature at the Barricades*, edited by Ralph F. Bogardus and Fred Hobson. University: University of Alabama Press, 1982.

———. "The Voice in *12 Million Black Voices*." *Mississippi Quarterly* 42, no. 4 (fall 1989): 415–24.

Neubrech, W. LeRoy. *American Southern Cypress*. Washington, D.C.: United States Government Printing Office, 1939.

Nicholls, David G. "George Wylie Henderson: A Primary and Secondary Bibliography." *Bulletin of Bibliography* 54, no. 4 (December 1997): 335–38.

Nixon, Herman Clarence. *Forty Acres and Steel Mules*. Chapel Hill: University of North Carolina Press, 1938.

North, Michael. *The Dialect of Modernism: Race, Language, and Twentieth-Century Literature*. New York and Oxford: Oxford University Press, 1994.

O'Daniel, Therman, ed. *Jean Toomer: A Critical Evaluation*. Washington, D.C.: Howard University Press, 1988.

Peters, Pearlie. "Women and Assertive Voice in Hurston's Fiction and Folklore." *Literary Griot* 4, nos. 1–2 (spring–fall 1992): 100–110.

Phillips, Christopher. "The Judgment Seat of Photography." *October*, no. 22 (fall 1982): 27–63.

Polk County, Florida, Publicity Department. *Polk County, Florida*. Bartow, Fla.: Polk County Publicity Department, [1928?].

Priebe, Richard. "The Search for Community in the Novels of Claude McKay." *Studies in Black Literature* 3, no. 2 (summer 1972): 22–30.

Propp, Vladimir. "The Nature of Folklore" (1946). In *Theory and History of Folklore*, edited by Anatoly Liberman, translated by Ariadna Y. Martin and Richard P. Martin. Minneapolis: University of Minnesota Press, 1984.

Puckett, John Rogers. *Five Photo-Textual Documentaries from the Great Depression*. Ann Arbor: UMI Research, 1984.

Quennell, Peter. Review of *Ollie Miss*, by George Wylie Henderson. *New Statesman and Nation* 9 (1 June 1935): 829.

Rahming, Melvin B. *The Evolution of the West Indian's Image in the Afro-American Novel*. Millwood, N.Y., New York, and London: Associated Faculty, 1986.

Ramchand, Kenneth. "Claude McKay and *Banana Bottom*." *Southern Review* (Australia) 4 (1970): 53–66.

———. *The West Indian Novel and Its Background*. 2d ed. London: Heinemann, 1983.

Rampersad, Arnold. *The Life of Langston Hughes*. Vol. 1, 1902–1941, *I, Too, Sing America*. New York and Oxford: Oxford University Press, 1986.

———, ed. *Richard Wright: Early Works*. New York: Library of America, 1991.

Raper, Arthur F. *Preface to Peasantry: A Tale of Two Black Belt Counties*. Chapel Hill: University of North Carolina Press, 1936.

Raper, Arthur F., and Ira De A. Reid. *Sharecroppers All*. Chapel Hill: University of North Carolina Press, 1941.

Reed-Morrisson, Laura. "'Money and Fun and Foolishness': Rethinking Work and Play in *Mules and Men* and *Their Eyes Were Watching God*." Typescript, University of Chicago, 1994.

Reilly, John M. "The Reconstruction of Genre as Entry into Conscious History." *Black American Literature Forum* 13, no. 1 (spring 1979): 3–6.

———. "Richard Wright Preaches the Nation: *12 Million Black Voices*." *Black American Literature Forum* 16, no. 3 (fall 1982): 116–19.

———. "The Search for Black Redemption: Jean Toomer's *Cane*." *Studies in the Novel* 2 (1970): 312–24.

Riis, Jacob A. *How the Other Half Lives: Studies among the Tenements of New York*. 1890. Reprint. Cambridge: Belknap Press of Harvard University Press, 1970.

Robertson, Edythe. "Young Bronx Printer Strides toward Fame." *New York Amsterdam News*, 31 August 1932, 2.

Rodgers, Lawrence R. *Canaan Bound: The Afro-American Great Migration Novel*. Urbana and Chicago: University of Illinois Press, 1997.

Rohlehr, Gordon. "The Folk in Caribbean Literature." In *Critics on Caribbean Literature*, edited by Edward Baugh. New York: St. Martin's, 1978.

Rowell, Charles. "Sterling A. Brown and the Afro-American Folk Tradition." In *The Harlem Renaissance Re-examined*, edited by Victor A. Kramer. New York: AMS, 1987.

Sánchez-Eppler, Benigno. "Telling Anthropology: Zora Neale Hurston and Gilberto Freyre Disciplined in Their Field-Home-Work." *American Literary History* 4, no. 3 (fall 1992): 464–88.

Scarry, Elaine. *The Body in Pain: The Making and Unmaking of the World*. New York and Oxford: Oxford University Press, 1985.

Scott, Emmet J. *Negro Migration during the War*. 1920. Reprint. New York: Arno, 1969.

Scott, James C. *Domination and the Arts of Resistance: Hidden Transcripts*. New Haven, Conn.: Yale University Press, 1990.

———. *Weapons of the Weak: Everyday Forms of Peasant Resistance*. New Haven and London: Yale University Press, 1985.

Scruggs, Charles. *Sweet Home: Invisible Cities in the Afro-American Novel*. Baltimore and London: Johns Hopkins University Press, 1993.

Sedgwick, Eve Kosofsky. *Between Men: English Literature and Male Homosocial Desire*. New York: Columbia University Press, 1985.

Shivers, Forrest. *The Land Between: A History of Hancock County, Georgia, to 1940*. Spartanburg, S.C.: Reprint Company, 1990.

Smith, Elizabeth Wiley. *The History of Hancock County, Georgia*. Vol. 1. Washington, Ga.: Wilkes, 1974.

Smith, Gary. "The Literary Ballads of Sterling A. Brown." *College Language Association Journal* 32, no. 4 (June 1989): 393–409.

Sollors, Werner. "Modernization as Adultery: Richard Wright, Zora Neale Hurston, and American Culture of the 1930s and 1940s." *Hebrew University Studies in Literature and the Arts* 18 (1990): 109–55.

Spero, Sterling D., and Abram L. Harris. *The Black Worker: The Negro and the Labor Movement.* 1931. Reprint. New York: Atheneum, 1968.

Spillers, Hortense J. "Mama's Baby, Papa's Maybe: An American Grammar Book." *Diacritics* 17, no. 2 (summer 1987): 65–81.

Spivak, Gayatri Chakravorty. "Can the Subaltern Speak?" In *Marxism and the Interpretation of Culture,* edited by Cary Nelson and Lawrence Grossberg. Urbana and Chicago: University of Illinois Press, 1988.

Spofford, William K. "The Unity of Part One of Jean Toomer's *Cane.*" *Markham Review* 3 (1972): 58–60.

Stange, Maren. *Symbols of Ideal Life: Social Documentary Photography in America, 1890–1950.* Cambridge: Cambridge University Press, 1989.

Stepto, Robert B. "Sterling A. Brown: Outsider in the Harlem Renaissance?" In *The Harlem Renaissance: Revaluations,* edited by Amritjit Singh, William S. Shiver, and Stanley Brodwin. New York and London: Garland, 1989.

Stoff, Michael B. "Claude McKay and the Cult of Primitivism." In *The Harlem Renaissance Remembered,* edited by Arna Bontemps. New York: Dodd, Mead, 1972.

Stott, William. *Documentary Expression and Thirties America.* New York: Oxford University Press, 1973.

Sundquist, Eric J. *To Wake the Nations: Race in the Making of American Literature.* Cambridge and London: Harvard University Press, 1993.

Taylor, Clyde. "The Second Coming of Jean Toomer." *Obsidian* 1 (winter 1975): 37–57.

Taylor, Patrick. *The Narrative of Liberation: Perspectives on Afro-Caribbean Literature, Popular Culture, and Politics.* Ithaca and London: Cornell University Press, 1989.

Thomas, H. Nigel. "Claude McKay's *Banana Bottom:* A Black Response to Late Nineteenth and Early Twentieth Century White Discourse on the Meaning of Black Reality." In *Nationalism vs. Internationalism: (Inter)National Dimensions of Literatures in English,* edited by Wolfgang Zach and Ken L. Goodwin. Tübingen: Stauffenburg Verlag, 1996.

Tillery, Tyrone. *Claude McKay: A Black Poet's Struggle for Identity.* Amherst: University of Massachusetts Press, 1992.

Todes, Charlotte. *Labor and Lumber.* New York: International, 1931.

Todorov, Tzvetan. "'Race,' Writing, and Culture." In *"Race," Writing, and Difference,* edited by Henry Louis Gates Jr. Chicago and London: University of Chicago Press, 1986.

Tolnay, Stewart E., and E. M. Beck. "Black Flight: Lethal Violence and the Great Migration, 1900–1930." *Social Science History* 14, no. 3 (fall 1990): 347–70.

Toomer, Jean. *Cane.* 1923. Reprint. Norton Critical Edition. Edited by Darwin T. Turner. New York: Norton, 1988.

———. *A Jean Toomer Reader: Selected Unpublished Writings.* Edited by Frederik L. Rusch. New York and Oxford: Oxford University Press, 1993.

———. *The Wayward and the Seeking: A Collection of Writings by Jean Toomer.* Edited by Darwin T. Turner. Washington, D.C.: Howard University Press, 1980.

Trachtenberg, Alan. "From Image to Story: Reading the File." In *Documenting America,*

1935–1943, edited by Carl Fleischhauer and Beverly W. Brannan. Berkeley, Los Angeles, and London: University of California Press, 1988.

———. *Reading American Photographs: Images as History: Mathew Brady to Walker Evans.* New York: Hill and Wang, 1989.

Tracy, Steven C. *Langston Hughes and the Blues.* Urbana and Chicago: University of Illinois Press, 1988.

———. "To the Tune of Those Weary Blues." In *Langston Hughes: Critical Perspectives Past and Present*, edited by Henry Louis Gates Jr. and K. A. Appiah. New York: Amistad, 1993.

Trotter, Joe William, Jr. "Introduction: Black Migration in Historical Perspective." In *The Great Migration in Historical Perspective: New Dimensions of Race, Class, and Gender*, edited by Joe William Trotter Jr. Bloomington and Indianapolis: Indiana University Press, 1991.

United States Government Printing Office. *Sixteenth Census of the United States: 1940: Population: Internal Migration 1935 to 1940: Color and Sex of Migrants.* Washington, D.C.: United States Government Printing Office, 1943.

Wagner-Martin, Linda. "Toomer's *Cane* as Narrative Sequence." In *Modern American Short Story Sequences: Composite Fictions and Fictive Communities*, edited by J. Gerald Kennedy. Cambridge, New York, and Melbourne: Cambridge University Press, 1995.

Wainwright, Mary Katherine. "Subversive Female Folk Tellers in *Mules and Men*." In *Zora in Florida*, edited by Steve Glassman and Kathryn Lee Seidel. Orlando: University of Central Florida Press, 1991.

Wald, Priscilla. "Becoming 'Colored': The Self-Authorized Language of Difference in Zora Neale Hurston." *American Literary History* 2, no. 1 (spring 1990): 79–100.

Wall, Cheryl A. "*Mules and Men* and Women: Zora Neale Hurston's Strategies of Narration and Visions of Female Empowerment." *Black American Literature Forum* 23, no. 4 (winter 1989): 661–80.

———. *Women of the Harlem Renaissance.* Bloomington and Indianapolis: Indiana University Press, 1995.

Wallace, Michele. *Invisibility Blues: From Pop to Theory.* London and New York: Verso, 1990.

Warren, Kenneth W. "Appeals for (Mis)recognition: Theorizing the Diaspora." In *Cultures of United States Imperialism*, edited by Amy Kaplan and Donald Pease. Durham: Duke University Press, 1993.

———. *Black and White Strangers: Race and American Literary Realism.* Chicago and London: University of Chicago Press, 1993.

———. "Delimiting America: The Legacy of Du Bois." *American Literary History* 1, no. 1 (spring 1989): 172–89.

Washington, Booker T., ed. *Tuskegee and Its People: Their Ideals and Achievements.* 1905. Reprint. Freeport, N.Y.: Books for Libraries, 1971.

———. *Up from Slavery.* 1901. Reprint in *Three Negro Classics*, edited by John Hope Franklin. New York: Avon, 1965.

Watkins, Patricia. "Is There a Unifying Theme in *Cane*?" *College Language Association Journal* 15 (1971–72): 303–5.

Watkins-Owens, Irma. *Blood Relations: Caribbean Immigrants and the Harlem Community, 1900–1930.* Bloomington and Indianapolis: Indiana University Press, 1996.

Webb, Barbara J. *Myth and History in Caribbean Fiction: Alejo Carpentier, Wilson Harris, and Edouard Glissant.* Amherst: University of Massachusetts Press, 1992.

White, Hayden. *The Content of the Form: Narrative Discourse and Historical Representation.* Baltimore and London: Johns Hopkins University Press, 1987.

Williams, Brett. "The South in the City." *Journal of Popular Culture* 16, no. 3 (winter 1982): 30–41.

Willis, Miriam DeCosta. "Folklore and the Creative Artist: Lydia Cabrera and Zora Neale Hurston." *College Literature Association Journal* 27, no. 1 (September 1983): 81–90.

Willis, Susan. *Specifying: Black Women Writing the American Experience.* Madison and London: University of Wisconsin Press, 1987.

Wirth, Louis. "Urbanism as a Way of Life." *American Journal of Sociology* 44, no. 1 (July 1983): 1–24.

Wright, Richard. "Blueprint for Negro Writing." In *Richard Wright Reader,* edited by Ellen Wright and Michel Fabre. New York: Harper and Row, 1978.

———. Introduction to *Black Metropolis: A Study of Negro Life in a Northern City,* by St. Clair Drake and Horace R. Cayton. New York: Harcourt Brace, 1945.

———. "I Tried to Be a Communist." Pts. 1–8. *Atlantic Monthly* (August 1944): 61–70.

———. "I Tried to Be a Communist." Pts. 9–13. *Atlantic Monthly* (September 1944): 48–56.

———. *12 Million Black Voices.* Photo direction by Edwin Rosskam. New York: Viking, 1941.

———. "12 Million Black Voices." *Coronet* 11 (April 1942): 77–92.

———. *Uncle Tom's Children.* 1938. Reprint in *Richard Wright: Early Works,* edited by Arnold Rampersad. New York: Library of America, 1991.

Zinn, Howard. *A People's History of the United States.* New York: Harper and Row, 1980.

Index

Abel, Elizabeth, 144n. 10
Adjaye, Joseph K., 144n. 8
Africa, 75–77, 117–19. *See also* Middle Passage
Afro-American Novel and Its Tradition, The (Bell), 4, 146n. 4
Agee, James, 155n. 28
"Agricultural Show, The" (McKay), 67
agriculture
   in Alabama, 1930s, 93–95
   in Jamaica, post-emancipation, 66–68
   mechanization of labor, 3, 86, 100, 120–24
   subsistence farming and modernity, 10–11, 16, 22–23, 33, 40, 82, 113, 132–33
   truck farming, 47–48
   See also boll weevil; migrant labor; plantation system; sharecropping
Alabama, 85–111
   agriculture, 1930s, 93–95
   Hannon, 103, 109
   Macon County, 93
   Tuskegee, 99 (*see also* Tuskegee Institute)
   Warrior Stand, 86
Anderson, Benedict, 3
Anderson, James D., 99
Andrews, Adrianne R., 144n. 8

Anthropology. *See* ethnography
atavism, 69, 73–76
autobiography, 44–46

Baby Lou and the Angel Bud (Henderson), 110
Baker, Houston, Jr., 5–6
Bakhtin, M. M., 87
Balcolm, Lowell Leroy, 88–90
   "Ollie," 88, 89 fig. 5
   "Ollie and Slaughter Returned to Their Plows and Continued until Noon," 88, 90 fig. 6
ballad, 69–70, 80
   "John Henry" (anonymous), 51–52, 61
   See also folk songs
Banana Bottom (McKay), 2, 63–83, 85, 113, 142n. 28
Beck, E. M., 152n. 43
"Becky" (Toomer), 33
"Beehive" (Toomer), 34–35, 37
Bell, Bernard W., 4, 24–25, 140n. 10, 141n. 12, 146n. 4
Benítez-Rojo, Antonio, 81, 149n. 30
Benston, Kimberly W., 13–14
Berman, Marshall, 137n. 37
Big Sea, The (Hughes), 1
Bildungsroman, 86–88, 100–103, 110
   of artist (*Kunstlerroman*), 24, 140n.12

Binder, Wolfgang, 118
Black Atlantic, The (Gilroy), 10, 137n. 37
Black Metropolis (Drake and Cayton),
    129
"Blood-Burning Moon" (Toomer), 33
"Blueprint for Negro Writing" (Wright),
    115
blues, 92, 153n. 44
    as commercial art, 61–62
    at the juke joint, 59
    and poetry, 13–15, 138n. 56
Boas, Franz, 145n. 18
Body in Pain, The (Scarry), 117
boll weevil, 28–30, 33. *See also* agriculture
"Bona and Paul" (Toomer), 36–37
Bone, Robert, 4, 136n. 13, 150n. 5, 154n. 15
Bontemps, Arna, 17
Boone, Robert, 151n. 22
Bottomley, Gillian, 139n. 67
"Bound No'th Blues" (Hughes), 15
Bourke-White, Margaret, 122
"Box Seat" (Toomer), 35–37
Boxwell, D. A., 144n. 14
Breitinger, Eckhard, 147n. 13
Bremer, Thomas, 148n. 21
Broadway, 61–62
Bronz, Stephen H., 147n. 11
Brotherhood of Timber Workers, 145n. 24.
    See also labor, unions
Brown, Sterling A., 4, 11–17
    "Convict," 12
    "Long Gone," 12
    "Mecca," 12
    "Odyssey of Big Boy," 12
    "Riverbank Blues," 13–14
    "Southern Road," 12
    Southern Road, 12–14
    "Tin Roof Blues," 12
Buell, Lawrence, 139n. 66
Buhle, Paul, 114
Butler's AME Zion Church, 99

Caldwell, Erskine, 122
Campbell, Elaine, 147n. 12
Cane (Toomer), 2, 21–41, 44, 85–86

canon formation, 6–7. *See also* tradition;
    vernacular criticism
Cappetti, Carla, 154n. 15
Carby, Hazel V., 3, 7–8, 46, 81, 136n. 30
Carew, Jan, 149n. 34
Caribbean, 67–68, 81, 149n. 26, 154n. 17
    and modernist literature, 149nn. 26, 28
    See also Jamaica; West Indies
"Carolina Cabin" (Hughes), 14
Carpentier, Alejo, 149n. 28
Cayton, Horace, 129
Chakrabarty, Dipesh, 9–10, 131
Chauhan, P. S., 147n. 13
Chicago. *See* Illinois
Chicago Defender, 107
Chicago School of Sociology, 148n. 16,
    154n. 15. *See also* sociology
Childs, John Brown, 135n. 3
Chinitz, David, 138n. 56
Christianity, 63–64, 68–71, 73–77, 83. *See
    also* Butler's AME Zion Church
citizenship, 137n. 39. *See also* nationality
"City of Refuge, The" (Fisher), 107–8
Clark-Lewis, Elizabeth, 142n. 30
class
    black middle-, 35, 39, 69–70, 77, 120
    black working-, 43–62, 114–15, 129
    elite versus popular culture, 1–4,
        120
    middle, 65, 115–16, 123, 129
    proletarian, 113–16, 119, 127–29
    See also labor; masses; peasants
Clifford, James, 45
colonialism
    in America, 119
    British 63, 66–68, 83, 132
Comaroff, Jean and John, 9–10, 131
Communist Party, 114–15, 128–29, 153n. 9,
    156n. 32
"Convict" (Brown), 12
Cooper, Carolyn, 70, 79, 149n. 30
Cooper, Wayne F., 148n. 13
"Cotton Song" (Toomer), 29–30, 37
Cudjoe, Selwyn R., 68
Cullen, Countee, 17

Davies, Carole Boyce, 149n. 26
"Daybreak in Alabama" (Hughes), 14
de Certeau, Michel, 43, 143n. 2
"Deer Hunting Story" (anonymous), 56
de Man, Paul, 137n. 36
"'De Reason Niggers Is Working so
    Hard'" (anonymous), 54
dialect, 13–14, 45, 128, 147n. 13
diaspora, 118. *See also* Africa; Middle Pas-
    sage
discrimination, 115, 128. *See also* Jim
    Crow; segregation
District of Columbia (Washington, D.C.),
    22, 34, 143n. 31
Dolby-Stahl, Sandra, 45
Dorst, John, 144n. 14
Doyle, Laura, 140n. 10
Drake, St. Clair, 129
Du Bois, W. E. B.
    and Booker T. Washington, 2, 5–6
    on education, 2
    Souls of Black Folk, The 2, 5–6
    and "Talented Tenth," 128
Dutcher, Dean, 142n. 30

education, 2, 38–39, 47, 64, 68
    agricultural-industrial model, 22, 82,
    99
Eldridge, Richard, 140n. 5
emancipation, 133
England, 70
Enlightenment, 4, 9–10, 118, 134
"Eroded Land, Alabama" (Rothstein), 124,
    125 fig. 9
essentialism, 4–7, 10–11, 83, 129
ethnography, 44–46, 61, 145n. 18
    and gender, 44–46, 144n. 11
Evans, Walker, 155n. 28
"Evenin' Air Blues" (Hughes), 15
Everglades Cypress Lumber Company, 47

Fabre, Michel, 153n. 8, 155n. 24
"Face" (Toomer), 30–31
Farm Security Administration, 122–27
    photographic archive, 58 fig. 3, 60 fig. 4,

96 fig. 7, 123 fig. 8, 125 fig. 9, 126 fig.
    10, 127 fig. 11
Faulkner, Howard, 140n. 10
Fauset, Arthur Huff, 135n. 10
Fauset, Jessie, 17
FBI, 124
Felski, Rita, 137n. 39
feminism, 137n. 39, 148n. 23
    and Zora Neale Hurston, 45–46, 61,
    144nn. 8, 11, 145n. 17
"Fern" (Toomer), 32–33, 86
Fido, Elaine Savory, 149n. 26
"First Colored Man in Massa's House,
    The" (anonymous), 56
Fisher, Rudolph, 17, 153n. 44
    "City of Refuge, The" 107–8
Fleischmann, Ulrich, 148n. 21
Florida, 43–62
    Bartow, 59
    Eatonville, 44–45, 47
    Everglades, 53, 60 fig. 4
    Loughman, 47, 50
    Polk County, 44, 46–51, 61–62 (*see also*
    Hurston, Zora Neale; *Polk County,
    Florida*)
Foley, Barbara
    on Jean Toomer, 28, 141n. 16, 142n. 24,
    143nn. 33–34
    on Richard Wright, 116, 154n. 13
folk
    as alternative modernity, 63–83
    and Bildungsroman, 85–111
    and class consciousness, 113–34
    and folklore, 43–62
    located historically and geographically,
    11–17
    and migrant labor, 43–62
    and modernism, 21–41
    in poststructuralism, 3–7
    and race, 113–34
    related to modernity and historicism,
    7–11
    as trope, 2–4
    in vernacular criticism, 3–7
folklore, 41, 43–62, 72, 132, 135n. 10

folk (*continued*)
　as alternative modernity, 63–83
　"Deer Hunting Story" (anonymous), 56
　" 'De Reason Niggers Is Working so
　　Hard' " (anonymous), 54
　"First Colored Man in Massa's House,
　　The" (anonymous), 56
　and recreation, 57–60
　and resistance on the job, 52–57
　"What Smelled Worse" (anonymous),
　　57
　"Why the Sister in Black Works Hard-
　　est" (anonymous), 53–54, 59
folk songs, 21–41, 51, 109, 111, 132
　"John Henry" (anonymous), 51–52, 61
　See also ballad
folk-urban continuum, 67, 148n. 16
Foner, Philip S., 114
Ford, Karen Jackson, 139n. 65
Frank, Waldo, 21
Frazier, E. Franklin, 117, 151n. 16, 154n. 15
"Freedom's Plow" (Hughes), 15–16
frolics, 96, 151n. 23
Fuss, Diana, 4–7, 136n. 29

Gabbin, Joanne V., 138n. 51
Gates, Henry Louis, Jr., 5–6, 135n. 2
Gayle, Addison, 156n. 33
Genovese, Eugene D., 43, 55, 62, 143n. 2
Georgia, 15, 50, 53, 123 fig. 8
　in *Cane* (Toomer), 21–41
　Greene County, 23, 27–28, 33
　Hancock County, 23, 28
　Sparta, 22, 27–28, 38, 140n. 5, 143n. 33
"Georgia Dusk" (Hughes), 14–15
"Georgia Dusk" (Toomer), 26–27, 29,
　31–32, 37
Gikandi, Simon, 82
Giles, James R., 148n. 13
Gilkes, Michael, 64–65, 81
Gilroy, Paul, 10, 13, 137n. 37
Gingertown (McKay), 67
Glissant, Edouard, 149n. 28
Golding, Alan, 140n. 10
Gordon, Deborah, 144n. 14
Grandel, Hartmut, 138n. 52

Great Depression, 82, 127
Griffin, Farah Jasmine, 143n. 33, 153n. 44
Grossman, James R., 107, 135n.9, 151n. 30,
　156n. 33
Guha, Ranajit, 137n. 38

Hakutani, Yoshinobu, 153n. 8
Hale, Anthony R., 145n. 14
Hampton Normal and Agricultural Insti-
　tute, 99
Harlem, 1, 82, 107–8, 153n. 44
　Riots of 1935, 120, 128
　See also New York (city)
Harlem Renaissance, 6, 63, 108, 147n. 7
　as Negro Renaissance, 1
　as New Negro movement, 40
　and terminology, 135n. 2
Harris, Abram L., 145n. 24
Harris, Wilson, 149n. 28, 154n. 17
Harrison, Beth, 145n. 14
"Harvest Song" (Toomer), 37
Hemenway, Robert E., 44–45
Henderson, Rev. George W., 152n. 33
Henderson, George Wylie, 17, 85–111,
　150n. 6
　Baby Lou and the Angel Bud, 110
　Jule, 2, 87, 101–11, 113, 152n. 33
　Ollie Miss, 2, 87–111, 113, 132, 142n. 28,
　　150n. 5, 151n. 13, 152nn. 31, 33
　" 'Thy Name Is Woman,' " 152n. 31
Henderson, Stephen E., 138n. 51
Henri, Florette, 142n. 30
Hernández, Graciela, 145nn. 14, 18
Herskovits, Melville J., 118, 154n. 16
Hill, Lynda Marion, 146n. 26
Hine, Darlene Clark, 142n. 30
historicism, 3–11, 17–19, 131–34
　and "hidden transcript," 43–44, 46,
　　50–52, 60, 62
　local history and world historical narra-
　　tive, 131–34
History of Hancock County, The (Smith), 28
Holt, Thomas C., 66–68, 79
"Homesick Blues" (Hughes), 15
homosocial desire, 15n. 36
　and mimesis, 101–6, 109, 152n. 36

and race, 104–6, 109
hooks, bell, 7, 145n. 14, 156n. 4
Huggins, Nathan, 136n. 13
Hughes, Langston, 4, 11, 14–17, 139n. 65
  Big Sea, The, 1
  "Bound No'th Blues," 15
  "Carolina Cabin," 14
  "Daybreak in Alabama," 14
  "Evenin' Air Blues," 15
  "Freedom's Plow," 15–16
  "Georgia Dusk," 14–15
  "Homesick Blues," 15
  "Juice-Joint, Northern City," 15
  "Migration," 15
  "Negro Artist and the Racial Mountain,
    The," 14
  "One-Way Ticket," 15
  "Po' Boy Blues," 15
  "Red Clay Blues" (with Richard
    Wright), 15
  "Restrictive Covenants," 15
  "Share-croppers," 14
  "South, The," 15
  "Visitors to the Black Belt," 15
hunting, 103–4, 109
Hurston, Zora Neale, 17, 43–62, 132, 150n.
  5
  "Deer Hunting Story" (anonymous), 56
  " 'De Reason Niggers Is Working so
    Hard'" (anonymous), 54
  "First Colored Man in Massa's House,
    The" (anonymous), 56
  "John Henry" (anonymous), 51–52, 61
  Mules and Men, 2, 43–62
  Polk County (with Dorothy Waring),
    61–62
  "What Smelled Worse" (anonymous),
    57
  "Why the Sister in Black Works Hard-
    est" (anonymous), 53–54, 59
Hutchinson, George B., 140n. 5

identity politics, 83
"Ideologies of Black Folk" (Carby), 7–8
Illinois, Chicago, 36–38, 127 fig. 11, 129.
  See also Chicago Defender

Industrial Workers of the World, 145n. 24.
  See also labor, unions

Jackson, Blyden, 150nn. 9, 14
Jamaica, 63–83
  peasant freeholds and economic capital
    in post-emancipation, 66–68
Jameson, Fredric, 17, 146n. 3
Jean Toomer, Artist (McKay), 24
Jehlen, Myra, 18
Jim Crow, 43–44, 137n. 38. See also dis-
  crimination; segregation
"John Henry" (anonymous), 51–52, 61
Johnson, Barbara E., 6–7, 45
Johnson, Charles S., 93–95, 102, 154n. 19
Johnson, Lonnell E., 150n. 5
Jones, Robert, 141n. 15
Jordan, Rosan Augusta, 145n. 14
"Juice-Joint, Northern City" (Hughes), 15
Juke Joint, 52, 59–60, 60 fig. 4, 62
" 'Juke Joint' and Bar in the Vegetable Sec-
  tion of the Glades Area of South Cen-
  tral Florida, February 1941, A" (Wol-
  cott), 59, 60 fig. 4
Jule (Henderson), 2, 87, 101–11, 113, 152n.
  33
Julien, Isaac, 16
Juneja, Renu, 146n. 2

"Kabnis" (Toomer), 38–40
Kane, Patricia, 150n. 5
"Karintha" (Toomer), 31–33
Kelley, Robin D. G., 99–100
  on deconstructing the folk, 3, 8
  on everyday forms of resistance, 43, 62,
    137n. 38, 154n. 20
Kennedy, Louise Venable, 103, 142n. 30
Kent, George E., 64–65, 147n. 7
Kerblat-Houghton, Jeanne, 141n. 15
Kerman, Cynthia Earl, 140n. 5
Kinnamon, Kenneth, 155n. 24
Kirby, Jack Temple, 22, 29
Klotman, Phyllis Rauch, 152n. 38
Kruger, Loren, 139n. 68
Ku Klux Klan, 110
Kutzinski, Vera M., 13, 139n. 4

labor
and education, 2–3
as erotic, 98
and gender, 95–98, 102–3
and race, 2–3
unions, 114, 145n. 24
See also class; migrant labor; peasants;
slavery
Lamming, George, 65, 146n. 2, 147n. 13
Land of Hope (Grossman), 107, 135n. 9,
151n. 30
Lange, Dorothea, 96
"Plowing Cotton, Georgia," 121, 123 fig.
8
"Small Tenant Farm Producing Peanuts
and Sweet Potatoes in Southeastern
Alabama, August 1938, A" 95, 96 fig.
7
Larsen, Nella, 17
Lawrence, Leota S., 65, 81
Lee, George, 17
Lee, Russell, "Street Scene under the El,"
126, 127 fig. 11
Lemann, Nicholas, 140n. 4
LeSeur, Geta, 147n. 12, 148n. 23
Levine, Lawrence W., 141n. 17, 155n. 30
Lewis, Earl, 142n. 30
Lewis, Edward E., 141n. 21
Liberator, 63
Linkon, Sherry Lee, 135n. 2
Locke, Alain, 13
New Negro, The 1, 3, 107
"Long Black Song" (Wright), 85–86
"Long Gone" (Brown), 12
Louisiana, New Orleans, 44
Lowe, John, 146n. 31
Lurie, Susan, 144n. 10
lynching, 31, 33, 39, 143n. 33
lyric, 24, 34

Marcus, George E., 45
Marks, Carole, 142n. 30
Marshall, Paule, 146n. 2
Martin, Odette C., 140n. 10
Marxism, 114–16
and aesthetics, 63, 115

masses, 1–2, 34, 115, 135n. 3. *See also* class;
labor
Mayor, Archer H., 146n. 24
McGee, Leo, 151n. 22
McKay, Claude, 17, 63–83, 132
"The Agricultural Show," 67
Banana Bottom, 2, 63–83, 85, 113, 142n.
28
Gingertown, 67
McKay, Nellie Y., 24–25, 141n. 12
"Mecca" (Brown), 12
mediation, 17–18, 26, 134
Meisenhelder, Susan, 145n. 15
Michaels, Walter Benn, 142n. 27, 154n. 16
Middle Passage, 116–19, 133. *See also*
Africa
migrant labor, 10–12, 23, 43–62, 86, 125,
132
Chinese, 64, 79
East Indian, 64, 79
migration, 10, 37, 85–111, 124–25, 135n. 9,
140n. 4
forced, 133
and gender, 30–34, 85–86, 101–5, 142nn.
29–30
from Georgia, 23, 28, 33
Great Migration, 3, 8, 87, 106, 120–21,
124–25, 133, 142n. 30
and historiography, 106–7
and narrative, 101–10, 121, 152n. 38
and rural modernity, 85–111
urban migrants, 1–3, 12, 15, 34–38,
126–28, 143n. 31
See also migrant labor
"Migration" (Hughes), 15
Mikell, Gwendolyn, 145n. 16
Miller, James A., 135n. 2
Mintz, Sidney W., 67, 148nn. 16, 19
Mississippi (state), 126 fig. 10, 140n. 4
modernism, 23–26. *See also* Caribbean, and
modernist literature
Modernism and the Harlem Renaissance
(Baker), 5–6
modernity, 137nn. 36–39
and alternative modernities, 17, 57,
63–83, 125, 132, 139n. 68, 141n. 17

and antimodernism, 63
and autonomy, 9–11, 23, 29, 37, 40,
    63–64, 68, 79–80, 85–111, 125
and Bildungsroman, 86–88
and form, 17–19
and modernization, 4, 8–11, 16, 22–25,
    86–88, 113, 116, 120, 129
as multiple, 9–10, 131
and narrative of national development,
    3, 10, 19, 131
and race, 3
as rural modernity, 85–111, 113, 133
and transition narrative of develop-
    ment, 9–11, 16–19, 25, 131–34
Modernity and Its Malcontents (Comaroff
    and Comaroff), 9–10
modes of production, 8, 11, 116, 132
Monson, Ingrid T., 154n. 18
Moore, Jack B., 156n. 34
Mules and Men (Hurston), 2, 43–62
musical, the, 61–62
Myth of the Negro Past, The (Herskovits),
    118

narrative, 133
and documentary voice-over, 121, 155n.
    24
and framing, 43–46, 57, 144n. 6
and "hidden transcript," 50–52
and voice, 44, 50–60, 80, 116, 120–21
nationality, 114, 117, 128–29, 131, 147n. 13
naturalism, 64–65, 80
"Negro Artist and the Racial Mountain,
    The" (Hughes), 14
Negro Novel in America, The (Bone), 4
Negro Question, 114–16, 128–29
Negro Renaissance. *See* Harlem Renais-
    sance
Neubrech, W. LeRoy, 146n. 24
New Criticism, 24–25
New Negro, The (Locke), 1, 3, 107
New Negro movement. *See* Harlem
    Renaissance
New Orleans. *See* Louisiana, New Orleans
New York (city), 38, 61, 63, 87, 100. *See also*
    Harlem

New York Daily News, 87, 150n. 7
Nicholls, David G., 150n. 7
Nixon, Herman Clarence, 155n. 28
North, Michael, 141n. 16, 147n. 13
North Carolina, 107
*Norton Anthology of African-American Liter-
    ature* (Gates et al.), 6
nostalgia, 23, 39, 63, 68, 83, 122, 133
"November Cotton Flower" (Toomer),
    29–30, 33

Obeah, 74–76
O'Daniel, Therman, 140n. 10
"Odyssey of Big Boy" (Brown), 12
"Ole Massa and John Who Wanted to Go
    to Heaven," 56
"Ollie" (Balcolm), 88, 89 fig. 5
"Ollie and Slaughter Returned to
    Their Plows and Continued
    until Noon" (Balcolm), 88,
    90 fig. 6
Ollie Miss (Henderson), 2, 87–111, 113,
    132, 142n. 28, 150n. 5, 151n. 13, 152nn.
    31, 33
One-Way Ticket (Hughes), 15
"One-Way Ticket" (Hughes), 15

pastiche, 25–26
pastoralism, 34–35, 37, 40, 53, 139n. 66,
    143n. 33
peasants, 66–82, 132, 137n. 38. *See also*
    class; labor; migrant labor
Peters, Pearlie, 144n. 8
Petry, Ann, 17
Phillips, Christopher, 155n. 27
photo-documentary history, 113–29, 155n.
    28
plantation system, 27, 29, 66–68, 79,
    117–19
    after demise of, 93–95 (*see also* Johnson,
        Charles S.)
    and peasant freeholds, 66–68, 82
    See also agriculture; slavery
"Plowing Cotton, Georgia" (Lange), 121,
    123 fig. 8
"Po' Boy Blues" (Hughes), 15

Political Unconscious, The (Jameson), 17, 146n. 3

Polk County (Hurston and Waring), 61–62

Polk County, Florida (Polk County, Florida, Publicity Department), 47, 48 fig. 1, 49 fig. 2

"Portrait in Georgia" (Toomer), 30–31

Post, Marion, "Tractors in Cotton Field, Mississippi," 124, 126 fig. 10. *See also* Wolcott, Marion Post

post-colonial studies, 4, 9, 11, 133, 137n. 38, 139n. 66, 147n. 13

"Postcoloniality and the Artifice of History" (Chakrabarty), 9–10

postmodernity, 45–46, 61

post-structuralism, 11, 131, 133
  critique of vernacular criticism, 3–7

Preface to Peasantry, A (Raper), 27–29, 33

Priebe, Richard, 146n. 5

prints, block, 88–90. *See also* Balcolm, Lowell Leroy

Problem of Freedom, The (Holt), 66–67

Propp, Vladimir, 57

Puckett, John Rogers, 155n. 25

Quennell, Peter, 151n. 13

race
  and class consciousness, 113–29
  and education, 2–3
  and essentialism, 4–7, 10–11, 14, 17
  and injustice, 86, 126
  and progress, 78, 87, 99, 113

Rahming, Melvin B., 147n. 12

Ramchand, Kenneth, 64–65, 147n. 13

Rampersad, Arnold, 14

Raper, Arthur F., 27–29, 33, 40, 117, 154n. 15

"Reapers" (Toomer), 29–30

recreation, 57–60

Redbook, 150n. 7

"Red Clay Blues" (Hughes and Wright), 15

Redfield, Robert, 148n. 16

Reed-Morrisson, Laura, 145n. 18

Reid, Ira De A., 154n. 15

Reilly, John M., 121, 140n. 10

Repeating Island, The (Benítez-Rojo), 81

resistance, 43–63, 67, 119, 145n. 15, 148n. 21

"Restrictive Covenants" (Hughes), 15

Riis, Jacob A., 155n. 26

"Riverbank Blues" (Brown), 13–14

Robertson, Edythe, 150n. 7

Rodgers, Lawrence R., 152n. 38

Rohlehr, Gordon, 65–67

romance, 64–65, 80–81, 94–95

Rosskam, Edwin, 121, 123

Rothstein, Arthur, "Eroded Land, Alabama," 124, 125 fig. 9

Rowell, Charles, 138n. 51

Rural Worlds Lost (Kirby), 22

Sanchez-Eppler, Benigno, 145n. 14

"Sawmill Workers Waiting for a Motor to Cool" (Wolcott), 56, 58 fig. 3

Scarry, Elaine, 117

Scott, James C., 43, 137n. 38, 143n. 2

Scottsboro Boys, Trial of, 121

Scruggs, Charles, 153n. 48

Sedgwick, Eve Kosofsky, 148n. 23, 152n. 36

segregation, 47, 49 fig. 2, 50, 145n. 24. *See also* discrimination; Jim Crow

sermon form, 121

"Seventh Street" (Toomer), 34

Shadow of the Plantation (Johnson), 94–95, 154n. 19

"Share-croppers" (Hughes), 14

sharecropping, 27, 29, 85, 93–95, 100. *See also* agriculture

Shivers, Forrest, 140n. 8

Sixteenth Census of the United States, 152n. 35

slavery, 55, 110, 114, 117–21, 133, 152n. 36
  in Jamaica, 66–67, 79

"Small Tenant Farm Producing Peanuts and Sweet Potatoes in Southeastern Alabama, August 1938" (Lange), 95, 96 fig. 7

Smith, Gary, 138n. 52
socialism, 114, 137n. 37
sociology, 118, 129. *See also* Chicago School of Sociology
Sollors, Werner, 150n. 3
"Song of the Son" (Toomer), 21–23, 26–27, 30, 37, 40
Souls of Black Folk, The (Du Bois), 2, 5–6
"South, The" (Hughes), 15
South Asia, 137n. 38
"Southern Road" (Brown), 12
Southern Road (Brown), 12–14
Spero, Sterling D., 145n. 24
Spillers, Hortense J., 152nn. 32, 36
spirituals, 109, 111, 132, 153n. 44. *See also* folk songs
Spivak, Gayatri Chakravorty, 137n. 38
Spofford, William K., 141n. 15
Stange, Maren, 122
Stepto, Robert B., 14
Stoff, Michael B., 147n. 12
Stott, William, 154n. 21
"Street Scene under the El" (Lee), 126, 127 fig. 11
Sundquist, Eric J., 135n. 2
Symbols of Ideal Life (Stange), 122

Tangier, 63, 82, 147n. 13
Taylor, Clyde, 141n. 15
Taylor, Patrick, 81
"Theater" (Toomer), 35
Thomas, H. Nigel, 148nn. 21, 22
Tillery, Tyrone, 148n. 13
"Tin Roof Blues" (Brown), 12
Todes, Charlotte, 145n. 24
Todorov, Tzvetan, 144n. 10
Tolnay, Stewart E., 152n. 43
Toomer, Jean, 17, 21–41, 131–32, 143n. 33
    "Becky," 33
    "Beehive," 34–35, 37
    "Blood-Burning Moon," 33
    "Bona and Paul," 36–37
    "Box Seat," 35–37
    Cane, 2, 21–41, 44, 85–86
    "Cotton Song," 29–30, 37

"Face," 30–31
"Fern," 32–33, 86
"Georgia Dusk," 26–27, 29, 31–32, 37
"Harvest Song," 37
"Kabnis," 38–40
"Karintha," 31–33
"November Cotton Flower," 29–30, 33
"Portrait in Georgia," 30–31
"Reapers," 29–30
"Seventh Street," 34
"Song of the Son," 21–23, 26–27, 30, 37, 40
"Theater," 35
Trachtenberg, Alan, 155nn. 27, 30
"Tractors in Cotton Field, Mississippi" (Post), 124, 126 fig. 10
Tracy, Steven C., 138n. 56
tradition, 4–8, 11, 13, 17–18, 131–32, 139n. 67. *See also* vernacular criticism
trickster figure, 55–56
Trotskyism, 114
Trotter, Joe William, Jr., 106–7, 156n. 33
Tuskegee Institute (Tuskegee Normal and Industrial Institute), 82, 87, 93, 98–100, 111, 152n. 39
    Trinity Church Boston Oratorical Prize, 99, 151n. 25
    See also Booker T. Washington
12 Million Black Voices (Wright), 2, 113–29, 155n. 24

Up from Slavery (Washington), 5
utopianism, 8, 35, 37, 64, 81–82, 110, 132

vernacular criticism, 11, 16–19, 131, 133
    critique of, by post-structuralism, 3–7
    See also tradition
"Visitors to the Black Belt" (Hughes), 15

Wagner-Martin, Linda, 141n. 16
Wainwright, Mary Katherine, 144n. 6
Wald, Priscilla, 45
Wall, Cheryl A., 45, 144n. 6
Wallace, Michele, 145n. 17
Ward, Mrs. Humphrey, 71

Waring, Dorothy, 61
Warren, Kenneth W., 7, 118, 138n. 47,
    156n. 5
Washington, Booker T., 132, 135n. 9
    and W. E. B. Du Bois, 2, 5–6
    on education, 2, 99–101
    and Tuskegee Institute, 98–99, 111
    Up from Slavery, 5–6
Washington, D.C. *See* District of Columbia
    (Washington, D.C.)
Watkins, Patricia, 140n. 10
Webb, Barbara J., 149n. 28
West Indies, 65, 147n. 13, 149n. 30. *See also*
    Caribbean; Jamaica
"What Smelled Worse" (anonymous),
    57
White, Hayden, 17
"Why the Sister in Black Works Hardest"
    (anonymous), 53–54, 59
Williams, Brett, 143n. 31
Willis, Miriam DeCosta, 144n. 12
Willis, Susan, 144n. 11, 151n. 15
Wilkinson, Doris Y., 150n. 5
Wirth, Louis, 154n. 15

Wolcott, Marion Post
    "'Juke Joint' and Bar in the Vegetable
        Section of the Glades Area of South
        Central Florida, February 1941, A"
        59, 60 fig. 4
    "Sawmill Workers Waiting for a Motor
        to Cool, Childs, Florida, January
        1939," 56, 58 fig. 3.
    See also Post, Marion
Worker's Dreadnought, 63
World War I, 115
World War II, 115, 128
Wright, Richard, 17, 111, 113–19, 132,
        153n. 9, 154n. 13, 155nn. 24, 31, 32
    "Blueprint for Negro Writing," 115
    "Long Black Song," 85–86
    "Red Clay Blues" (with Langston
        Hughes), 15
    12 Million Black Voices, 2, 113–29, 155n.
        24
Writing Culture (Clifford and Marcus), 45

You Have Seen Their Faces (Caldwell and
        Bourke-White), 122